Return or The Mother

RETURN TO LOVE

SHARON MCERLANE

BOOK 4 of *The Grandmothers Speak*

Net of Light Press

Return of the Mother: Return to Love
© 2021 Sharon McErlane
All rights reserved.

Book 4 of the series "The Grandmothers Speak"

Published by Net of Light Press, 6/30/21
www.netoflight.org
www.grandmothersspeak.com

ISBN: 978-1-7374903-0-2 (paperback)
ISBN: 978-1-7374903-1-9 (eBook)

Cover painting by Nicholas Roerich

Book design/layout: Timothy W. Brittain

Printed in the United State of America

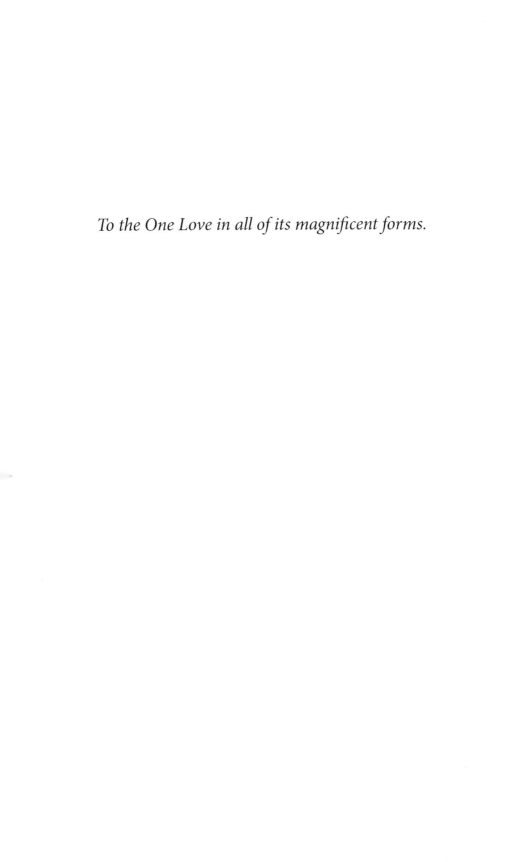

To the One Love in all of its magnificent forms.

CONTENTS

INTRODUCTION

The Grandmothers begin this, their fourth book, with a brief review of their message—why life on earth is out of balance, their purpose in coming at this time and the work that must be done now. As I gathered material for this introduction, I noticed that their language was sharper, more abrupt than usual. There is an urgency to this introduction. They are calling us to step into the work at hand and to *do it now.*

The Grandmothers Speak:

"For more than twenty years, we, the Great Council of the Grand-mothers, have been sharing our messages with you. Teaching, dem-onstrating, and prodding you to action, and in that time many of you have responded. You have grown in power and presence.

"All over the world, numbers of people now meet to share our messages, practice our teachings, and help one another to come awake. This is as it should be," the Grandmothers said, their heads nodding in unison, "and now we will offer more to those who want what we have come to give. There is another layer of learning avail-able," they said, "and if you listen to what we have to share, we will lead you through the darkness of the times you are in.

"For many years," they said, "woman has lived cut off from her position of power on earth. Long ago, when she was removed from her station in life, she became separated from her essence. Deprived then of her inherent power, woman, who had been the hub of life's wheel, was forced to live offset from her center. Forced to live with-out power. Woman was pushed to the side so-to-speak," they said, "and although the denigration of the Feminine Principle occurred thousands of years ago, its effects are still felt today. From that long-ago time until now, woman has been unable to sustain a position of power in human life.

"It is the female of the species that anchors life on earth; the female gives birth, tends to the young, nurses the sick and cares for the dying. The human female supports life through all its stages—birth, through death. She is the natural hub of the wheel for the human family. But when patriarchy supplanted her and claimed this position for itself, it removed the hub.

It was then that the wheel began to spin out of control. And it was then that the pattern of life energy on earth began to fragment. Where once had been an anchor of stability, security, and generosity—yin energy at the hub—now was only a collection of aggressive yang. The removal of woman from her position at the wheel of life created grief for all beings, not only human beings and life on earth began to suffer.

"When patriarchy diminished woman's role in society, the reservoir of yin energy for the planet was also diminished. This created a vacuum, an empty space, and into this empty space flew random particles of energy. This in-coming energy was seeking, active (yang) in nature, not holding and receptive (yin), and over time it magnetized like-energy to itself. This was how yang energy built up within what had previously been a core of yin.

"Yang is always active, so as more and more yang particles came together, they created a strident, churning mass of agitation. And what had previously been home for the holding, nurturing power of yin now became filled with aggression.

"As the process continued, earth filled with more and more yang while the supply of yin dwindled downward. Life on earth then became dominated by energy that was not only one-sided, but strident and increasingly violent. This is where you are today," the Grandmothers said, their faces grim.

"In order for life to flourish, these two poles of energy must come into balance with each other. But for far too long woman, the natural reservoir of yin for this planet, has been absent from her center position. When she was removed as the hub of the wheel and lost alignment with her essence, the energy on earth also went out of alignment. And because the void that was created when yin was removed, became filled by yang, today, instead of harmony between yin and yang, earth holds what amounts to a double dose of yang.

"Today, *all* is change, fast movement, and violence. And since creation was not designed to be one-sided like this, *everything* on earth is out of balance. Plants, animals, water, air, human society—everything has been deeply affected by this lack of harmony.

"This condition now exists all over the earth," the Grandmothers said, "and the obvious solution is to return to balance. But how? We, the Great Council of the Grandmothers, have begun our work by helping women return to their center point," they said. "We have shown women and men how to align with the energy of yin. Our first three books, *A Call to Power: The Grandmothers Speak; Our Love Is Our Power;* and *Casting the Net,* are filled with examples of how to do this.

"Woman does not yet know it," the Grandmothers said, "but she carries a reservoir of strength within herself. Because *she* is a holding tank of yin energy, it is her nature to be potent. *Human women hold yin for all life on this planet.* A woman carries within herself the power to support life," they said. "And once she fully understands this, she will be able to line up her essence and return to her original position at the center of the wheel of life.

"Because of her built-in capacity to store yin, woman can easily align with it. And let us assure you that this power we speak of is not *power* as you think of it today. This is not '*power over*' or '*power in order to....*'. NO!" the Grandmothers declared. "This is the power that feeds and supports life. It is a force for good, an unselfish, life-affirming force.

"Because the male of the species is designed differently and does not carry inside himself the capacity to store yin, he cannot help woman with her task of returning to center point. His role in returning the earth to balance is different from hers. His task is important, but ancillary to hers. Man can support woman as she returns to center, but the first piece of work belongs to her. As she re-aligns herself with yin, she will benefit from man's support, but she alone must take this step into power. Woman must take this step and until she chooses to do so, life on earth will continue to be out of balance.

"With a few exceptions, at this time in history, men are no longer able to lead," the Grandmothers said, catching my eye to be sure I was following them. "We understand that what we say here may surprise you," they said, "but we say it because at this time, vast numbers of human males are fragmented—not whole within themselves.

The excessive energy of yang that has for so long run life on earth has weakened them. And strangely, in spite of the many years of persecution and denigration that woman has endured, she is still whole. This is why when women hear our call to step forward into this work, they take that step. They do it because *they can do it.* They were born for this moment. Women!" the Grandmothers called out, "Trust yourselves!

"Once a woman aligns with her center point of yin, her actual design becomes that of a container. *She who holds,*" they said. "She who holds life. She who holds and is at the same time held by life. Woman naturally carries a reservoir of yin, and *this energy in turn holds her.* This is why woman's ability to share understanding and compassion is so vast. *This* is the power of yin.

"The innate capacity to give and receive love is inborn in woman. Woman is able to bring forth life, most nurturers are women, and more females follow a spiritual path than do males. Woman is one with the Feminine Principle of life; she is one with the Great Mother, one with the container and sustainer of life." And standing tall, the Grandmothers declared, "**Woman IS.**

"We know that what we are telling you may sound foreign, but we promise that if you pay attention to what we are saying, you will be able to do great good. If you follow our guidance you will soon have the joy of watching your own life expand. And," they smiled, "as your energy expands, every living thing on earth will benefit.

"Because you ARE a reservoir of yin, each time you tap into that reservoir, you have a calming effect on everyone you meet. By living from the center of yin within yourself, by following the path of yin, *you become a walking blessing upon the earth.* We, the Great Council of the Grandmothers, have come to return yin and yang to balance and we will begin this work with women.

"And now, a word about men," the Grandmothers said. "The male of the species needs your love—especially at this time, especially while the energies on earth are shifting so radically. He also needs your respect and understanding. Spiritually, most human males are *younger* than are most females, and if you can bring yourself to think of them like this, it will help you understand them better. Because you carry such a great deposit of yin inside, you *can* love them. You can love them in spite of the damage human males have done in the world. And once you see them as they truly are," they said, "you will also be able to accept them.

"Both sexes have suffered from the great imbalance of energy on earth," the Grandmothers said, "and, in recent times, their suffering has grown even greater. When woman lost her connection with her center point, when she lost her grounding in yin, she became weak. For thousands of years she was treated as a possession, degraded and deprived of human dignity. This went on for so long that even today many women find that they have no 'legs' to stand on. Their energy sometimes wavers and collapses. Most women today do not know their own strength," they said, "and because so many of them live in an incapacitated state, they are by far too weak to claim it.

"But man has also become weakened by the gross energy imbalance on earth," the Grandmothers said. "Yang energy, churning in a state of constant aggression, devoid of its partner, yin, becomes frantic and wild. It splits off from itself and fragments and when it does that, it grows more and more out of control. Many men today are stuck in a state of constant reactivity, run by random energy. They are frantic and starved for the anchoring presence of yin.

"To calm the crazy play of energy on earth today, and help the planet return to balance, woman must reclaim her position at the center point of life. *Woman must return home to power.* This is the first step toward balance.

"The container of life must again claim her place at the hub of the wheel of life. And until women make the decision to step up and 'center in,' life on earth will be lost. Without the holding, anchoring power of yin, the world itself will be lost.

"It is time now for the Mother," the Grandmothers said. "Time for earth to once again fill with the Feminine Principle. *You have waited long for this moment.* And we tell you," the Grandmothers said, "now is the time for *The Mother's Return*."

AUTHOR'S NOTE: For this book to be written, the Grandmothers had to speak it to and *through* the author. But when the Grandmothers speak here, they are actually speaking *to* you, the reader. So, please remember that when the Grandmothers say, "You," they mean *you*.

Dear reader, this book is yours.

GRATEFUL ACKNOWLEDGEMENT to the following people who continue to propel the Grandmothers' work forward and who helped bring this book to fruition.

Thanks to Cathy Landrum for editing *Return of the Mother, Return to Love*, and to Tim Brittain for designing the book. To Nadia den Aantrekker and Kate Rogers, who work tirelessly to get the Grandmothers' messages out into the world. And to our team of translators who make the messages available everywhere.

Thanks to Grandmothers' Beacons all over the world who share the Grandmothers' teachings and anchor the Net of Light on earth, and to the Regional Coordinators who support them. Thanks to the Grandmothers' Council for its faithful guidance and support and thanks also to the organizers of the many Net of Light Gatherings that are held around the world. And most of all, we are endlessly grateful to the beloved Grandmothers themselves, whose example lights the way for us in all that we are and all that we do.

CHAPTER ONE

Who and What are the Grandmothers?

For over twenty years now, thousands of us have been hard at work with the Great Council of the Grandmothers. These divine teachers, who represent all races and cultures of humanity, show us what it is to be powerful as women, what it is to be balanced as human beings.

The Grandmothers shoot straight from the hip. They are patient; they are profound and at the same time, full of fun. And over and over, they explain why our world today is out of harmony and what we can do to correct this. The Grandmothers are joyful and share with us their message of uplift and service. Today hundreds of Grandmothers' groups meet around the world to practice their teachings and live their message.

The Grandmothers first appeared more than twenty years ago, and their arrival upended the life I'd known until then. They showed up one day as I walked the dog beside the beach and announced, **"We have come to return the world to balance and we will do this primarily through individual women."** Soon after they first appeared, I called women together and we began to work with them—journeying, meditating, and inviting others to receive their teachings. They taught us how to uplift the earth by working with the Net of Light. We passed their Empowerment on to one another, and since then, the work with them has never stopped. Now thousands of us are involved.

The Grandmothers have come at this time to call humanity to power, to teach us how to turn the imbalance on earth back to balance, and how to magnify the power of the great Net of Light that's holding the earth steady during these unsteady times. Their first three books, *A Call to Power: The Grandmothers Speak; Our Love is Our Power;* and

Casting the Net, show us how to partner with them to elevate both ourselves and our planet. And because their work is on-going, so too is ours. Here then begins the Grandmothers' fourth book.

Many ask if the Grandmothers have ever told me their names, and to this I always say 'no.' Truthfully, I've never been interested in their names or in any personal information on them probably because I don't think of them as separate beings. From the first moment I saw them, to me they were simply 'the Grandmothers'—a council of wise women. Not separate individuals, but a unit.

One day I posed that question to them, and they responded by smiling benignly. Then, squeezing themselves in close to one another, they said, **"We are one in our purpose. We make up one body."** Then they moved in even closer. **"We *are*,"** they declared, and the looks on their faces told me *it's the coming together* of these seemingly 'individual' Grandmothers that's important. Together they make up one being, *the Grandmothers*—here to teach and work with us.

Those of us who are drawn to their message also form a unit when we gather together to learn from them. In fact, much of what we do with the Grandmothers we end up doing together. Songs, ceremonies, meditations—it's a *we* thing—and, as it's turned out, this 'work' with them is joyful as well as companionable. And, since we, too, tend to function as a unit, there's little if any hierarchy within our organization.

When I journeyed to the Grandmothers to ask them to explain more about this, they greeted me and said, **"You're at last discovering that you're not alone in this world but are an integral part of something. You're a moving piece of something wonderful. You're not what others may have said you are,"** they shook their heads, **"nor are you what you've thought you are. In fact, you aren't a separate entity at all,"** they said and burst into laughter at seeing the look of surprise on my face. **"You are part of a flowing, growing sea of energy,"** they said, **"a sea of energy that's busily moving matter in a new direction. You're no 'small potato' as you like to say, a separate someone of not much consequence. NO!"** they laughed. **"You're one with the Net of Light, an eternal, endless being—greater by far than you've ever imagined.**

"We're watching you as you make this discovery," they said, smiling and nodding to one another. **"We see that many of you are start-**

ing to come awake now, and you're doing it at the same time. We take delight in observing as you discover this truth about yourself. You're thrilled each time you catch a glimpse of your own magnificence, your expanding understanding and your ever-widening reach of love. And the joy you feel when you come upon this discovery is magnified many times over because you are making it together. You're coming awake together, feeling greater happiness," they said, "experiencing a sense of community and a feeling of communion. As you come together like this, we watch you and see joy being multiplied many times over." With tears in their eyes the Grandmothers said, "The happiness that you feel as you awaken to this oneness is also our happiness.

"You will continue to grow like this," they assured me. "You'll keep on growing in communion with one another and in communion with us. You'll keep on learning, stretching, and being stretched." Then they stood back and observed me. "You can start looking forward to greater harmony in your life now," they said. "Start looking forward to sharing more joyous times with one another.

"We see you!" they laughed. "We see you laughing together, singing together, and crying together, and we're so happy for you that we want to sing, too. You know the song," they said, smiling as they watched me out of the corners of their eyes. "Oh, how we love you, oh, how we love you!" they sang, and this beloved song filled my heart to overflowing. "Thank you, Grandmothers," I said.

After I'd dried my eyes and mulled this journey over for a few minutes, I sat up and looked around the room. "Well," I said as I stretched and yawned, "I guess that takes care of *that* question." I was feeling what the Grandmothers had shared with me inside my body now—a peaceful, companionable feeling—with myself and everyone else. And I realized that this feeling wasn't new to me. I'd actually been sensing it for a long time. "All of us," I said to myself, "who call on and work with the Net of Light have formed a family now, and every time we come together, waves of love and understanding automatically start flowing between us. And, as we've come more and more awake to the presence of the Net of Light, it's awakened in us too. Working together with the Grandmothers the way we do, we're forming a living, breathing unit of love and life. We're not really an organization," I said then, "we're more an organism."

I shook my head in amazement when I heard myself say that. I'd never expected to experience such an all-encompassing, **One Love.**

This journey to the Grandmothers had clarified something for me. Now I knew without a doubt that all of us are part of the great Net of Light; that whenever we come together at a Grandmothers' Net of Light Gathering, we form both a human *and* a divine connection. I'd never thought it possible to make a connection like this, let alone be able to experience it, but every time our local Net of Light group met there was an undeniable feeling of 'home' inside each of us. And in this home place there were no rules that we were expected to follow, no hierarchy we had to adhere to, and nothing we *had* to do. *Only love.* This 'home' was *filled* with love.

As these thoughts continued to flow through my mind, I realized how much this new way of being meant to me, meant to every one of us. "Oh!" I sighed as I let go a big breath. "This is it! I'm having a holy moment. A real one."

"It's time to bring men and women into harmony."

The next time I journeyed to the Grandmothers, before I had a chance to ask them anything, they said, **"It's time to bring men and women into harmony together. Time for men to become involved in this work."** "Men?" I questioned. "Why men?" Ever since they first appeared, I'd thought the Grandmothers' work was only for women and, even after a few men became interested in it, there were only a few of them, so nothing really changed. In my opinion the subject was hardly worth considering. "So, what are they talking about now?" I asked myself.

My face must have registered my surprise because the Grandmothers fastened their eyes on mine and said, **"The egg…. It goes back to the egg."** I stared at them, my mind racing. "The egg? The egg? What…?" Then I remembered how they'd once used an egg to explain the principles of yin and yang—feminine and masculine energy. They nodded to me emphatically.

"The inside of the egg," they explained, **"is the nourishing part, the life-bearing part. The inside is yin,"** they said. **"And the outside of the egg, the shell, is yang—it's the covering that protects the yin. Start thinking of women and men like this, and as you do, pray for**

understanding of the *actual* role of women and men. Don't look at the bad behavior you see today," they said, "but ask to understand the *underlying pattern of harmony* between the sexes." "I will, Grandmothers," I nodded to them, my eyes big. And after two or three days had gone by when I'd thought of little else, I journeyed back to them, determined to learn more about this subject of women and men.

Asking and praying about this question had made me aware of how *really* interested I was in it. I was eager to understand how to perform the Grandmothers' work with, and in the company of, men. Maybe it *was* time to bring the sexes together. **"We will guide you in this,"** the Grandmothers said, a far-away look in their eyes. **"Men need an understanding of yin and yang. Your husband, son, and many others need this. Let the possibility of doing this work with men percolate inside you for a while. You have other tasks before you now, so let this one cook slowly on the back burner while you go ahead and do the other things at hand. And pray,"** they said. **"Your prayers will keep enough focus on that back burner."**

"Okay, Grandmothers," I said, deciding to leave the subject to them and instead tackle the work before me. I trusted they'd bring me back to it when the time was right. It was about then that I had a *very* interesting dream.

A Naked Virgin Mary

In this dream, I was somewhere at a Net of Light Gathering, working with a group of women, and, as we meditated, several of them looked into a mirror and saw the Virgin Mary. But each time they glimpsed Her in the mirror, She was naked. In the dream, we began to discuss Her strange way of appearing, for none of us knew what to make of Mary showing up naked. One woman described the unclothed Mary as being in her 'pre-vessel' form, and after she said that, I heard myself say, "This is important. We must look at this idea of the Virgin not being clothed."

After I woke up, I thought more about the dream and realized that it was only patriarchy, after all, that had hung shame and wantonness (as if that in itself were bad) on being naked. "The word 'virgin' only denotes a pre-sexual state," I said. "This business of connoting shame is patriarchy's invention." Then I remembered the statues of Lakshmi, Parvati, and other forms of the Goddess that I'd seen when I was in India. These goddesses weren't always clothed and there was no shame there.

As these thoughts tumbled through my mind, I realized I wanted to explore this subject more. "When She's unclothed," I said, "She's pure shakti, pure life force…. not present for the benefit of man, but primal—Herself only. In Her unclothed state, She's not there to please men, to arouse men, to procreate, or 'do' anything. She simply IS." And then I remembered that the first time I met the Grandmothers, they'd told me, **"The feminine principle is first. Yin is primary."** And I recalled that when the feminine and masculine aspects of God are invoked in India, the first one called on is the feminine. And I'd witnessed this many times. *First is the Mother.*

It was interesting that, in this dream, we never discussed the fact that the women had looked into a mirror and seen, not a reflection of their own selves, but a reflection of the Virgin Mary. Because Mary was naked, we'd immediately jumped to *that* subject, not noticing that in looking at our own reflections, we had instead seen the Mother of God. This had slid right by our awareness and afterward, when I continued to reflect on the dream, it slid right by mine too. It took me some time to come upon this truth that had all the while been hiding in plain sight. Who was it who had actually been looking into that mirror and who was the one who was reflected there?

"We are breathing with you."

Shortly after this dream, I journeyed to the Grandmothers to ask for a message we needed to hear at this time. We put out a Net of Light newsletter every few weeks, and since it was time for a new message, we needed their direction.

"We are not distant from you," they responded as they bored their eyes into mine. **"We are not apart from you. In fact, we are so present, that at this moment we are breathing you. At *this* moment,"** they repeated and I swallowed hard, wilting a bit under the intensity of their gaze.

"You are one with us. You hold the power of the Divine Feminine," they reminded me. **"You are the pure, loving energy of yin and so are we. You are *that* just as we are *that*."** I looked up at them when I heard this, the naked Virgin Mary dream flashing in my mind. Here again was that theme—we are one with God. We are divine.

"Close your eyes," the Grandmothers said and gave me a secret smile. "Call on us, and let yourself drop into deep contact with us. We are always with you, but you've forgotten this. And because you've forgotten, you continue to pray, beseech, and beg us or other forms of God to hear you. *We hear you*," they said, leaning so close to me that our noses almost touched. "We hear you loud and clear. How could we not when we're present inside you? At this very moment, we're breathing you," they laughed. "Can anyone be closer than breath?

"Why do you persist in believing that God is distant from you?" they asked me, their brows furrowed. "Separate from you? Above you? Somewhere off in the distance? Where do these crazy ideas come from?" they asked, lifting their palms skyward. "They don't come from us," they said. "So where *do* they come from? Who tells you, you are separate from God? And why do you believe such a miserable fantasy?" I could only stare at them, open mouthed. "Where DO these ideas come from?" I asked myself.

"We know the truth," they said, their heads nodding up and down, "and deep in your heart, you also know the truth." Now I leaned forward in anticipation. I couldn't wait to hear what they were going to say next. "The truth is this," they said: "*It is not possible for God's creation to be separated from God. Creator and creation are always linked. God, in whatever form you love, is with you at every moment of your life.*" And having said this, they silently regarded me.

Finally, they said, "Stop this charade of separation!" and wagged their fingers in my face. "After all," they said, "we stand with you, sit with you, sleep with you, ride in the car with you, work with you, laugh and cry with you. We are *always* with you, so when you persist in telling yourself that you're all alone, you couldn't be more wrong."

Then they took a step away from me, and with playful looks, said, "Let's start having some fun together. Why not?" they asked, daring me to disagree. "Begin by acknowledging our presence with you," they said. "Do this right away, and, once you've done it, keep on doing it. Do it all day long," they said. "We're *always* with you'; *don't you get that?* And since we're always with you, you might as well start paying attention to us.

"Talk to us, sing to us, complain to us, love us, and allow us to love you," they said. "We're here all the time. Of course, if you insist

on it, you can continue to ignore us," they rolled their eyes, **"but if you'd rather enjoy yourself, we could start having some wonderful times together. And we could get busy doing the things that need doing."** Then they flung their hands in the air, threw back their heads and shouted, **"Enough of this separation nonsense!"**

Later that day, after I had more time to think about what had transpired on this journey, I said to myself, "Boy, sometimes the Grandmothers are right in your face with these truths, and sometimes they're just the opposite—really subtle." This time they hadn't been subtle at all but had reminded me that by holding myself separate from them, separate from God, I was preventing myself from melting into the oneness of yin. After I thought about that for a while, it came to me that if the Grandmothers are in fact with me all the time, in me, breathing me every moment of my life, the fiction of being apart from God is just that—fiction. THIS is why in the dream of Mary none of us even noticed that instead of our own face in the mirror, we'd seen the face of the Mother of God. This *is* who we are.

In the years that I'd worked with them, the Grandmothers had always talked about yin, and now they were showing me its primal nature. The first time they appeared as I walked beside the beach, they told me, **"Yin is first,"** pointing out that before we can have anything else, we must have the bedrock of the Mother. **"Yin is,"** they had said, and now, all these years later, it was finally dawning on me that *yin is the state of being at one with the Mother.* We are yin; we're the Divine Mother Herself. That's it. That's the 'truth' the Grandmothers wanted to share.

"Love is not a subject to be understood."

After this message, almost a month went by before I returned to them again. There were Net of Light Gatherings coming up to prepare for, songs to put together and messages to write, so, instead of journeying, I let myself fold into these tasks and kept busy with them for quite a while.

I'd taken the Grandmothers at their word and now included them in *everything* I did. This gave me the pleasure of their company all the time, and I was beginning to register the happiness that came from living every day with them. As it turned out, this way of living suited me fine.

So, I happily immersed myself in my work and remained immersed in it—until again I felt that familiar nudge to return to them. The Grandmothers were calling. It was time to learn more.

"We're going to talk to you today about love," they said as soon as I saw them, peering at me over the tops of their noses. Today they were wearing colorful dresses, and now they began to dance together, weaving an in-and-out pattern together as they spoke to me. "Yes, Grandmothers," I said as I watched them dancing, thrilled to be with them again. **"This topic of love,"** they said, **"is one of which you have little understanding,"** and when I heard this, I stood up a little bit straighter. Now I *really* wanted to learn.

"Though you say the word 'love' many times a day, sing about it, long for it, and wonder about it, you don't understand it," they shook their heads as they spoke. **"Most people never will,"** they said, looking hard at me to be sure I got their point. **"And that's not important,"** they added. "Not important?" I echoed. "What do you mean, 'not important'?" **"What *is* important,"** they replied, giving me a cool look, **"is that you *live* it, that you *live* love.**

"Love," they explained, **"is not a subject to be understood. It's not something to strive for, worry about, regret, or fear. *Love is*,"** they said, and as they spoke, they spread their arms so wide I thought they might lift off. **"Love is the force that holds your planet in its orbit. And it's the only thing that will truly give you pleasure. You don't have to understand it,"** they shook their heads, **"and it's a good thing you don't, because rare is the person who does. We repeat,"** they said, **"*love is*. You move into a state of love each time you're willing to open yourself to it. That's all there is to do. Your willingness to open to love without needing to understand it automatically invites love in,"** they said. Now I was hanging on their every word.

"It's the ego that demands to understand love," the Grandmothers said, **"the ego that questions love and tries to codify and explain it. 'Should I love that one?' it asks. 'Are *they* worthy? Am *I* worthy?"** The Grandmothers laughed uproariously and said, **"Love *never* asks why, nor does it hold back. Love simply gives itself, gives itself at every opportunity."**

Then taking my hands in theirs, they looked deep into my eyes and said, **"We assure you that if you want to be happy, you must follow love's lead. Let go of all your judgments, hesitancy, and fears about it.**

You need to make the decision to love and then plunge into it. Plunge in no matter what, plunge into love everywhere, and plunge in at all times." "Yes, Grandmothers," I whispered, overcome by the image of myself 'plunging' into one unknown after another. I wondered if I had the courage for that.

"First love your own dear self," they said, and as they spoke, they reached out to me and wrapped me in a tight hug. Rocking me back and forth with them, they held me close to their breasts and said, **"Have compassion for the innocent one you are and then have that same compassion for your fellow wanderers on earth."** And when they said this, the truth of it, the truth of *everyone's* innocence, hit me in the heart. And it felt so BIG, so noble, so godly that it made me cry.

"No one 'deserves' to be loved," they shook their heads as they continued. **"If that were so, not one of you would pass the qualifications test. You deserve to love and be loved simply because you are who you are. That's enough,"** they said, their heads nodding. **"You are who you are and so we love you.**

"Please begin now to relate to yourself like this," the Grandmothers said, their eyes full of compassion. **"Let go of the harsh judgments you've held about yourself and then do the same for others. Who you are *deserves* to be loved and *is* loved,"** they said, **"and your neighbors, friends and even (*and especially*) your so-called 'enemies' deserve this same love. So,"** they smiled sweetly, **"should you decide that you want to be happy, simply make the decision to love. *No matter what!*"** they added, making a hammering motion with their fists. **"And once you make that decision,"** they laughed, **"life will present you with an endless stream of opportunities to love. In fact,"** they said, **"you can be sure that one will appear today."**

This lesson on love gave me a lot to think about. **"Plunge into love,"** the Grandmothers said. **"Choose love with no qualifications whatsoever. Be open to the possibilities all around you."** "Yikes!" I said to myself. "This stuff is not for the faint of heart."

"Don't be afraid when these people die."

It was about this time that Nelson Mandela died. I remember because I was on the lookout for the possibilities to love that the Grandmothers had stirred up in me when I heard the news of his passing. For me,

Mandela had been an example of love in action, and so I felt a wave of sadness when I heard that he was no longer with us.

I remember thinking, "Now we've lost another of the truly Great Ones, those who come to earth now and then and grace us with an example of the reach of love. There had been only a few examples like this in my lifetime, and each time one of these people left the earth, I grieved. *"Who's left to guide and inspire us now?"* I'd ask myself. I remember feeling like this when Mother Teresa died. These great-souled ones are rare, and when they go, we know we've lost something.

"**Don't be afraid when these people die,**" the Grandmothers said to me, interrupting my musings. "**Love will always fill the gap. When a five hundred-watt bulb burns out, one hundred five-watt bulbs immediately flick on. You may hardly notice these smaller bulbs at first, but a plethora of small bulbs lights up the darkness just as well as one large one. And when they beam together into the Net of Light, they *really* light up the darkness.**

"**There's no dearth of light and love on your beloved planet today,**" the Grandmothers said, "**and there never will be. When the Great Ones pass on, they are immediately released to spread their light into the cosmos, to broadcast it over a wider range than was possible for them when they were here on earth. No longer confined to the limits of one small form, the light of these Great Ones can radiate farther and wider.**

"**As their light moves outward, it illumines the universe (including the earth). And the moment that happens, your sometimes more modest lights come together to dispel the darkness around you, to encourage and empower one another, and to light the path for those who will come after you. You're one of the lights we're talking about,**" the Grandmothers said, "**and many of you are glowing far brighter than you think you are. You may measure at ten watts, twenty-five watts, or at a hundred watts or more, but whatever your potency at this moment,**" they said, "**you are burning clear and true and your power will increase over time.**

"**It's your job to shine your light,**" they said. "**It is also your delight. Shining is your nature,**" the Grandmothers said, "**because, after all, shining is what a light does.**"

I loved what they'd said about this and found myself returning to this message over and over again.

"Male and female, female and male. These are only roles."

The yearly Net of Light Gathering in California would be coming up again soon, and people were flying in from around the world for it. When the opening day arrived, we were surprised to find several men, friends of a Net of Light group leader, waiting for us at the front door of the Gathering. And they'd come bearing roses! We'd had no idea they were coming, and when the men told us they'd come because they wanted to 'live the Grandmothers' message,' we cried.

Men had participated at the Net of Light Gatherings in Europe, but only four or five had ever come to one in America. In fact, in America it was rare for a man to even attend one of our monthly meetings. Having this group show up like this was so unexpected that as soon as the Gathering was over, I went to the Grandmothers to ask what it was all about.

The Grandmothers seemed to study me for a moment and then, giving me a knowing look, said, "**All** are divine," drawing the 'all' out. "**All,**" they repeated. "**Male and female, female and male. These,**" they explained, "**are only roles, a type of 'clothing' you put on when you come into an incarnation on earth. But now it's time for you to move beyond this old familiar 'clothing' and stop fully identifying yourself with it.**

"**Fasten your hearts to us or to any form of Divinity that you love,**" the Grandmothers said, "**and this will help you move beyond the limited societal and self-imposed roles you've been playing. You've been conditioned to believe in these roles,**" they said and shook their heads, bemused, "**but *you are beyond roles!* Neither man *nor* woman!**" they said. "**You're not limited in *any* way. You are divine. That's your true identity, so put your heart and energy into *that* and claim it. Listen to our teachings with your heart,**" they said, and they patted me gently. "**We've come to move you further along the path than you have yet gone. We've come to lead you to who you truly are. Do you want that?**" they asked, their eyes bright as they peered into mine. I then looked back at them and dumbly nodded, "Yes."

"**Good!**" they said, rubbing their hands together as if to say, "Well then, let's get started." "**You can use our teachings or any teachings that appeal to you to raise yourself to the truth of your own being.**

There are many paths to the Divine, but we're here to teach you something specific. We're telling you that in essence you are not a man or a woman. That is not *you*. You are not limited to any role," they added; "It's time for you to let roles go and claim your divinity."

After they spoke these words, there was nothing but silence for a couple of minutes while I simply breathed and attempted to take it all in. Finally, I heard myself say, "Okay, Grandmothers, I think I get what you're telling me. I get what you're saying and…at the same time," I shook my head as I continued to think it over, "I know most people don't think like this. Neither women nor men," I said. "Nobody thinks like this. Everybody sees themselves as their gender just the way I've always seen myself. So how?" I began, "how can we reach women and men with this message? If we're going to do this, we'll need some practical directions from you."

"We'll talk about the men first," they said, letting me know this was where we would start. "Men need to feel loved," they said. "They need to feel *deeply* loved. They need to feel like they've come home, and once they get this sense of homecoming," they said, "they'll be able to let down the defenses they've been carrying." "Yes, Grandmothers," I agreed, listening intently. "I can see that would help, and I know they have a hard time being vulnerable and letting down their defenses. But is this really for us to do?" I asked. "How can we as women make it easier for them to do that? How can we help them experience being loved like this? I mean, this can't be a sexual or a romantic love," I said. "Not that, but rather loved with a compassionate, overreaching love."

"Enfold them," the Grandmothers responded. "Accept men as they are at this moment…not for anything they've done or anything they will do, but for their very being. This is what they need," they said. "Accept them just as they are as human beings, at this moment in time. Receiving this sort of acceptance from women, especially from older women," the Grandmothers said, "will mean a great deal to them."

As they were speaking, suddenly I saw a man who was sitting in a circle with a group of women. He was surrounded by them, and the women were holding him as they mothered him and flooded him with love. And as I watched this scene unfold, the hardness around the man began to melt away. His face softened and I saw tears start up in his eyes.

"I see what's happening in this scene, Grandmothers," I said, "and what's happening here is good, but is there more than this?" "**Of course,**" they said, "**much more. But first of all, you must ready and steady your own heart for this work. Women will be the leaders in this,**" they said. "**It can be no other way. Because women *can* more easily access love, you will be the ones to be our instruments. For example,**" they said, "**should a man show up at one of your meetings, go to him and welcome him. Quietly flood him with love and acceptance and welcome him in. However, always use discrimination as you communicate with men.**

"**In some ways you will be the mothers here,**" the Grandmothers said, and I felt myself startle. "The mothers?" I asked. "**The mothers and the big sisters,**" they explained, "**the ones more practiced in living in love. In order for a change to occur between the sexes, you must reach out to men. This is something that women *can* do,**" they nodded, smiling benignly, "**especially older women. You *can* take them in, in a non-sexual, non-competitive way. You can embrace them in your heart.**

"**At their core, these men are like younger brothers to you,**" the Grandmothers explained, "**younger brothers who are worn to the bone by the ravages of yang energy. Younger brothers who long for peace. Help them discover peace within themselves,**" they said. "**And, if at times they act inappropriately, remember who *you* are. You are the elder; you are the wiser one. Should that happen, then take charge of the situation and bring them up short. Remember,**" they said, "**most of them are *younger* brothers—not yet grown up.**"

"I see some possible difficulties with this, Grandmothers," I said. "Men are accustomed to dominating, to trying to take over and 'be the boss' even when they don't know what they're talking about. Often they're blinded by their egos," I said. "What do we do when that happens?" "**Expect this to happen at first,**" the Grandmothers said, "**and stand steady when it does. When a man strays from the path, return him to our teachings. Sometimes you will need to set firm limits with him.**" And shaking their heads back and forth, they said, "*You must lead. It can be no other way.*"

"When you say '*you*' here, Grandmothers, are you talking to me, I asked them, "or are you speaking to all women?" "**We are speaking mostly to you now,**" they said, "**but also to the women in our groups.**

Great numbers of them have accrued enough power at this time to be able to deal with men as men begin to try their wings with our work." I waited to hear more then, but this was all they would say about the subject and soon they let me know that our time together was at an end.

After this journey was over, I found myself thinking about it all the time. "Ugh!" I groaned. I wasn't the least bit eager to jump into this one. "This is a formidable task the Grandmothers are laying before us, and we've only begun to scratch the surface of it. Ugh!" I said again as I shivered. "I'm sure they'll tell us more about it in the future…as we go, I guess," I added. "*I sure hope they do.*" And because the thought of working with men like this continued to haunt me, before the week was out, I returned to my wise teachers to learn more.

"Men are only at the bare beginnings of comprehending the power of yin."

A young man came to dinner at our house the other night, a businessman in his thirties who's developing his family business. He is the son of an old acquaintance and he turned out to be what was once called 'a man of the world', a man who knows the ins and outs of business and politics across the globe. Smart, driven, a type-A personality, he talked about himself and his world the whole evening.

Afterward I mused about such an extreme case of self-involvement. The young man had been oblivious to anyone but himself. "Yang," I said to myself, "when it has no connection to the energy of yin really can't help itself nor can it be of any real help in the world. In fact, extreme self-involvement like this is bound to do damage." What I'd seen in this young man was out-of-balance yang energy seeking for something outside itself. He'd spent the whole evening pushing and thrusting himself outward on us with no concern for anyone or anything else. "This guy was not concerned or even aware of his own ground of being," I said to myself. The young man, I reflected, wasn't grounded in his humanity. He didn't actually experience his connection to others. In his mind, Roger and I were just there as an audience for him while, head up, he was busy charging onward. "Why," I asked myself then, "why this endless pushing onward?

"Of course, he wants money and power," I mused. "After all, that's all he talks about. But *why* is he craving money and power? Why is he oblivious to his humanity and to those around him? Why is he selling himself and others so short? What does he imagine all this money and power is going to do for him?

"Grandmothers," I said the next time I went to them, "about the men," and I was so focused on the subject I don't think I even said hello to them before I launched into it. "About what you said last time, Grandmothers," I said, "It's been much on my mind since then, and I want to learn more about it. I *need* to learn more," I said with a beseeching look, and they nodded their heads in understanding.

They held my eyes with theirs for a moment, and then they began to speak slowly and clearly, their eyes, willing me to understand. **"Men are only at the bare beginnings of comprehending the power of yin,"** they said. **"As yet they have but little wisdom,"** they shook their heads in compassion, **"and so they need your guidance. The man who came to dinner was lost. He is locked in a prison of yang striving. And the men who surprised you by showing up at the Net of Light Gathering in California have a lot of enthusiasm but little understanding of the Feminine Principle. And even less understanding of their place in it,"** they added, their faces serious. **"Those men will need you to lead them,"** they said, and stared pointedly at me. I swallowed hard when I saw their look. I wasn't sure I wanted this job.

"For a long time, men have been 'in charge' of the affairs of the world," the Grandmothers said. **"And because they're accustomed to thinking of themselves that way, they won't easily let go of the reins."** "Yes, Grandmothers," I said, sighing, "I know."

"They are accustomed to leading," they said, **"and will expect you to defer to them. But no more,"** they said, their faces unsmiling. **"Not at this time. Do not look to men to lead you. Do NOT look to them to lead,"** they repeated, their faces severe. **"Most of them are only boys,"** they explained, **"well-meaning boys, but boys nonetheless.**

"Listen to the men who say they are interested in our work. Listen to them a bit," they said, **"then step in and guide them. And then listen some more. Some of them think they know more than they do,"** the Grandmothers said. **"This is what out-of-control yang energy has done to men. It's made them arrogant. Don't be fooled by their 'take charge' attitude,"** they said, **"and don't be beguiled by charm or chivalrous ways,"** and now I recalled the men at the Gathering with their arms full of roses. **"Ask them about their *understanding*,"** the Grand-mothers said, eyeing me pointedly. **"Ask them what they're *learning* from our books. Always give them an opportunity to learn, and remember that's what they're there for—to learn. From us and from you,"** they said.

"Grandmothers," I said as I thought this over, "what part do men actually have to play in your work?" I was starting to wonder what this might be. Did they even have a role to play? **"A part that does not sit at the center of the work,"** the Grandmothers responded, **"a part that sits off to the side. As women, you must continue to go deep and you must go far with your growth. The in-depth work of infusing yin back into the earth is not for men to do, and as women open more to yin, men won't understand exactly what it is you're doing. At this point, dealing with the energy of yin is beyond their understanding, so you must do this job of deepening and you must do it alone.**

"Men can support you with encouragement and by 'guarding your back," the Grandmothers said, **"but the work of infusing yin into the planet is for women to do. Don't expect men to understand it. You will need to give up that desire. It is not for men to go deep into this work the way you must,"** they said. **"Don't try to explain it to them either. That's not necessary,"** they shook their heads. **"Just love them and ask for their help when you need it.**

"Let them support you with silent strength and when they're not working at supporting you, let them work with one another, build-ing trust among their brothers. For the most part, women already trust one another, so you needn't do the work of trust-building that men must do. Simply continue to nurture the woman-to-woman bond that already exists and together keep on moving forward. *Men are ancillary to our work*," the Grandmothers said. **"They can be very helpful. They can help make your work easier, but they're not neces-sary to the task at hand."**

"How then, Grandmothers, can we utilize men in this work and honor them in the process?" I asked. "We don't want them to feel overlooked and left out, and we can't let them into the work until they really 'get' it." **"Yes,"** the Grandmothers said, **"we know."** They paused then, seeming to think all this over, and then they said, **"Ask them to be present with you for particular ceremonies and activities. Ask them to 'hold the field' of yang energy in balance, to be a witness** and stand steady. Ask them to stay connected to the Net of Light. All this will educate them about the powerful love of the Mother. And, if they can do these things, they will provide a matrix for other men to plug into.

"As men hold the Net of Light, witness the work you women are doing, and, at the same time, contain and regulate the energy of yang that's moving through themselves, they will provide an example to many," the Grandmothers said. "They'll also become touchstones for countless beings within the invisible network of light that's supporting the world. Many men will benefit from the work that these men will do, and many women will breathe a sigh of relief that there are men like them, willing to work in a selfless way for the good of all. Then the Grandmothers said, "We remind you again that with this work women must lead. It can be no other way."

"Speak Truth."

I thought about this subject all the time. I couldn't get it out of my mind, and finally, on New Years' Eve, I journeyed back to the Grandmothers. "Grandmothers," I said, "the work you gave us when you first appeared was about the energy of yin and about bringing balance back to earth. Of bringing *everything* into balance. And, one struggle right now, one thing that's out of balance, is the relationship between men and women. I've asked you about this before and you haven't given me much. I don't understand why you haven't gone into this before, but I'm going to try again.

"There's great upheaval right now," I said, warming to my subject, "and women are speaking out about men who have harmed them. There's a lot of anger and a lot of push back. And, at the same time, Grandmothers, what all of us really want is balance and harmony, real harmony. However," I said, "we don't know how to get there. But because you are able to see us as we really are, I'm going to ask you something. Given the lack of understanding today between women and men, what is the most important thing for we women to learn? How can we have a better relationship with men and, at the same time, have a better relationship with one another?"

"When you speak to men and also when you speak to one another," the Grandmothers said, "speak from your heart. Speak the truth in a clear way, speak it in a kind way, a non-defamatory way. And when you open your mouth to speak of difficult issues, think of voicing the truth so that all generations can hear it. Speak only what you would be proud for those in the future to hear. And when you speak, think of the good that you want to take place on earth, not only for yourself but for all beings.

"If you think like this," they said, "your words won't wound as they otherwise might. You will be heard, and you won't waste your energy in anger and lashing out. Speak the truth. Speak it as a WOMAN—as *a woman of power*, which is what you are," they said, giving me a long, steady look. "A real woman— one who seeks the highest good for all beings.

"Whenever you come from this unselfish place," they said, "people will hear you. Be brave," they said, and then they stood quietly, studying me. "Say the things that are hard to say," they said and as I gazed back at their sober faces, I realized that what they were telling me now was of great importance. "Speak these things for the good of all," they continued. "Voice them for the good of your so-called enemies, for yourself, for the generations to come, and for those who came before you. Speak from this place of deep connection with all life. As you do this, you will honor all beings. People will hear you. They will listen and pay attention.

"In the past men have not listened to women," the Grandmothers said, shaking their heads. "They have ignored you and demeaned you, and you in turn have often ignored one another, sometimes even demeaned one another. And, as to lashing out at men," they added, wincing at the words, "don't waste your time on that any longer! Speak the truth clearly. Come forward with it," they said, and, after a thoughtful pause, added, "Stand up and be counted. Step forward and speak what needs to be said. Don't cower and hold back. And don't boast and call attention to yourself. Simply speak the truth— straight up!

"You are living with us now," the Grandmothers said, and I looked up at them in surprise. "We are with you now every day," they said. "You call on us constantly, and we respond. We are so deeply linked that now God is in your breath, in your blood, in your every thought, word and deed. And when this is the way you live, when this visceral connection with the Divine is present in you, the truth will always come out. You won't need to plan what you will say. It will simply come out of your mouth. Easily!" they declared. "Clearly! And at every moment," they said, their heads nodding up and down. "The Divine," they explained, "which is what you really are—IS truth. And truth must be expressed.

"We are happy that you've come to this place at last," they said, "very happy for you to experience what you call 'speaking truth to power.' This is what is needed now. In speaking truth to power, you will find the great love, the great service that seeks the highest good for all.

"Truth is rolling forward now," they said, lifting their arms expansively, "rolling up and rolling forward. And you are part of that momentum," they said and then began to hum. "Hummmmmmm," they droned for several seconds. Then they sighed contentedly and added, "We are happy for you. You have worked hard to get to this place of power. You've been stalwart and brave and true, and it shows!" they declared. "We salute you."

"Oh!" I said as I bid them goodbye. "I feel so happy, Grandmothers. I feel so filled with goodness, filled with happiness and peace and gratitude. Filled with all of it," I said, wrapping my arms around myself. "Amen, amen, amen," I whispered under my breath. "Grandmothers," I said, "you are magnificent."

"Change of this magnitude will require an entirely new way of living."

After these last few journeys to the Grandmothers, I felt that maybe, just maybe, I was on a roll with this subject of women and men. It had been awhile since the Grandmothers had shared this much information with me about the difficulties between the sexes. Some puzzle pieces were starting to fit now. So, maybe, I thought, this is a good time to try again to learn more from them.

"Grandmothers," I said the next time I stood before them, "you've shared a lot of valuable information lately, and it's been really helpful. However," I said as I thought it over, "as a woman, my relationship with, as well as my understanding of men, is still lacking something. I'd like to learn more about the divide between the sexes. I'd like to understand more. Please let me try again."

They didn't respond but only stood there, looking at me, so I took in a breath and plunged ahead. "Women," I began, "feel let down by men. I often feel like that," I admitted, "and so do others. Many times, we're shocked by their selfish behavior. We get angry at them for the way they treat us; we don't trust them. And yet the only thing this anger and distrust of them does is create a greater sense of separation. So, Grandmothers," I said, "how can we as women take a realistic view of men and still like them? How can we see them the way they are, warts and all, and still be able to help heal the wounds between females and males?"

"**This is a big order,**" the Grandmothers said, and slowly shook their heads. "**You're asking a lot—a lot of yourself and a lot of us.**" But Grandmothers," I said, "I wouldn't be asking this of you if I already knew the answer. I'm asking because I really *want* to relate to men with respect. I love men, even like most of them, but their behavior as a gender is terrible. They are doing a lot of damage.

"Yes," they said. "**They are. They're lost. They don't know how to be men now; they're not sure what that even means. A lot of them are still acting out old roles that used to work for the male gender but aren't valid any longer. Many of the old roles that men would like to return to aren't valuable for society now. For example, today's world has little need for hunters and classic warriors. And, on top of that, today machines do most of the tasks that men used to do.**

"**Though many of the so-called nurturing tasks that women have always performed, like nursing and teaching, are still open, the classic men's tasks have been drying up. There's not much left for men to do. Little REAL work,**" they said. "**Numbers of men occupy themselves by moving money around, buying and selling, and working in the technical industries. Those occupations are still viable. Other men provide law enforcement and military service, and some work in construction. These are some of the classic male work roles, but few of these fields are expanding.**

"**Men today see their world shrinking, and this causes some of them to try to turn back the clock, hoping to return to a simpler, more traditional, more 'manly' way of life. They're frightened of all this change, frightened of what's become of the world they've known. You can see them contracting in fear as they try to dominate those around them (mainly women) and lash out at anyone they** see as an 'enemy.' Dictatorships are sprouting up all over the world today as 'strong men' grasp at power, hang on for dear life, and bully those 'beneath' them." The Grandmothers took in a breath and said, "You are asking a lot with your question.

"This is a time of change… Great change," they said. "You haven't seen the likes of this before. Change of this magnitude will require an entirely new way of living," they said, "so, you must be patient with yourselves. And you must be patient with men, too. If you can remember that men are frightened—deeply frightened—you will be better able to deal with them. We have told you that you can't look to men to lead you now because at this time, they are not capable of that. Instead of looking to them to show you the way, for guidance, you must turn within yourself.

Constance and Tim

We end this chapter with a letter from a Net of Light Beacon in Southern California. Constance and her partner, Tim, had just returned from a trip to Italy, and what struck me most in this letter was the way the relationship between Constance and Tim seemed to work. Here was an illustration of how yin and yang *can* work together.

She wrote:

> "This is something that may interest you. We just returned from visiting a friend in Italy. In the weeks prior to our departure, I had a dream about my Italian friend, Silvia's, ancestors and realized that I needed and wanted to know more about how to communicate with ancestors in general. This surprised me as I'd never had much interest in working with Ancestors—even though they show up routinely where we meet to do spiritual work at our home. But that dream about these Italian ancestors set off a cascade of events that began to prepare us for our trip to Italy.
>
> "In the days before we left, it was uncanny how the Grandmothers' books opened up to where I needed to learn more about the Ancestors. There was also a big surge in spreading the Net of Light, giving empowerments, and in communicating with the Ancestors in the spiritual meetings at home. But this time Tim, my partner, joined me in these activities, whereas in the past I've usually done them on my own—which can be depleting. As we prepared for the

trip, we got a foreshadowing of how it feels to share these gifts when the embodied masculine joins in the process.

"A week later, in the midst of the excitement of exploring Italy, I forgot all about this preparation, but then, one morning in Florence, Tim and I decided to walk over to a historic, yet still active, synagogue near our hotel. I had visited it almost ten years ago, but on this morning, we were among the very few people there.

"We had to walk up four flights of stone steps to visit the small museum on the top floor and I was the first to enter and quickly became intrigued by the artifacts of my Jewish faith. Tim entered right behind me and the minute he did, he was stopped in his tracks by a heavy density that enveloped him. This man, who never complains, told me he felt such a heaviness in his chest, he thought he was having a heart attack. We looked at one another, and intuitively knew that this was not true, but that he was perceiving the heaviness of the space we were in.

"While he held those physical sensations in awareness, we both began spreading the Net of Light, calling to our ancestors and the ancestors of the land. His physical discomfort slowly dissipated as more ancestors than we could count lined up before us. After asking if they wished to receive the Grandmothers' Empowerment, I began passing empowerments to the feminine, and the cloak of comfort to the masculine until I recalled that they could then pass it on to those who were standing behind them. They seemed so eager and interested to receive this energy, as well as eager to assist us. It was mind boggling to witness them passing the empowerment on down the ancestral line to what seemed like infinity.

"It was equally fascinating to experience this in tandem with my partner. In his masculine, Tim held this space in security and stability so that I was free to communicate with the ancestors. He provided safety, protection, and support, while also holding the heaviness that existed in that space. This would have been a very different experience without his presence. Here was balanced Feminine and Masculine in Unity Consciousness, spreading healing Light to the world. Not only was it easier to work in this way rather than doing it on my own, it was more balanced, gratifying and unified.

"Tim and I then went downstairs to the main sanctuary, and saw that there were still bayonet holes in the Ark of the Covenant where the Nazis had violated this sacred space during WWII. We continued to spread the Net of Light and witness the Ancestors continuing to pass on empowerments. We ended our visit by casting the Net of

Light at the Holocaust memorial in front of the synagogue, commemorating all those who had been killed during the War.

"As we left the area, two Jewish women sold us loaves of traditional Jewish bread, challah, that is used in Friday night Shabbat services. A gift of sustenance. Then we passed by a young, fully armed guard, standing in front of the synagogue, a reminder of the imbalance in the world that we were now infusing with Love.

"A few hours later, in the Florence train station as we prepared to leave, I went through a major emotional upheaval—traumatic and overpowering. Tim and I dealt with it as best we could, and my tears rained down throughout the long train ride. It felt like this was related to the experience at the synagogue, and how my body and psyche had been triggered and were now releasing. Thankfully, the next day was scheduled as a rest day.

Do we really know how this type of experience affects us on so many levels? I'm not sure, but being with each other helped, and we grew as a couple."

Gratefully,
Constance and Tim

Chapter Two

"All over the earth, destructive energy is rising to the surface."

The next time I went to the Grandmothers, I was terribly upset. There was a health crisis raging in Africa that was killing thousands of people, and there were daily blood baths all over the Middle East. Suffering and upheaval were taking place all over the globe, and I was so upset by it all that this time I went to my teachers for reassurance. I needed something to lift me up, encourage me and help me keep my head on straight. The Grandmothers, however, had their own view of things on earth.

"**The world appears to be spiraling downward,**" they said to me and nodded impassively. "**Wars, terror, and violence are springing up all over the earth and fear is having a field day.**" "Yes, Grandmothers," I gulped, "that's pretty much it," and when I spoke, one of them wrapped an arm around me to comfort me. "**Although all this and more is happening now,**" they said and gave me a look full of compassion, "**we assure you that *things are not as they seem*. When we first appeared, we told you about the times that were coming.**" Looking at me over the tops of their noses, they said, "**and now they're here. This is it.**

"**All over the earth, destructive energy is rising up to the surface,**" they said, "***and this is no accident*. It's coming up to be transmuted and eliminated,**" they explained, **and while this is going on, we ask you to stand steady, observe it as it shows itself, and give thanks that at last, it's coming to the surface. Dark energy has repressed the love and life on your planet for a very long time,**" the Grandmothers said, shaking their heads sadly, "**so this rising of evil *must* occur. We're** asking you to bear witness to it as it shows itself and hold the Net of Light for your planet."

I'd been listening with great intensity, and now I saw the dark energy they were talking about. It was lying still, deep down in the muddy bottom of a lake, while off and on a finger of it oozed its way up to the surface to swirl the waters. I had a sense that until recently, this oozing mass had been dormant—sleeping at the bottom of the lake. But no more! Now there was movement beneath the mud and I shuddered as I watched its snakelike ripples rising.

"Call on us or on any form of the Divine you love," the Grandmothers said, interrupting my horrified fascination, "and call on the Net of Light. The radiance of the Net will hold you safe as all this rises up to the surface. You can let yourself fall back into the embrace of the Net of Light now. Allow it to hold you," they said. "And, as you give your fearful feelings over to the Net, remember that its golden strands are holding everyone and everything on earth. It's even holding this nasty ooze you're watching," they said and I shuddered again. "Every time you call on the Net of Light, it automatically takes over," the Grandmothers explained, "so you can count on it to steady and uplift *everything.*

"Work slowly and purposefully with all that's rising into awareness now. It's coming up to be released," they reminded me, "so each time you become aware of some rising darkness, call on the Net of Light. If you approach this work like this, in a patient way, you'll be able to magnify the power of the Net for yourself and for every living thing. So, each time a new horror is revealed," they said, "call on the Net of Light.

"As all this seeming destruction takes place on earth, we will cherish and protect you," the Grandmothers said. Then they motioned me over to them. "Sit with us now," they said, and reaching out their arms, they drew me onto their laps. "Take time to be with us now," they said. "Take time to allow us to love you. Take time for that," they said and held me close to their breasts as they gently stroked my back.

"While all the suppressed pain on your planet rises to the surface, we will comfort you. You are not alone. No!" they shook their heads. "We are with you at every moment of your life. We'll attend you day and night. We are," they smiled, "the very breath in your body.

"It will be new for you to work with us patiently like this because you've spent most of your life in a rush. *'Keeping busy,'*" they said with rueful smiles. "**After all,**" they added, "**you've been conditioned to chase after the things of the world. Chase after money, after ideas, thoughts (both 'good' and 'bad' ones),**" they said, "**and yet in the long run, all this chasing does is make you tired. It makes you feel lonely and afraid.**" They shrugged their shoulders then as if to say, 'Well, what do you expect?' and added, "**Take a break from that now, and instead, spend some time with us. We're here,**" they gestured, opening their arms wide. "**We stand before you, behind you, and beside you. At this very moment, we're holding and enfolding you.**"

They stepped back then and regarded me for a moment. "**The things of this world are insubstantial at best,**" they said, "**so why spend so much energy pursuing them?**" And when they said this, my mouth dropped open. I didn't know how to respond. "**We know you've been taught to chase after the things of the world,**" they laughed. "**You've been trained to do that,**" they shook their heads, "**and so you persist in it even though the world *'out there'* is falling apart. But focusing your attention *'out there,'*"** they said, "**especially at a time like this, is robbing you of peace, robbing you of strength.**"

"**If you just sit quietly with us and call on the Net of Light, and do it for only a few minutes every day, you'll feel much better,**" they said. "**If you do this, you'll experience our love, and the feeling of being loved will buoy you up. Then, as you allow love to flow back and forth from us to you, from you to us, the way love naturally does, this flow will allow us to take all your worries away.**"

It's simple," the Grandmothers said. "**We promise to take care of everything for you. When you came into this life, you arrived carry-ing with you the presence of Divinity. The Divine permeates every part of you—your mind, your feelings, your body and thoughts. It permeates the very air you breathe. At every moment you are *that* close to us, *that* close to every form of the Divine,**" they said, pinch-ing a thumb and finger together to illustrate. "**But you don't know it,**" they said and shook their heads. Their eyes filled with tears then at the thought of my suffering, at the thought of all human suffering.

"**Practice just sitting with us now,**" they said. "**Think of looking into our eyes while you feel our arms around you. Do this and then rest in this *'receiving place'* for a while. We promise that each time you drop into this receptive mode, all the things you long for, all the** things you want—both material and non-material—will be taken care of. It will happen that way," they explained, "because every time you relax like this and let go, you allow us to take over. It's as easy as that. It's those old habits of worry, all the *'trying,'* that gets in the way of you receiving your heart's desire. We're standing right here, and we're ready to give it to you," they said, gesturing broadly, "so start practicing receiving. Start letting go of all that trying," they said. "Do it for just a few minutes every day."

Then they said, "Many years ago we told you: 'You do the living and we do the giving' and when you heard that, you laughed. Well…," they smiled mischievously, "since we never tell a lie, you can count on those words. So go ahead and try it!"

After this journey was over and I'd returned to my ordinary life, I thought a lot about what they'd said. I knew the Grandmothers were right about me needing to take time to be with them, so finally I said to myself, "Oh, what the heck! I'll try it." But knowing myself the way I do, I realized that I would need to do this first thing in the morning. Sit down with the Grandmothers *before* I began my day; otherwise, I'd get absorbed in something and forget about it. "This will take some discipline," I said to myself, and as it turned out, I was right. Setting aside time to practice like this did take discipline, and… the discipline paid off. After just three days of starting my morning with receiving from them, I was calmer and more focused. I also noticed that I was spending less time worrying, less time spinning my wheels. And I was enjoying myself more.

I probably did this morning practice for at least a month before I allowed my attention to become pulled away by other things. And after that I didn't always begin the day with this exercise, but since I now knew what a difference it made, whenever I found myself getting distracted, irritable, or anxious, I quickly sat down with the Grandmothers. And each time I did that, because of the generous beings they are, they accepted me with open arms.

"Saturate your days and nights with the presence of the Divine."

The next time I journeyed to them, as soon as I saw them, I said, "Grandmothers, all of us who are involved in this work with you need confidence in ourselves. We need to know that we *can* magnify the power of the Net of Light, that we *can* stay the course during these rough times we're living through. I was once again feeling the negative bombardment of the news—worrying about where our country was heading. Worrying about where the world was heading. "I know this is a sort of general request for me to make to you," I apologized, "but it's the best I can do right now, so I'm leaving the rest up to you."

"**Wait on us,**" they replied, not missing a beat. "**Wait on the Divine,**" they said. "**As soon as you wake in the morning, think of us, or of any form of the Source you love. And,**" they said, "**if you wake in the middle of the night, make use of that time too, by turning your hearts and thoughts to the Divine. Then keep them there!** *Begin to fuse yourself with divinity.* **At this time on earth, don't attempt to live apart from us even for a moment,**" they said and gave me a severe look. "**To stay steady within the shifting energy on earth now, to keep yourself in a stance of power, you must align with divinity. Every day!**

"**Life will attempt to distract you from your focus, and sometimes it will succeed. But,**" they emphasized, "**as soon as you recall your intention to be at one with the Source, then return your thoughts to us. Your alignment with divinity will keep you safe and sane during these unsafe, insane times.**

"**After you've called on the Divine, then go out and live your life,**" they nodded encouragingly. "**Do the things you want to do. Don't hold back from anything that feels right to you, but before you act, get in the habit of thinking of your connection to the Divine.**

"**Post little reminders to yourself to turn within, and place them where you'll see them. Place sacred pictures or objects in your line of vision at home, put reminders on your phone, play sacred chants, songs, and prayers in the car and where you work. Quietly at work,**" they smiled. "**Call on us before meals, before bedtime, and upon awakening.** *Saturate* **your days and nights with the presence of the Divine.**

"**Take time to feel our love for you, and once you've felt it, then silently pass that love on to others. This will be easy for you to do because generosity is part of your nature.** "**So,**" they said, "**go ahead and express the purity of your heart and enjoy yourself while you're at it!** The connection you build with divinity at this time will set up a force field around you that will protect you from the negative energy that's rising all over your planet."

Then, holding their arms out to me—to us, the Grandmothers said, **"We will do this with you. After all, you are NOT alone! We're all on this adventure, so we will ride out this storm together."**

"All is changing. Nothing will be the same. Nothing!"

Not long after I received this message, I began to feel that something new was on its way to me. It was just an inkling I had, a vague feeling, but it kept returning to my mind. Two dear friends from Holland were due to arrive for a visit soon and together we'd planned a road trip through the Southwest—Joshua Tree, Sedona, Montezuma's Well, and the Grand Canyon. And because it had always seemed to me that the Grand Canyon was somehow connected to the lower world, I decided to go to Bear, my helping animal spirit, to ask him about the purpose for this trip.

It had been several months since I'd last visited him, and as I thought about that I began to wonder if he would be there to meet me. And, as these thoughts came to mind, again I sensed it was time to move in a new direction with the Grandmothers' work—time to go to new territory. A feeling *was* building. It was time for me to learn more, to go where I'd never been before. Excitement, along with a swell of commitment, was rising inside me.

I fastened my mind on Bear, telegraphed him that I was coming, and, the next thing I knew, I was falling down my opening into the lower world. Down and down I plunged until at last, shooting my arms over my head, I dove headlong into the familiar river there, quickly hauled myself into a canoe and paddled like mad to reach the shore. But this time as I ran the canoe aground, I realized that I was holding my paddle up before me like a French voyager from long ago who was trying to steady himself.

Bear was waiting for me at the water's edge. He had his paws on his hips, and as I fastened my eyes on his beloved face, I said, "Bear, at last I'm ready to learn more. Please teach me the purpose of this trip to the Southwest. Why do I feel such an urge to go there?"

He motioned me to follow him, and then he lumbered away. Today he was walking upright on two legs and as he went forward, he looked a little like a cartoon bear. Nevertheless, I followed in his footsteps, walking behind him for what seemed a very long time. In fact, it went on for so long that I began to worry that maybe nothing special would come from this journey after all. Maybe I was just going to follow and follow and not really get anywhere.

As we trudged onward, I was watching his every move when suddenly a flock of birds flew in between us. They were a brilliant blue color, graceful and vivid, but again, almost cartoonish in appearance. I was wondering what all this was about when in a flash everything around me grew bright—very bright. "It feels like I'm inside a Disney movie," I said, and when I looked around to see what else was appearing, a rumbling sound began—a rolling roar was rising up from the Grand Canyon itself. Soon there were tremors and the ground began to shake as if in an earthquake, and then a fierce wind began to blow. To howl! "The earth is shaking!" I cried, "and it's starting to storm." Then I gasped and the word, "Wow!" escaped me as I was blasted by a hot flash. Now I was burning up.

"**Changing and changes,**" a deep voice intoned. "**All is changing and nothing will be the same. Nothing!**" it declared, and after a pause, "**You need to prepare.**"

"Prepare? Prepare?" I gulped. "What does that mean?" Now, not only was I hot, I was frightened, and, not knowing what else to do, I began to repeat my question for this journey, chanting it over and over again. "What is the purpose of this trip? What is the purpose of this trip?" Repeating and repeating it until at last, the voice replied, "**Preparedness is the purpose of this trip.**"

"Uh...," I stammered, "Uh, I don't think I know what that means." "**You will learn,**" it said, and when I heard that, I wasn't hot any longer; now I was shaking with cold.

Then Bear spoke. "**You need to begin now,**" he said. "**Begin to harmonize yourself with the earth. Walk barefooted on Her, talk to the Mother, drum for Her, and sit expectantly and wait for Her.**" I think he said more than that, but somehow, I wasn't able to retain it. I must have gone into a state of shock then, as the last thing I remember him saying is, "**WAIT!**" and then, "**Go slow, go deep. Go into sacred territory.**"

"I will!" I promised him when the drumbeat finally stopped and the journey was over. " I'll go into sacred territory. I'll do all of that."

Though I still didn't understand why, clearly this up-coming trip to the Southwest was somehow important. Babs, Lilium and I would leave for the Southwest in November and since it was now only July, there was plenty of time to prepare for it. Perhaps Bear would be my guide and companion for this new phase of the work.

"This garbage has no value in itself. It has nothing to teach you."

About ten days after this journey to Bear, I fell into a hole. That's exactly how it felt. Before that happened, I was just going about my life, business as usual, when suddenly I felt simply awful—physically and emotionally. It began with a jumpy, sickish sensation that built for several days until at last I took myself to a chiropractor and then to a homeopath. After their treatments I felt a little bit better, but I was still unstable—vulnerable and uneasy inside my skin. Waves of fear were playing havoc with my mind as well as with my body, and as fear literally ran through me, I was spending a lot of time in the bathroom.

When I pulled myself together enough to take a journey to the Grandmothers, as soon as I saw them, I broke down sobbing. "I'm at my wit's end," I wailed to them. "There's so much garbage coming up in me now that I can hardly stand it, Grandmothers. I feel dreadful, and whatever this stuff inside me is, it just keeps on coming. It's subterranean goo of some kind," I said to them, "and it just keeps on surfacing. And," I said, "as far as I can tell, what's coming up in me doesn't have much to do with my everyday life. There's nothing in my life now that's causing this. These are old wounds of some kind, states of consciousness from long ago," I said to my teachers, and as I spoke the words, I wondered how I knew all this. But I did.

The Grandmothers listened to me and nodded understandingly. **"The work you did with the chiropractor and then with the homeopath set this old material free, so it's quickly rising up now to be eliminated. It's nothing for you to worry about, nothing to take ownership of,"** they assured me. **"It has no value in itself,"** they said, shaking their heads, **"none at all. It has *nothing* to teach you,"** they said, **"so you're right in calling it garbage. Just let it continue to rise and allow yourself to be transformed.**

"And take care of yourself," they said. **"Go to bed, rest, eat, do the**

simple things and keep to yourself. You needn't tell anyone about what you're going through right now as they can't help you anyway," they shrugged. "**Simply let all this stuff rise up, and when it shows itself, don't judge yourself or anyone else for it. Can you let go of the judgment and let go of the asking 'why?'**" they asked. "**Can you simply let it be and abide in us?**" "Yes," I said to them. "That's what I want to do. Abide in you. I've already tried to figure it all out, Grandmothers," I explained, "and I can't, so there's nothing left for me to do *except* abide in you."

"**Good!**" they said and smiled, and now I noticed that Bear was nodding his head in concert with theirs. "**Rest and wait upon us…wait upon the Divine,**" they said, smiling at their turn of phrase. "Okay," I promised them, "I will."

So, I watched and waited, waited and watched, and as I did, I couldn't help but notice that the nasty stuff that was rising up in me probably wasn't so very different from the nasty stuff that was rising up all over our planet. Everyone and everything on earth was now in the process of being transformed—with no exceptions. I didn't like my own personal parade of ugliness, and it surely didn't feel good, but whatever was going on with me was far beyond my puny likes and dislikes. So, I tried my best to let all of it go and simply stick with the watching and waiting part. This, I told myself, I could do.

"You will be moving into contact with elemental life. Go there."

The watching and waiting experience finally passed as all things do, and it wasn't very long after the flotsam and jetsam settled down that I ended up taking an unexpected trip to northern Indiana where I'd grown up. My brother had invited me to come for a visit, and I went, eager to share some time with him.

It was good to see him again, and together we made the rounds of all the old places—the woods near our childhood home, the lakes, and our hometown itself. One day he took me to a Carmelite monastery near where he now lived. This monastery had been dug and built right into the earth, rather like an elaborate cave, and as we climbed up and down all over this place, it came to me how important it is to salute the sanctity of Mother Earth wherever we may be. So, as I entered the doorway of this shrine, I called on the Net of Light and asked that this much loved holy place be a radiant point on the Net. And as I felt the cosmic connection between the Net of Light and the monastery taking place, I understood that linking the earth with the Net of Light needs to be done by all of us—wherever we are. Then I remembered that early on the Grandmothers had told me, "**There is no mundane world. The earth itself is sacred.**"

Making lighted connections is important for we human beings. And when later I went to the Grandmothers, they again confirmed this. "**You are link pins in the great *Game of Light*,**" they said. "**It's time to play now, and everyone who wants to, is welcome. It's a good thing to do,**" they smiled, and laughing, added "**Really, it's the only game in town.**

"**Until recently humanity has been asleep to the fact that earth is sacred and that human beings, too, are sacred,**" they said. "**You've been taught that you're 'unworthy', that you're 'not enough', and you've believed it!**" they cried, incredulous. "**It's not true! You *are* enough,**" they said. "**You *are* worthy, and what's more, you have a job to do. It's time to re-connect earth with the Net of Light. Every-where!**" they cried, "**and *you are here to do that.***

"**Earth Herself is sacred. She has always been sacred,**" they said. "**And you're here at this time to be a link pin, a conduit for the Divine. You're the middleman,**" they laughed, "**needed to make the connection between earth and heaven, between the so-called 'mun-dane' and the Divine. *You're the link*. And since there is no other,**" they lifted their eyebrows in emphasis, "**it's time for you to get to work.**

"**Wherever you are, the earth under your feet is sacred. Earth is a life-giver and as such, She is full of light. But for a long time, earth has been burdened by mankind's negativity, so at this time She needs to be reconnected with divinity. Humanity needs to reach out and connect Her with the Net of Light.**" "*Humanity* is supposed to do this?" I asked, and the Grandmothers laughed at the shocked look on my face. "**You will be relieved to learn that it's not as difficult as it may seem,**" they said.

"**Begin this work by asking us to show you a specific place on earth that's calling out for this sacred connection,**" they said. "**An area that wants to be revivified. Often it won't be a large place," they explained, "**just a point on the earth that's ready.**

"If it happens to be near you, go there, and if you can't do that, go to it in your mind. Make the connection with this place, then move into your heart and call on us or on any form of the Divine you love. You'll then experience your lighted link with us and your connection with those who work with the Net of Light. Then, from your heart, cast the Net of Light to this spot on earth, and experience as the Net anchors itself deeply. It will do that," they said, smiling and nodding to me.

I nodded back at them, and as I did, I recalled how a group of us had once worked with the Net of Light in this long-distance way. About six years ago, the Dutch Beacons had begun to meet in an old government building in The Hague. The building was well situated for public transportation and had spacious rooms, but something about the energy of the place wasn't right. As soon as they moved into this building, the Beacons started having miscommunications and power struggles among group members, and this was something they'd never before experienced. As we sat together around the dinner table one night, they spoke at length about this problem and, at one point, mentioned that during the Second World War, this building had been a regional headquarters for the Nazi army. Bingo!

As soon as I heard that, we called on the Grandmothers who directed us to get out a map, call on the Net of Light, and get to work. So, we pulled our chairs up to the table, placed our hands on an open map of Europe, fastened our hearts to the Grandmothers and called on the radiant Net of Light. Our goal was to anchor and amplify the presence of Light at this once darkened place. I remember that several of us broke into a sweat as soon as we began to work like this. For several minutes we sat in silence, our hands immobile on the map, calling on the Net of Light and asking it to bless and uplift this place. We repeated this exercise several times that day, and from then on, there was no more trouble at this meeting place.

After that experience with the map, we understood that we could use this long-distance method to lift *any* place on earth. Anyone could work with a map, a globe or a facsimile of the earth as we'd done with The Hague, or simply think of and magnify the holding power of the Net of

Light wherever there was a need. I looked up at the Grandmothers as all this came back to me and they smiled back. Message received.

Turning their attention to the present moment, the Grandmothers said, **"When the three of you travel to the Southwest in November, we will guide you. Be aware that we'll be with you as you drive,"** they said, **"and pay attention to the pull of the earth and the presence of divinity with and around you. The earth *is* sacred. She stands ready to communicate with you wherever you are. So, let the land speak to you as you travel,"** they said; **"listen as it calls to and teaches you. Listen and learn,"** they said, their heads slowly nodding. **"The specific places you visit on this trip are less important than the overall presence of the land,"** they said. **"The land will teach you of the part it plays in the panoply of life, so let the land lead.**

"Relax into the embrace of the earth," they said. **"Relax and let yourself vibrate with it. Open yourself to the natural world. Hum with the stars,"** they said. **"Listen and learn, listen and learn. You will take this trip again later on your own,"** they added, **"but this experience with Babs and Lilium will be valuable. The three of you are going on this journey to get your circuitry honed. You think you're making this trip as service for the land, as service for the Ancestors, and you are,"** they said, **"but you're doing it primarily for your own growth. Take the journey,"** they said. **"Listen and learn.**

"And while you're making the drive," the Grandmothers said, **"do it mostly in silence. Stop the car periodically and sit in the quiet of the great spaces there. And after you've done that for a while, then give and receive feedback from one another on what it is you're experiencing as the land communicates with you. As you take this trip, don't be in a hurry,"** they said, **"but take the time to communicate with the land and then with one another. Treat this drive as a sacred journey because that's what it is.**

"As you travel, you will be going beyond the ordinary, going beyond man-made society. You will be moving into contact with elemental life. Go there," they said.

Joshua Tree and Sedona

Joshua Tree National Park covers a vast tract of desert in Southern California where miles of scrubland alternate with rounded

monument-like rocks that suddenly tower up out of the sand. It's a pro-
foundly silent place where Babs, Lilium and I were able to make deep
contact with the earth and the stars. As we drove into the park, several
times we left our car and walked over to a group of boulders to pray
and cast the Net of Light for the earth and all Her beings. Quiet and
a deep peace lay over this place, and as we sat in the wash of silence,
we were graced with one of those sacred moments in nature. Here we
anchored the Net of Light to earth, and here each of us received a personal blessing from the Great Mother. It was an auspicious beginning
to our journey.

We took a short detour off the road from Phoenix to Sedona to stop
at Montezuma's Well, a deep pool of water in the midst of this arid
land. This unexpected source of water had been used to irrigate crops
in ancient times, and off to the side of the pool was a pathway. We followed it to a water course that had been built into the cliff there with
small, hand-placed stones. Here we met a park ranger who told us that
this water course had been built hundreds of years ago by an unknown
tribe, and that the people living in this area today still refer to this as
the Hopi 'Place of Emergence'.

Many years earlier I had read the *Book of the Hopi* and now I
recalled this 'Place of Emergence,' the legendary opening in the earth
where people emerged from the darkness of the third world into this,
the fourth. The *Book of the Hopi* had not said where this place was, and
there were no references to a 'Place of Emergence' in our guidebooks,
but it perhaps we had inadvertently stumbled upon it here.

As the ranger spoke about it, we caught one anothers' eyes, and
nodding our agreement, deciding that we would take her at her word.
We thanked her for this information and made our way down the trail
until we found a place where we could stop and meditate. There the
three of us linked our hearts with the Net of Light and asked the Net
to connect itself with this ancient power place and bless all beings who
had ever stood in this place. I remember that as soon as we called on
the Net of Light, a powerful wave of energy flooded in, lined up with
us and anchored us to the land there. Surprised by the strength of this
response, we shared with each other that perhaps this actually *was* 'the
Place of Emergence' after all. In silence we then turned and headed
back to our car, a bit stunned by what had occurred on this 'detour' to
Montezuma's Well.

Later that day, after we'd arrived in Sedona, we performed a simple ceremony at two vortexes there, but remembering what the Grandmothers had said about holding our focus on the entire presence of the land rather than only on specific areas, we kept up an ongoing communication with the earth. And we carried on this two-way conversation from us to the land, from the land to us, the entire time we were in Sedona.

Wherever we went—Bell Rock, Cathedral Rock, Courthouse Rock, the Chapel, in the car, at dinner, in bed—we magnified and anchored the Net of Light. A herd of wild pigs greeted us as we walked to our room, and from then on, it felt like wherever we went, we were welcomed by the land—grounded, spiritually fed and re-charged by it. The soil of this Red Rock area was giving to us, and it quickly became clear that this was the real reason we'd come to Sedona. To receive the anchoring embrace of the land.

Because of what the Grandmothers had told us before we left for this trip, as we drove around, we became more and more powerfully connected to the land and because we were connected like this, we were easily able to receive from it. And the land in turn was able to receive from us. As we wandered through Sedona, we could feel the Net of Light at work—inside us and all around us—strengthening the rocks, the trees, the animals and ourselves. The great red vistas spoke to us and we spoke back. The blessing of the Net of Light was now activated simply because we were there. And as all of this was taking place, the Net of Light, via its strands, was carrying the potent energy of Sedona throughout the cosmos. We were conduits and we felt the light pouring into and through us. The experience of being a conduit like this was so moving that when it was time for us to leave Sedona, we'd formed such an intimate connection with the red earth country that it literally hurt us to drive away.

The Grand Canyon, however, was a different story. There, a fierce wind was blowing. Hard, so hard that when we reached Mather Point on the South Rim of the canyon, we decided we'd better work with the Net of Light from inside the car. And when, while sitting in the car high above the canyon bottom, we magnified and anchored the presence of the Net, I felt the energy of blood as well as a great power climbing up the walls of that canyon. The warrior Mother Herself was climbing those walls, and as she came forward and made herself known to us, I gasped. She was fierce and potent—almost scary in her power and as we huddled together in the car, trying to stay warm, She 'marked us' as her own. She gazed deep into my eyes then, and I shook with cold and fear as I understood that somehow I, too, was to become a warrior. I had no idea then what this meant, but all three of us were deeply moved by this unexpected contact with Her.

Several weeks after our Southwest trip was over and my Dutch 'sisters' were on their way home again, I returned to the Grandmothers who greeted me and acknowledged that our journey through the Southwest had been a rousing success. Then they got down to business.

"You Are the Light Switch"

Wasting no time on pleasantries, the Grandmothers spoke. **"The Net of Light has come forward at this time to turn the world from darkness to light, to help humanity move from contraction into expansion."** "Uh, yes, Grandmothers," I said, surprised by how quickly they'd jumped into this subject. But they waved my hesitation aside and said, **"The Net of Light will help you open both your mind and your heart. And,"** they added, watching me out of the corners of their eyes, **"while this opening inside you is taking place, remember that *you are the light switch*. You are the switch,"** they repeated, **"for yourself and others."**

"What?" I asked, "I don't understand, Grandmothers. What does it mean...I'm the light switch?" But they continued to look at me and held their silence, so, I stopped talking, too, and holding my breath in anticipation, I simply gazed back at them. For a few minutes, they continued to regard me like this, and so I, too, continued to wait.

"When you call on the Net of Light," they said at last, **"you automatically move your consciousness from fear to love. You turn your thoughts from 'no' to 'yes,'"** they explained. **"And as soon as you do that, you let go of contraction and instead open to expansion."** They smiled at me and nodded knowingly. **"Each time you call on the Net, you not only connect yourself to its field of radiance; you connect everyone else too! By your decision to activate it, you turn the Net on. YOU turn it on. *YOU are the light switch*,"** they said, and when they saw my bewildered look, they waved their hands as if to say, 'Oh, never mind.' But then they relented. **"Well, okay,"** they said, **"we'll explain a little more.**

"The strands of the Net of Light weave throughout the cosmos," they explained; "**they link everyone and everything together. And, because this is the way it works, each time you think of the Net of Light, you connect with and automatically touch everything in the universe. You are able to make all these links by simply** *thinking* **of the Net of Light!**" they exclaimed. "**It happens instantly!** *Here indeed,*" the Grandmothers said, "*is the power of thought in action.*

"**It is true that today you are living in difficult times,**" they said and nodded understandingly at me, "**but even so, you needn't sit around waiting for a great being or some special teaching to come forward to save you and your planet. You can help save your planet and yourself right now!**

"**When just one of you calls on the Net of Light, you amplify its power to lift and bless. Every time you call on it!**" they cried. "**And when groups of you come together to work with the Net, miracles occur. This isn't magic,**" they said; "**it's the law of nature. And what's more,**" they added, "**it's not even difficult. This is simply how the Net of Light works. You ARE the light switch,**" they said, now regarding me like proud mother hens.

"**Your scientists are just beginning to explore the Net of Light,**" they said**. "Although they don't call it the Net of Light, they call it the Cosmic Web.**" "Yes, Grandmothers," I said. I'd heard this. In 2015 when Roger and I had been in Los Angeles, we happened to wander in to a film about what astronauts had learned from the Hubbell telescope. We were sitting in an Imax theater at the Los Angeles Museum of Natural History when photographs of the Net of Light came up on the screen, and as soon as he saw them, Roger began to nudge me. I took in a breath when they came on the screen and when the narrator said, "Science has now discovered the largest living construct in the Universe—this cosmic web of dark matter connects all life throughout the cosmos," I started to shake. This *was* the Net of Light! Many years ago, the Grandmothers had called us together and taught us how to work with the Net of Light or Cosmic Web, and now scientists had 'discovered' it. I sat crying in that darkened theater, stunned and overwhelmed with joy. The Net of Light wasn't just a spiritual construct; it was real in *every* way!

As the memory of that moment came back to me now, the Grandmothers smiled and asked," ***Shouldn't you, like the scientists, also be*** *spending time exploring the Net of Light?"* I cocked my head at them, unsure of what they were getting at. **"All it takes to activate the power of the Net is your willingness to connect with it,"** they said, **"and your willingness to allow it to support you."** Then they rocked back and forth on their heels a few times and said, **"The Net of Light will support you and everyone else. And it will do it every time!**

"What?" I wondered, "are they asking of me? I'm already working with the Net of Light."

"The Net is a gift to you and to the world," they said in response. **"A precious gift, given to humanity to use,"** they said. **"So, use it!"** I watched them now as they spoke and wondered exactly what they had in mind. How did they want us to use it? But, giving me a knowing look, all they said was, **"You can't over-do it."**

CHAPTER THREE

"What we have come to bring goes far beyond the limits of religion."

Around this time, I began to hear disturbing reports from a Net of Light group leader in Eastern Europe. Someone over there was saying that the energy of the earth was evil and because the Net of Light works with the earth, it too was evil. The Grandmothers were evil and I was especially bad because I was teaching all this. This person declared that I was out to cause harm and hurt people. "Holy mackerel, Grandmothers," I said, "what in the world is *this* about?"

In response, they gave me such a long, slow look that I felt weighed and measured by them. Then they said, **"You know that there is great power in the land of Eastern Europe. Great power,"** they repeated, and I leaned forward, intent on what they were saying. **"The Mother,"** they announced, **"has dwelled in that part of the world throughout human history. She has been worshiped there from time out of mind. The Great Mother has played a central part in the lives of the people in that area of the world—always,"** they said, giving me a meaningful look. **"Of course, She is present everywhere,"** they added, **"but She is especially comfortable where she has long been worshiped. For millennia She has been revered in this part of the world and today, in the form of the Blessed Mother, She's still honored there.**

"With the arrival of Christianity," the Grandmothers explained, **"patriarchy attempted to oust her. But though the fathers of the church tried, they were unable to get rid of Her. So, as was done in many other parts of the world, the powers that be in Eastern Europe substituted the Blessed Mother for the Great Mother. Today She continues to be revered in Eastern Europe, in the form of Mary.**

There She is wedded to the land. Love of the Great Mother pulses in the blood of the people in Eastern Europe for to them She is not a symbol or an idea. She is real.

"Because of Her strong presence in the land there, the patriarchal structures in Eastern Europe are frightened by our arrival," the Grandmothers said. "They fear the message we've come to bring because it awakens people to the actual *presence* of the Divine Mother. It makes Her even more real. You see, what we have come to bring goes far beyond the limits of religion," the Grandmothers said. "It is elemental, and it is powerful. It is the living truth, and *that*," they said, "is the last thing patriarchy wants to encounter, especially in a place where the Mother's presence is already strong.

"And the Net of Light!!!" the Grandmothers cried out, laughing so hard that they rocked back and forth where they stood. "The Net of Light!" they repeated, holding their sides and howling. "The Net of Light does away with all hierarchy and separation. Absolutely does away with it!" they cried. "Within the radiant Net, all are One! Able to connect with the Source! Every time a person thinks of the Net of Light, their sense of separation from God melts away. Within the Net, people feel their union with the Source; they know their oneness with the Light.

"And when one opens to the Great Oneness, where's the need for priests and pundits then?" they asked. "Once a person recognizes their connection to the One Love, society's strictures and habits fall away. This movement into Oneness that we bring threatens those who would set themselves above others," the Grandmothers said. "Their kingdoms, systems and hierarchies, their control over others become superfluous.

"What you're witnessing in Eastern Europe now is the play of fear—fear is rising now in those who are caught up in the vestiges of patriarchy. People who are wedded to the old power systems are afraid of letting them go and as they try to hang on to their old ways, they try to make others afraid too. They are using fear to fend off our message, reasoning that if they can make people afraid of the One Love, they can continue to feel important and in control.

"But it won't work," the Grandmothers said, grimacing as they shook their heads. "It's impossible to hold back the flooding in of the light. The Net of Light is here now," they said, "and it's relentlessly connecting all of life. Even those that are presently caught up in fear will finally open to the love and light within the Net. Even their fear will drop away.

"Just go forward and do your job," the Grandmothers said, and they waved a hand in dismissal. "Don't be distressed by all this drama. It's nothing! Go forward. Carry our message wherever we send you. Darkness is falling away now and we promise that it will continue to fall away. Follow us," they said. "We know what we're doing and so too do you."

They looked me in the eyes then and again they seemed to measure me. an "Call them in," they said. I looked up when I heard this, my eyes big with surprise. What? Call *who* in?"

"Call out to those who are able to hear," the Grandmothers said, "and tell them that the time is now. Ask them to rely on our presence within themselves and to also rely on one another. Ask them to link with each other in sisterhood, in brotherhood. Call these people forward. They are the Family of Light," the Grandmothers said, "and as such, they are needed to hold steady now, to step up and most of all, to listen. Tell them to listen within, to listen to the silence," they said. "The Mother is coming. She is returning to earth."

I goggled at them when they said this, hardly able to believe I'd heard them right, but they smiled a smile of understanding and continued. "Even though She has been absent from most of the earth for millennia, the Great Mother is present in the cultures of Eastern Europe. She was nearly erased from the consciousness of humanity, but *'nearly',*" they laughed, "wasn't enough. She adhered," they said. The energy of Yin did not go away; it only went underground. And that's what it did in Eastern Europe. It went underground, but today it is rising to the surface. And now it is present once again, present within each woman and also present in many men. It is time," the Grandmothers said, holding my eyes with theirs, "to call that up now. Use this bit of pushback from Eastern Europe as a springboard for moving forward with this work," they said. "Let it propel you.

"Begin meeting now in groups of like-minded people to talk about the Mother, to explore who She is, to sing Her songs and enjoy being held in the energy of the Divine Feminine. You have been deprived of Her embrace for far too long," they said, "so long that at this moment, many of you are struggling to understand what we are talking about.

"**'*Divine Feminine? What's that*' you ask. We understand your confusion,**" the Grandmothers said, smiling with compassion. "**The Mother was removed from recorded history, removed from nearly all aspects of the world's religions. Her statues were removed from public squares and Her name from everyday discourse. This removal took place several thousand years ago,**" the Grandmothers said, their faces severe, "**and it was done deliberately. However, no matter how misguided people may sometimes be, no matter how confused they become, mankind is not capable of removing one half of creation. *The Father is, the Mother is*,**" they declared. "**And,**" they held me with their eyes, "**She is back.**

"**What we are sharing with you now may shock you,**" they said. "**You may find yourself turning away from it, and if you do feel that way, be sure to ask yourself '*why?*' Why does it seem *strange* that there would be a Mother of the world? The answer to this question is simple,**" they said. "**You have been conditioned to doubt Her existence, to doubt that there can be anything other than a Father. For thousands of years, humanity has been shaped by patriarchy. Dominated by patriarchy. And for those thousands of years patriarchy controlled all of human history.**

"**But something new is happening now,**" the Grandmothers said. "**The energy on your beloved planet is changing. Amidst all the strife and upheaval that is taking place today as the old systems on earth begin to topple, there is a new wind blowing. The Mother is returning. And not a moment too soon,**" they said. "**It's time for you to get to know your Mother.**"

"This is the 'guts' of life, the stuff of life."

When the Grandmothers said, "**It's time for you to get to know your Mother,**" I believed them—believed them and *wanted* to get to know Her. "They're telling me… the Mother is back," I said to myself, "and if this is true, then there must be more work for me to do. I'm ready to do it," I said, and inspired by the strength of my desire two days later, I journeyed back to them.

This time I purposefully journeyed using the Circle of Stones, and included in my request for help, the Holy Man who had worked with me for so long, and Bear. For this journey, I was looking for as much help as I could get, and, with this in mind, I set my intention, thought of each Grandmother sitting before a large stone, took in a breath and walked in between those stones. Then I stood, facing them in the center of their circle, and said, "Grandmothers, I'm calling you, calling the Holy Man, Bear and all those who've guided us in this work for more than twenty years. For the good of all, I'm asking to be shown the next piece of work we are to do, the next piece we are to learn. I want to work more, to work harder," I said. "I want to learn the next lessons you are ready to teach and pass them on.

"The world is in crises now," I continued, "and because I love everything and everyone on earth, I want to serve with all I have in me. So, I ask you, Grandmothers, you who came and gave us such joy and so much learning—for the good of all, what is the next lesson? I come to you with my heart open," I said, fighting back tears, "and I come in humility because I don't know what the lesson is. But I know the need is great."

I dropped to my knees then, and the Grandmothers put their hands on me in blessing. My head was down at their feet, and as I took in a breath, the Grandmothers declared, **"Yes!"** And at that moment, my left eye began to twitch, and when I felt that twitch and saw Bear standing right behind the Grandmothers, I burst into tears. "Oh!" I exclaimed as he let out a roar.

My eye kept on twitching, so I took in a few deep breaths and attempted to calm myself. Then Bear began to dance. He was up on two legs, shuffling his massive paws in deliberate movements and I understood that this dance he was performing was making a connection with the earth. And as I watched him stamp and step, I could feel a grounding taking place within my own body. "Okay, Grandmothers," I said as I again recalled the purpose for this journey, "what is the next lesson?" And when I asked this time, my energy quickly dropped down into rhythm with the drum. **Bom ba bom ba bom ba bom.**

"Whoof!" I exhaled as the cadence of the drum beat its way into my chest. Pounding into the center of my body, now it was bringing up a burning sensation around my heart. "Ooh!" I shivered as I felt the burn, and then "Clearing, clearing," I crooned slowly. "It's drawing out all the stuck garbage from my chest—lots and lots of things, piles of it," I said in amazement.

"Graugh! Braugh! Waugh!" Bear growled as he leaned in over me to pull this stuff out of my body. And then he began to pull things out of his own chest too, and as I watched him working like this, I understood that what I was looking at now, what I was seeing as *his* chest, was actually *my own*. In working on himself like this, he was actually pulling these things out of me! For some reason, he was performing this action *for* me, even *as* me. "W...o...w," I exhaled, drawing out the word. "What IS this?" But I realized that strange as it might seem, what I was seeing really was *Bear as me*. Now I couldn't take my eyes off him, and as I stood there, transfixed, he growled and flung away all the things that had previously been stuck inside me.

Chills were running all over my body as I watched him work. He was so fierce in his determination, roaring and pulling dark objects out of his chest, working so hard at it that it brought tears to my eyes. I began to sob then and watching him, I cried and cried. "I don't know why I'm crying like this," I said to myself, and as I spoke the words, I could hardly get them out. "It must be the oneness," I said at last. "This must be what I'm seeing. He's so committed, so devoted to doing this work for me," and now my voice caught in my throat. "This must be what the Native Americans call 'the give away.' The great selflessness. This must be what I'm seeing."

As I watched him continuing to dance and fling off objects, I said, "He's showing me that there's no separation between him and me, no separation at all. In a way, he's sacrificing himself for me," I said, choking as I was overcome with feeling; "and as he does this, he's showing me that all is one, *that all is love*. And I *feel* it," I said, tears in my voice. "I feel this great love right here, right now in my body," I said, and my fingers touched my heart. As Bear continued to dance like this, I marveled at his greatness of heart, crying and crying all the while until finally I wore myself out.

After a period of silence, I began to breathe slowly and evenly again, and when at last I had quieted down and could feel myself centering in again, I became aware of the big trees that were standing all around us. Towering above and beside us. I also became aware that Bear was now dancing by starlight. It was night time, and as I watched him stamp, sway and gesture against the dark sky, an entirely new thought came to me.

Suddenly it was clear that all the ideas we have about God and the Goddess, and all that we believe about the different spiritual paths on earth, are actually pretty paltry. 'Spindly' to use Bear's word—minimal and weak. The things we believe in don't come near to touching the truth of the matter. They're just descriptions of that truth, and not very good ones at that. "Wow!" I said to myself. "Where did *this* thought come from?" But before I could consider it further, **"Yes,"** the Grandmothers said, nodding their heads emphatically. **"This is correct,"** and I looked at them with a question in my eyes. *'What is all this about?'* **"Enjoy all the legends on earth, all the myths and stories you hear,"** they replied, **"but don't go chasing after them. You are correct in thinking that reality lies FAR beyond these legends.**

"Instead of attaching yourself to legends and stories of one kind or another," they continued, **"open instead to the presence of truth."** There was a long pause after they said this, and then the Grandmothers showed me that because we work with the Net of Light and because the Net operates through us, we are *always* connected with the core of truth. We are always connected with its presence. We're linked with the core truths of the different forms of God and the Goddess, with the core truths of all myths, legends, and spiritual stories. Because of our connection with the Net of Light, we are always aligned with the truth, and so the peripheral, non-essential stuff we encounter along the way can easily drop off. The truth in all the legends, myths, and traditions of the world is held steady within the Net of Light. **"Throughout time and space,"** the Grandmothers said, **"the Net of Light forever holds the reality of existence.**

"We have given you the Net of Light," they said and smiled at me benignly. **"The Net does many things,"** they said, **"and one of them is to provide a short cut for you. The Net of Light is the Source,"** they said. **"It is the Truth, and because it is, it will always take you straight to itself. There is no protocol you need to follow when you work with the Net of Light, and there are no intermediaries between you and the Net. When you call on the Net of Light, you are calling on the Source—pure and simple. And,"** they said, **"the Source always responds—immediately.**

"With the Net of Light, you needn't worry about arcane traditions. You don't have to follow a particular religious regimen, protocol or a specific set of rules. Working with the Net of Light is simple and direct. Every time you call on it," they smiled, "it will take you straight to the Truth, straight to the Oneness of life. You move beyond all the so-called limitations of time and space. Within the great Fabric of Being of the Net of Light, everything is connected.

"So, Grandmothers," I mused, "at this very moment I'm being held in the Net of Light, aren't I? I'm breathing it in. I'm at one with it. I'm resting in it," I said. They looked at me with love, and I realized that I was feeling the Net's strands rising and falling within me now, moving inside me with the vibration of the drum. "I'm breathing with it," I said to the Grandmothers, "and it's breathing with me."

"Yes," they answered. "The Net of Light makes up the Fabric of Being of the Universe. It is the 'guts' of life, the Force. What life is made of. The Net of Light is not about ephemeral things, the things that come and go," they explained. "It's not about fizzle and fluff— surface activities. No!" they said. "The Net of Light forms the sinews, the *deep* connections. It makes up the underpinnings of your existence. The foundation. It is both the warp and the woof.

"When you first began to work with it," the Grandmothers said, "you felt the Net of Light supporting you. You felt it holding you and you used it in turn to hold others. All of that is true," they said. "It is the nature of the Net of Light to nurture and support, but we want you to notice now that in addition to holding and being held by the Net, you ARE the Net of Light. You *are* part and parcel of the underpinning of life, the baseline format and structure of everything that lives. You *are* the framework itself. You," they repeated, "are the framework."

I was staggered by what they were telling me. "I am the framework of life?" What does that mean? I wondered. I wasn't sure I understood what they were saying. It seemed far too big and way too complex for me to grasp. And yet … there was truth in all this. I could feel it. Maybe the Grandmothers would teach me more.

"Because of your steadiness, because you didn't give up and walk away, at this point you are able to do this work."

After this lesson with the Grandmothers, over and over again I found myself thinking about the great power of the Mother and the resurgence of the Divine Feminine that was taking place on earth now. Something big was surfacing. So, one night just before bed, I asked the Grandmothers to teach me the purpose of their work at *this* moment in time. By now I was well aware that their work was constantly evolving, so I wanted to know what was coming next, what we should focus on as we proceeded with their message. And in the middle of the night they woke me from a sound sleep.

I sat up with a start, awakened by chills that were racing up and down my body. "Wow!" I whispered. "Something's coming!" Quickly I grabbed hold of the notebook I keep beside my bed, and immediately the Grandmothers spoke.

"We came to empower you," they said, responding to my question, **"*so you could do this job.* Without the Net of Light and the community that has grown up around it,"** they said, **"IT WOULD BE IMPOSSIBLE TO DO WORK OF THIS MAGNITUDE."** And when I heard this, tears welled up and poured down my cheeks. "Yes, Grandmothers," I whispered, awash in gratitude for the power and reach of the Net of Light. "I know," I said. "I know."

"The purpose of the work at this time," they said, eyeing me intently, **"is to amplify the Net of Light for yourself and for all life. The Net will cut through all the confusion and resistance on earth."** And, after they said this, they stood tall and added, **"We are the Great Council of the Grandmothers,"** and when they made this pronouncement, the cascade of chills that was already pouring through me doubled.

"You and all those who have joined with us have stayed with this message for over twenty years now," they said and peered at me from under their raised brows. **"And because of your steadiness, because you didn't give up and walk away, at this point you are able to *do* this work. You have 'stayed the course,'"** they said, and, hearing this, more tears started. **"Steadiness like this in the world you are living in is no small accomplishment,"** they said, **"and we, the Grandmothers, along with all forms of the Divine salute you. We rejoice in what you**

have become, are becoming, and are yet to become. You are magnificent!" they declared. "**We are proud of you.**

"**Now,**" they said as they gave me a fierce look, "**together you can do the work you were born to do. Now you can truly serve your planet and ALL life on it. You are opening your hearts, and because these opening hearts work in synch with the Net of Light, you are helping open the hearts of millions. When you said, 'yes' to being part of our mission, you became placeholders for these millions, each of you a '*hub in a wheel*' for countless others.**

"**Each time you take your glorious place on the Net of Light, so too can they,**" the Grandmothers declared, throwing back their heads in triumph. "**Over time we've taught you how to send this work beyond the so-called boundaries of time and space, so that today the reach of the Net of Light is endless. This 'work' you are part of is ENORMOUS,**" they said. "**If you could see yourselves as we see you now, you would drop to your knees.**

Keep on keeping on, brave hearts," they said, "**and follow where we lead. We will never fail you,**" they held me with their eyes. "**Together we are sharing this magnificent adventure and there is yet more to come. Keep on saying 'yes',**" they urged me, us. "**Keep on opening your magnificent hearts.**"

This message rocked me to my core. Their words, "**...without the community that has grown up around it (the Net of Light), IT WOULD BE IMPOSSIBBLE TO DO WORK OF THIS MAGNI-TUDE...**' kept echoing in my mind.

Back in 1996 after the Grandmothers first showed up, I felt very much alone. I was overwhelmed by what they were teaching me, plus I wasn't capable of sharing their message in a way people could understand. I couldn't find the right words to describe what was happening to me so I was lonely and scared—especially scared of the mission they were sharing. In those days I could never have imagined that a strong community would grow up around the Net of Light. And as I think back on all the growth that's taken place since those early days, I still can hardly believe it.

"This is almost too much for me to take in," I said as I reflected on what the Grandmothers had just said. "All I can do is marvel at what's transpired since they first appeared, know there's more coming, and just keep on keeping on."

Knitting the Strands in the Net

Four days later, I decided to journey to Bear. I wasn't sure why I was going to see him, but it felt right somehow, like the next thing to do. So, I journeyed to him the way I usually did, and after greeting him, I was soon walking along beside him, both of us upright, with my hand on his back. For some reason, this time I was not to ride on him but to walk the way he walks, observe the way he observes … basically, I was to be as much like him as I could. So, I aimed for that, and together we walked along like this for quite a way until at last we came to a cave.

Once before Bear had taken me to a cave. That was a year or so after the Grandmothers had first appeared. But this cave was different from that one. The first cave had been his 'looks within place,' and I remember that there'd been just enough room inside it for the two of us whereas this cave was roomier. Plus, there was a thick pile of straw spread over the floor where Bear and I could comfortably lay down and look up at the sky through an opening in the cave's roof. The night sky above us was patterned with stars, and as I took them in, somehow, I understood that it wasn't just the sky I was looking at. I was also looking at the Net of Light.

"**Umph,**" Bear agreed, and with his massive, but sensitive paws, he began to show me how to move among the stars and also how to alter the strands in the Net of Light. How to make the strands fine—very fine. I watched him as he worked like this and hesitantly at first, I began to emulate his movements so that together we practiced 'knitting' the strands of the Net closer and closer together. Knitting them very close indeed and leaving only tiny spaces between them. "**Finely spaced,**" Bear said as we worked, and when he gave me a long, serious look, I understood what he was telling me. This, a pattern of more tightly woven strands, was what would help hold Eastern Europe steady at this time.

As we wove this closely knitted pattern into the fabric of the Net of Light, it came to me that somehow this weaving work was also tied into an area in Southern California. There was a link here, not only with Eastern Europe but also with the small community of Idyllwild in the southern Sierra Nevada Mountains of California. Here the strands of the Net also needed to be finely woven. "**Hold this image of the closely woven Net of Light throughout Eastern Europe and then tie it into**

this continent through the small town of Idyllwild," Bear said. "What do these places have to do with each other?" I wondered, but I did as he asked and kept at it for quite a while. Soon, however, I grew sleepy, so sleepy that this was all I could recall of that journey.

I was disappointed to have fallen asleep and to have perhaps missed more that Bear was going to teach me, but when I made my good-byes to him, he told me to come back again soon and that he'd teach me more. So, I would return.

"The opposition you are experiencing is in direct proportion to the importance of the work you are doing."

Four days later, I was back. "Bear," I said as soon as he appeared by the river in the Lower World, "four days ago you told me to come back and said you'd tell me more about the Net of Light as it is at this point in history. Before that you showed me how fine and closely woven the Net was in certain places and told us to work with it that way to help Eastern Europe. I'm here again, Bear, and if you have a further message, I want to hear it. Please teach me."

"Look!" he said, and he turned and pointed upward to the sky over the northeastern part of Europe. Lithuania, Latvia, Russia and Poland. I looked to where he was pointing and saw that the sky there was packed full of stars—so full, I wondered if they were in fact stars. "Are those stars or is it the Net of Light I'm looking at?" I wondered. So, I kept staring at the sky until I noticed a movement in the heavens. "Oh!" I gasped, "the sky gods, the ones from long ago, are moving around up there, moving around in the firmament. It looks like they're rearranging themselves!" I said to Bear, stunned that such a thing could be possible. "And," I continued, "as they do this, they're forming new patterns in the sky." I looked up at him then, wondering if I had this right, but he didn't say a word, just patted my hand to reassure me that what I was seeing was indeed there.

"This new arrangement of the old gods will set up the Net of Light differently in this part of the world," I said. "It'll make the Net stronger and more all-pervasive." The words were coming out of my mouth now—tumbling over themselves—explaining ideas that I had absolutely no understanding of. I listened to what I was saying and marveled at it. Somehow what was unfolding in the firmament must be clear to some aspect of me.

"The control mechanisms of the patriarchal institutions of the past diminished the power of the Net of Light in this part of the world," I said as I continued downloading information, "diminished the strength of the Fabric of Being that holds all life together. Patriarchy wanted this power for itself, wanted to hold it all and titrate power down to those lower on the chain of command. It did NOT want power to be spread out freely for everyone to access and share."

I watched then as the gods and goddesses of the old cultures of Europe took new positions in the heavens and began to redistribute power in order to make it available for all to access. "These Devic beings," I said of the sky gods, "are able to do this because the indigenous ways have not entirely disappeared in this area of the earth. There's still enough of a human connection with the elemental powers of earth and the old nature-based gods to enable a link to be made here. And from the link in this part of the world, strength will pour into the Net of Light and connect to other parts of the earth as well."

"What can we do to help as this change takes place?" I asked Bear and the sky gods. **"Speak carefully about this subject so as not to alienate people and send them into fear,"** the gods replied. **"Fear of the old ways of relating both to the Divine and to the Earth,"** they explained. **"Patriarchy instilled this fear in people,"** they said, **"so you must tread carefully now.**

"The Earthly–Divine linkage must be made again," the gods said. **"This deep connection must be renewed. Here is a place for you to begin a more intensive way of connecting, and from here the connection will spread into all surrounding areas. Think often of the link between Eastern Europe and that small town in the mountains near you.**

Then they said, **"The opposition you are experiencing now from some in Eastern Europe *is in direct proportion to the importance of the work you are doing*. Don't be afraid when something like this happens but understand *why* you are being opposed. The Devic and elemental kingdoms on earth need and want to participate with the Net of Light. These beings are also lining up in England and in Ireland, so confide what we are telling you here with the Net of Light team in the United Kingdom and ask for their help."** "I will," I said.

"Is there anything more you want to share with me now? "Is there more we can do?" "**No**," they replied. "**This is enough for the time being.**"

"Neither patriarchy nor the energy of yang are naturally inclusive. They are exclusive."

This message from the old sky gods had a deep effect on me. It made sense that in the midst of Eastern Europe where the Mother has been honored for time out of mind would be a place where patriarchy might feel most vulnerable. Everything the sky gods and Bear had told me made sense, and I wanted to know more. I let a week go by so that I could fully assimilate what they had shared with me, and then unable to wait any longer, I returned to the Grandmothers, and this time Bear was there, too—waiting with them.

Reading the eagerness on my face, the Grandmothers immediately spoke. "**It's time to include the old nature gods in our work,**" they said. "**These gods and goddesses from long ago link the Devic kingdom to the Divine as well as to earth. These sacred beings need to be included in the work you are doing with us. You can call these gods and goddesses by their specific names,**" they said, "**or you can think of them in a general way. Whatever you call them,**" they said, "**they will respond, but, for them to enter in with you, you must first invite them. The elemental kingdom will provide invaluable healing for the earth,**" the Grandmothers said. "**These beings will help restore harmony to your planet.**

"**From ancient times until now, the religions of patriarchy have feared these gods, Devas, and elemental spirits,**" the Grandmothers said. "**They've feared them because these holy ones work with and for the earth. Patriarchy has always wanted an exclusive grip on earth's treasures and has tried to use the earth for its own ends. Therefore, patriarchal systems have no wish to share, nor do they know how to work with others for the common good. You need to recognize that these systems and the people who align themselves with them are by nature self-serving.**

"**Patriarchy,**" the Grandmothers explained, "**is constructed on a hierarchical model. Power coming from above and moving downward,**" they gestured, "**so patriarchy always serves what sits at the top—itself—only itself. Because they follow this linear pattern,** patriarchal systems are well suited to the energy of yang as the energy of yang, too, is linear. Unless yang has learned how to harmonize with yin, it holds itself apart, and, like patriarchy, avoids working with other energies. Neither patriarchy nor the energy of yang are naturally inclusive. They are exclusive," the Grandmothers said. "So, as you come to the end of this period of yang domination on earth, you will find that the old patriarchal systems no longer work.

"Your world is coming to the end of patriarchy now," the Grandmothers said. "Patriarchy's structure is too narrow and fixed for the times that are approaching. Today life on earth requires a harmonious movement of yin and yang, a balanced flow between these energies. Patriarchy has become stagnant.

"To speed the process of harmonizing yin and yang and bring about a balanced state on earth, human beings must return to working with the Devic realm, with the spirits of nature. So," they said, "whenever you call on and connect with the Net of Light, also call on the Devic realm. Invite the ancient goddesses and gods all over this planet; invite the little people and all earth spirits to align with the radiant Net of Light. Let them amplify its power to hold and bless life. We ask you to do this," the Grandmothers said, "for yourself and for everything that lives."

"You are experiencing a winnowing of sorts...."

The Grandmothers had given me a lot to chew on with these last few journeys, and chew I did. But...it was hard to know what to do with all this information. Sky gods, weaving the Net of Light finer, Devas, and elemental spirits. The Grandmothers were stretching me and boy, did I feel it! It was a bit overwhelming, actually a lot overwhelming. Who in the world could I tell about the sky gods moving around in the heavens? Or weaving the strands in the Net of Light closer together? I was starting to feel alone again, like I was out on a limb somewhere—all by myself. So, I decided I'd better take some time off, slow down and take a vacation from journeying for a while. Just for a while I'd do the 'normal' things in life—go shopping, see a few clients, paint and putter in the garden and watch the news with my husband. Watch the news....

After about ten days' worth of slowing down AND watching the news each night, I realized I wasn't feeling all that good, that I was, in fact, somewhat depressed. I was beginning to doubt myself again, to even doubt the effectiveness of the Grandmothers' work. I think it was that daily immersion in the news. What was taking place in our country now was really discouraging me. One shameful, inhumane action after another. It seemed like so many politicians were now taking the low road and when I looked at all of it together, it made me so sad.

When I noticed that my thoughts were moving in the direction of depression, I journeyed to the Grandmothers but my mood was so heavy that I didn't feel heartened by anything they said. And after that, I really began to doubt myself, just the way I had when the Grandmothers had first appeared to me. Was I kidding myself with all this information from the Grandmothers? Who was I anyway to be getting these messages?

The next day I realized how uncomfortably familiar these thoughts I was having were, so I went straight back to the Grandmothers. But this time I said, "Grandmothers, I'm stuck. I admit it. I'm circling the drain. Please show me how to stop this downward spiral I'm in now and move forward. Maybe I've been watching too much news," I admitted, "but this *is* a very hard time for our country as well as for the world. However," I said, "*this* is the time we're living in, so I need to get used to it. I don't want to waste one more minute of my life bemoaning the horrors of it all—stuck in the mud. I want to move forward. And I want to do it NOW!"

I looked up at them then and saw how they were looking at me, their faces full of compassion and understanding. And when I saw that, I said, "I think I need to cry." And so, I did. I sobbed quietly for a few minutes, and when I noticed how heavily I was breathing, I realized that something in me had changed. There was something else besides just sadness about the world going on—something more than I knew.

As soon as that thought came to me, no longer was I just standing with the Grandmothers. I was moving. Doing something. I was swimming! I was actually swimming! Fascinated by what I was experiencing, I watched my body as it cut through the water, a silvery flash. I was a fish! I was a seriously swimming fish, and when I looked around in the water, I noticed how crowded it was in there. So many fish with me that I had to navigate carefully, and I watched myself sliding past them, bouncing off their bodies as I made my way upstream. I was part of a school.

"It's tough-going here," I said to myself as I noticed that I was swimming against the current. I could feel the pressure of the water pushing me back as I kept surging forward. My arms or fins or whatever they were, were slicing through the water as I plunged onward and onward. Then I heard the surprise in my voice as I said, "But everybody else, well, almost everybody else, is going downstream, with the current." Again, I looked around, observing the fish in the water with me, and they seemed to be just floating along. "It looks like this swim is easy for them," I said, "but swimming up-stream like this is *not* easy for me. I guess I'm like a salmon," I said as again I felt the pressure of the water on me as I made my way upstream, "climbing up the falls.

"I really *am* a salmon," I said in surprise, as I leaped out of the water, jumping into the light above me. And when I said that, I could hear in my voice how tired I was and how heavy my breathing was. The continuous plunging forward was hard, hard work. **"You were born to make this run,"** the Grandmothers whispered to me, and when I heard their words, I blew out a little gasp and began to sob. "There aren't many other fish around me now," I said, "and I'm working awfully hard. I'm leaping and leaping to get up stream. It's tough work," I said. "I don't have companions or someone to follow except for this urge inside me that keeps pushing me on." Then, still swimming, I realized I'd begun to shake with fatigue, but before I could collapse, I heard the Grandmothers cry, **"Go to God, go to God, go to God!"**

"Yes," I declared, "yes, I will," and the next thing I knew, I had again leapt out of the stream into the *clear* air. And for a moment, all there was, was just me and that brilliantly clear air. Again, I was *jumping and climbing* upward and upward… farther and farther. I could feel the effort this was taking, and again I heard my own heavy breathing.

Then the Grandmothers spoke. **"For life to continue now,"** they said, **"certain ones have to make this journey. Brave salmon,"** they said, and added, **"be like the salmon. You long for a clear pool to swim in, to swim in together with your own kind. But there is no clear pool yet,"** they said, **"and there is no 'own kind.' You have to plunge ahead alone now; you have to go forward. Climb! Climb!"** they cried.

I continued to leap, to swim, and as I struggled on, I was puzzling over what they'd said when suddenly my thoughts were interrupted by the drumbeat—the insistent beat of the drum. The drum didn't stop, and as its rhythm flooded my awareness, everything inside me began to slow down, to calm down. The drum was bringing me back to the peace of the water, to the peace of the earth. Bringing me back to the peace of this moment on this planet where I live.

"You are experiencing a winnowing of sorts now," the Grandmothers said. **"It's time for you to let go of your allegiance to the group and to also let go of any attachment that you have to our work. It's time now for you to simply go forward,"** they said, **"to go forward because there's nowhere else to go *but* forward."**

"Nowhere else to go but forward," I said to myself, and as I spoke the words, I heard the wisdom in them. "Go forward," I said to myself. "Don't think of the whys and wherefores of it. Just do it because it's lying there to be done. Well, why not?" I said to myself. "What other place is there to go, but forward?"

The Grandmothers were challenging me. They were telling me to accept my aloneness, to let go of my attachment to the past, my attachment to friends, to my work, to being part of a community. To even let go of *their* work. To everything really. "I am to be like the salmon, just as they said. That's my job. I'm here to go forward now—no matter what," I said. To myself I muttered, "I'm sort of on a mission."

"Drop into the Earth."

The next time I contacted the Grandmothers was on a beautiful Sunday in late spring. The sun was shining, the garden was bursting with bloom, and the dog and I were luxuriating at the kitchen table. I'd just finished eating breakfast and was reading the morning paper, determined to stay positive even though I was looking at the news, when the Grandmothers showed up. **"Stop what you're doing right now,"** they said to me, **"and think of your connection to the earth. No,"** they said as I uncrossed my legs and sat up straight, **"not your connection to the floor or to the chair, but to the earth Herself. Earth underlies everything,"** they reminded me, **"the house, the car, the road—everything. And it's time for you to renew your kinship with Her, the Mother who nurtures and supports you.**

"Just for a moment," they said, wagging their fingers in my face, **"pull back from that eternal busyness in your mind. Stop what you're doing now and call on the Net of Light."**

"Okay, Grandmothers," I said, closed the paper, and quickly did as they directed. Then they said, **"Turn to your heart and become aware of your body. Feel the weight of your body."** I took in a breath when they said this and focused inside myself, under my breath muttering, "Orders are sure flying thick and fast here." But ignoring me, the Grandmothers said, **"Drop into the weight of your body now and keep dropping down until you feel yourself at one with the earth. Feel it!"** they commanded. **"You aren't separate from the earth. You're not alone. You're linked with your Mother. Always."**

"Relax and let yourself sink into the earth. Go ahead," they said, and making fanning movements with their hands, they motioned as if to hurry me along. **"Drop down now through the soil, through the rocks, sand, and all the layers of strata below you,"** they said. **"Start exploring down there—start moving around inside the earth."** "Okay, Grandmothers," I said, "okay," and I began to do as they'd directed. I would look around in here and explore a bit.

The first thing I noticed was that it was cool inside the earth—not cold, but comfortably cool—and this surprised me. It felt good in there, and then I noticed that there was light inside the earth, enough light to actually see by. It wasn't dark the way I'd imagined it would be, and as I turned my head and began to look around, I realized that I could see everything! How could this be? I wanted to ask the Grandmothers how this was possible, but before I could get the words out, they began to point out my surroundings.

"Look at the colors and forms that surround you here, and let yourself take it in. All these colors," they emphasized, **"all these textures. You're breathing in from the earth Herself now,"** they said to me; **"you're taking in what She is giving you. Breathing in the colors, the light, everything!"** they said with enthusiasm. **"Let yourself open up to what She has to give you,"** they said, and I nodded 'yes' to them and took in a nourishing breath. **"Peace,"** they said, smiling and nodding, **"steadiness, healing, rest, nourishment, minerals, and much more. She's giving it all,"** they said, smiling happily at me. ***"She is ever-giving.* The Mother takes joy in sharing all that She has,"** they said, **"so receive it now and rest in Her embrace."**

I felt myself giving over as they spoke, felt my body letting go of the rapid pace of life I was so accustomed to, dropping everything, really. It was such a relief to let go of it all. Weight was beginning to drop off me, sloughing off my shoulders, hands and arms, cascading off the back of my neck and rolling down my spine. Aughhhh," I groaned happily as I watched it all go. "Wonderful. This is wonderful."

"**It's time for you to move away from the machinations in your brain and move into your own deep intelligence,**" the Grandmothers said. "**When you're grounded in your being, when you're connected to the Net of Light and to Mother Earth, you will automatically feel good. And when you're scrambling around in your mind, racing from thought to thought, from image to worry, worry to image, you won't.**

"**So, keep on dropping down like this,**" they said, "**keep on diving ever deeper into your own essence. Keep on connecting with Mother Earth. You're not a fragmented human being!**" they exclaimed. "**You're not someone racing from stimulus to stimulus, someone who's run by fear and agitation. No!**" they grimaced as they shook their heads. "***You are great.* You're one with all of life. That is who you are. Own that!**" they said. "**Release the worry now. Release the fretting, the fuming and the despair, and instead, let yourself be held. Feel yourself being held. Right this minute,**" they said, "**move into the deep stillness at your core,**" and… "A h h," I groaned as I felt myself settling into this place within me. "A h h," I said again as I breathed in deeply, and "Y..e..s..s..s," the Grandmothers crooned.

"**You're one with the radiant Net of Light that cradles all of life,**" they said, "**so call on the Net, and do that often. Get into the habit of dropping down into the Net of Light and feeling your connection with the Great Mother. Move into oneness with the earth, and in this place of oneness, rest while She fills you. She will do that each time you open to this place within you.**"

I lay down on the carpet after this journey was over and stayed there—just breathing and lying still, very still. I was going over what the Grandmothers had shared and letting myself soak it in, and, as I mulled it over again, something they'd said in *A Call to Power: The Grandmothers Speak,* came back to me. "**We will fill you full. Let us,**" they'd said then, and I realized that at last, I was ready to let them.

"The power rising from the land at this time is the power of creation."

Several Net of Light Gatherings were coming up soon. In another two months, we'd be in Europe, holding our first Gathering in England. Our yearly event in California had just finished, and now it was time to get ready for a round of meetings in various places on the globe, one following after another. The Grandmothers had asked us to anchor the Net of Light in every country we were called to, and, shortly after they'd made this request, events had begun to stack up. A group of us would be traveling to all these places together, and since the Gathering in England was coming up soon, we needed to know what the Grandmothers had in mind for it. So, I went to them to find out.

"**This Gathering in England will anchor our work in the United Kingdom,**" they said. "**At present there's a fragmentation and a sense of division in the United Kingdom.**" They looked thoughtful as they spoke. "**The people there need to feel themselves as part of the One Love; they need to experience their own power. As you work with the Net of Light, you will tie the various parts of the United Kingdom into one whole, and as that happens, these people will get a sense of their own power.**

"**Not long ago, England was seen as a great world power,**" the Grandmothers said. "**Like other cultures,**" they explained, "**Britannia also had her moment on the world stage, but then the old ways there began to fold in upon themselves and collapse. Well,**" they shrugged, "**such things are transitory, and today the image of 'power' in the United Kingdom has shifted. And what happened in England in the last century is today taking place all over the earth. You're seeing it now,**" they said, "**as the 'established' power centers in the world everywhere begin to fail. And because the United Kingdom experienced this power shift first,**" they said, "**it has much to teach the rest of the world.**

"**We encourage everyone who comes to this Gathering in the English countryside to let go of the old perspectives on power they may still carry with them and instead, open to the uprising of elemental power in this area of the world. Nature is truly coming awake there, and your job will be to help the people at this Gathering recognize that. Teach them how to tune into the up swelling of love and good-**

ness rising from their land. Help them fill with it. *The power rising from the land at this time is the power of creation,"* the Grandmothers said. "Heaven and Earth are coming together.

"What we are saying is true," they fixed me with their eyes. "It's real. The Divine power that permeates and connects Heaven and Earth is real whereas the old, human ways of 'power' were never real. Nor were they truly powerful, they shook their heads. "This was patriarchy at work. Throughout history what human beings called 'power' was never natural nor was it God-given," the Grandmothers explained. "The sort of 'power' you are accustomed to is and was man made, contrived," they said. "Its identity was built on dominance and subjugation. Ask the people of the United Kingdom to let any attachment to this old version of power go now," the Grandmothers said. "We promise that they won't miss it. There is something far better waiting for them.

"Encourage them to open," they said, "to open to the wellspring of connection that's rising up to meet them now. It's the Net of Light, the Cosmic Web that's calling, the Net of Light that connects and unifies everything on earth. The radiant Net of Light and Love that links all life is calling them home.

"Always," the Grandmothers said, launching into a new subject, "the place where you find yourself living is the place where you have been planted. *This* is the place where you are to send down roots and grow. Accept your connection to the land where you live," they said. "Embrace your connection to Mother Earth in this place and drop anchor where you stand. Do that," they said, "and once you have anchored yourself, call on your ancestors. Then, through the Net of Light, link with them, so that together you can relate with the land. At every moment you are held within the Net of Light," the Grandmothers reminded me, "so there *is* no separation. No separation of time or place." And eyeing me fiercely, they said, "It's time to come home—to come home to the Net of Light, to the land, to the ancestors, and to one another.

"The Divine is present here and now," they said, and I noticed that they'd shifted themselves into a long line and were now standing shoulder to shoulder, as one body. "The Divine is present in the *real things* of life," they said, speaking as one, "and because it is, the Divine is there inside your heart. *Always* in your heart. So, let the scatter of all those mental constructs you've carried around with you drop away now and instead focus completely in your heart. Make the choice to live from your heart and make it now," they said. "Why not? What are you waiting for?

"Your heart," they explained, "will teach you wisdom, and wisdom will satisfy you in ways that knowledge never could. Try it," they said, cocking their heads as if to dare me. "We ask you to come home to wisdom and anchor yourself inside the radiant Net of Light. The Net of Light holds the earth, holds all life, and holds you. So, let yourself be held," they said. "After all," they smiled, "being held like this is your birthright."

"The places you will visit on this trip are points on a strand of light."

Not only would there be a Net of Light Gathering in England, the week before that, there'd be one in Latvia and another in Lithuania. Somehow the Grandmothers had lined up three different Gatherings in the north of Europe and these would take place one after another. We were wondering why these three had come together at the same time, so one day I journeyed to the Grandmothers to find out.

"The places you will visit on this trip are points on a strand of light," was the first thing they said, and then they demonstrated how Latvia, Lithuania, and the United Kingdom lined up geographically. And when they showed them to me like this, I said, "They look like beads on a string."

"The cultures in Latvia and Lithuania are each specific," the Grandmothers said. "The culture in the United Kingdom is also intrinsic to that place, but in addition to this, in the U.K. you will find a collection of cultures from around the world. The work you will do at these three sites will be specific to each place and will enable the Net of Light to lock into these specific countries and their people, connecting Heaven and Earth right there." And while they were speaking, I watched as a large knot formed at each point on the strand.

"At this time, it's possible for the Net of Light to penetrate these places on the globe," the Grandmothers said, "and that's why you're going to these particular countries. You're going to hold light steady so the Net can anchor itself and soak into these areas. As the Net attaches there, it will soften the hardened crusts on the land. It will also soften and repair the Net of Light itself," they said and when I heard this, my eyes grew big. "What did they mean by this?

"In recent history the Net became limited as to what it could do in this part of the world," the Grandmothers explained. "There were many factors that caused the Net of Light to become restricted here, and consequently, it became thinned out in this area of the world. Weakened," they said. "But after these Gatherings in Latvia, Lithuania, and the United Kingdom, each of them will be able to fully anchor the Net of Light. And this anchoring in of the Net will enable each place to provide a landing base for more love, light and power to tie into this part of the Eastern Hemisphere.

Then the Grandmothers said, "Begin now to work with the Sami," and I sat up in surprise. "The Sami?" I asked. All I knew about the Sami was that they are indigenous people in the far north of Europe and that they work with reindeer. "Work with the Sami," they repeated, "and work with the indigenous peoples of Russia, too. Simply call on them, and while you're at it, also call on the Celtic peoples. The Sami and the native peoples of Russia are still strongly linked with their land. They continue to practice the ways of their ancestors, so be sure to include them in the work you will do. And call on them in a deliberate way," they said, holding my eyes with theirs. "Begin now to share this information with the different organizing teams for the Gatherings so that together all of you can call on the indigenous peoples of these regions.

"The singing and dancing in Lithuania will do untold good," the Grandmothers said, "also the singing in Latvia. The old songs of these countries will call up the ancestors of their land who will then be able to work with you. This ancestral participation will make what you've come to teach go more smoothly.

"Until recently, many people in Latvia and Lithuania still worked on the land each day, and many of them still know the old songs and dances of their ancestors. These people continue to be in touch with the Devas, the gods of nature, and will, therefore, be able to recognize and open to the elemental spirits of their land. Our message of the One Love will be easy for them to grasp," they said, "and the ancestors of the land in Latvia and Lithuania will amplify the power of the work you will all do together. There will be much joy at these Gatherings," the Grandmothers said, and I saw that as they spoke, their eyes were filling with tears.

"The work you will do in England will be a bit more difficult," they said. "It will be challenging for some people there to open to the spirits of the land as such concepts are not part of their everyday life. The United Kingdom is not yet as strongly connected to the land itself," they said, "but soon it will be.

"If, as you work, you return again and again to your purpose of connecting to the land along with linking Heaven and Earth, it will help everyone. It will remind you of why it is you've come together. Each person at the Gathering will feel their connection to the earth and will then be able to focus on their own purpose. And each time they do that, they will curb the wanderings of their minds.

"As you move from Gathering to Gathering, call on us ceaselessly," the Grandmothers said. "Call on all forms of the Divine as well, and include the ancient gods of the Baltic countries. It's good that the work in Latvia and Lithuania will come before the work in England. The ancient gods of those two countries are still known and revered by the people there, so they will be able to assist you with the work you will perform for all of Northern Europe. The participation of the old gods of nature will help firmly anchor the Net of Light in this part of the world."

"Thank you, Grandmothers," I said to them. "Thank you for explaining all of this. I feel clearer now about what we are supposed to do on this trip. It means a lot to me to have a better understanding of exactly why we're going to these three places."

While the Grandmothers listened to me, I noticed that they wore thoughtful looks. "**Something happens when you come together to work for the greatest good,**" they said, "as you do at these Gatherings. **Something happens when you gather like this to selflessly work with and through the Net of Light.** *Something happens* and many of you are now becoming aware of that particular 'something.'

"In the last two years, you've witnessed a power that you never dreamed possible. Power is building now," they said, their bodies rocking back and forth as they nodded thoughtfully. "*It will continue to build,*" they said, "**and** *you* **have a great deal to do with this build up.**

"It is the heart-to-heart connection you make in the Net of Light that broadcasts the actual power of the Net. The link you make through your own hearts sends the Net of Light deeper, wider and more fully—into you, into all forms of matter, and far out into space.

"Waves of power rise up and roll outward from these Gatherings," they said, and when I heard this, I let out a little cry. "These waves of power form concentric circles of healing, and as they fan out, they bless everything they touch. It's the purity and love in your own heart that propels them," the Grandmothers said, and I began to choke up.

"*You* have become generators of power and purpose," they said. "It is YOU who are our hands, minds, words and hearts here on earth. Together with us, each one who responds to our call is doing critical work. YOU!!!" they said, their eyes piercing mine. "Do you understand the importance of the role you are playing? We are working together in partnership," they said. "And this is how it must be.

"Whenever a Net of Light Gathering takes place anywhere in the world, people from many nations attend it. And whenever people come together to work selflessly for the All, every nation on Earth is blessed. All peoples, animals, plants, bodies of water, all land-masses, ancestors, *all life,*" they emphasized, "is blessed. And because you gather for this purpose, each of you has begun to FEEL this power. Trust it," they said, and like a traffic cop, they held their palms up, straight before me. "It is real. It is not your imagination," they chuckled.

The Grandmothers had told me 'it is Not your imagination' many times in the years that I'd worked with them. Said it so often that 'it is not your imagination' had become a humorous touchstone for us in this work. Each time my mind began to wrestle with something it viewed as too audacious to be believed, I'd hear myself saying, 'This must be my imagination.' Once again, my mind was trying to deny that what I was hearing and seeing was real. "No," the Grandmothers repeated to me, shaking their heads and bringing me up short. "It is *Not* your imagination. Everyone is responding to the vast increase in love that's being generated at these Gatherings, and you are no exception. What you are experiencing is happening. It is real.

"The work we do with you will *always* expand," they said. "It will *always* push away any boundaries you may have imposed on it. Our work will *always* go deeper, wider, farther and farther than you can possibly imagine. This is the way it is," they said and shrugged their shoulders, "so you might as well get used to it. There is *no limit* to the work we have done and will do together. That's the way it's supposed to be," they smiled, "because there *is no limit* to the good that we can do together.

"Each day your heart is opening wider," the Grandmothers said and smiled happily at the thought. "You are growing in community, growing in communion with one another. And as this happens, you are making us very happy," they said, grinning broadly. "So, prepare yourself," they said and lifted their heads expectantly. "At these Gatherings in Latvia, Lithuania and England, you will weave this happiness into these three countries. You will weave it into the entire northern area of Europe."

CHAPTER FOUR

"We have songs for everything having to do with nature."

The first Net of Light Gathering would be in Latvia. We arrived in Riga in the middle of the night and though at this hour the airport there was almost deserted, Kaspars, our Latvian friend, was waiting to greet us. "Welcome to my country!" he cried and threw his arms around us. Dragging our luggage behind, we followed him out into the night and after a long drive in a jet-lagged stupor, we arrived at a hotel beside a lake somewhere out in the countryside. There we quickly fell into bed. We'd see Kaspars the next day. He'd been talking about bringing the Grandmothers' work to Latvia for several years and now he'd finally done it. So, tomorrow we'd meet with his people and share the Grandmothers' message.

After some bleary-eyed sight-seeing the next morning, followed by a brief nap, that evening we were ready to meet the Latvians. About fifty men and women had come together and were waiting for us in an upstairs room in Riga. Like Kaspars, most of them appeared to be in their early forties and, from the way they were looking us over, it was clear that they'd come to hear about the Grandmothers only because Kaspars had asked them to. So, as we began the evening's program, the atmosphere in that room didn't feel very warm and inviting. The people who'd come were reserved and some of them looked downright distrustful of these Americans who'd suddenly been dropped into their midst. The unspoken question in the room appeared to be, 'What *is* this stuff?' and 'Who are these people and what's this woman talking about?'

Although they were polite, most of these people were clearly uncomfortable and unfortunately, this atmosphere of distrust was familiar to me. The first time I'd brought the Grandmothers' message to Lithuania the atmosphere in *that* room had felt a lot like this one. Then too there had been a distrust, a 'show me what you got' attitude in the room. My guess was that the distrust went back to the Russian occupation of both of these countries. Distrust of us, the American enemy.

When I recognized the familiar feeling in the room, I stood up a bit straighter, smiled at them, thought of opening my heart more, and soldiered on. And because the people who'd gathered in this meeting room loved Kaspars, they were brave enough to stick it out. But when at last we began the ceremony of the Grandmothers' Empowerment, at last everyone came alive. When we embraced them and wrapped them in the caul so they could feel the physical embrace of the One Love, their hearts opened. Many of them flooded with tears then, and as soon as that happened, their mistrust melted away. From that moment on, they took us into their hearts. In fact, right then and there a troop of them decided that the next day they would drive us out into the countryside and show us the *real* Latvia.

The next morning, twelve of us took off together—a caravan of one American and three Latvians per car. But best of all, these people were singers! And as we traveled from place to place, they sang us the ancient songs of their country. "We have songs to start the rain and songs to stop the rain," they said, "and they work! God is in all our songs and God is a friend, someone we can talk to." As we drove through the countryside, it was one haunting melody after another—God was working in the fields with a farmer, God was answering a woman's question, and God was looking in through a window at a family gathered together around a table.

Now and then we stopped to gather wildflowers along the roadside that they would later dry to make tea, and, on a grassy hillside with an old farm in the distance, we lay down amidst the wildflowers that nodded high above our heads and watched the clouds floating by. No cars on the road, no planes in the sky, no telephone wires, no man-made noises of any kind—only the hum and trill of bees and birds going about their business.

Our next stop would be an old stone farmhouse where the greatest poet of Latvia had once lived and where a now famous physicist lived. Here we would be served a lunch, prepared by the physicist's wife.

Flowers lined the driveway to the farm, roosters were strutting and crowing in the garden, and everything was in bloom. Fruit trees, berry bushes and flowering shrubs. And when I walked into the rustic room at the farmhouse where we were to have lunch, I choked up. Here the table was laid with a white cloth. It was heaped with food and flowers, and from a lone window light poured in onto the ancestral pictures on the walls of the room. The cascade of light from that wooden window filled the room with such peace and serenity that as I stood there, I burst into tears. It was the timeless beauty of the place, and the feeling I had that this room was full of my own Polish ancestors! Because that morning I'd realized that Poland was only right next-door.

The people who had brought us to this home then began to sing their thousand-year-old songs. These aren't the usual love songs we're accustomed to, but are poignant philosophy. For example, when we held hands and stood around that table for grace, grace went—'God I cover this table with white,'—then named the specific god who sat at each corner of the table, and ended by asking God to 'cover my family and home'. And this was sung in a haunting, minor key. 'God' was here; God was near and dear, and as these people sang to us from their hearts, I choked up again, but this time, so did everybody else.

The food they served us had been grown on that farm and, taking the food and the magical atmosphere of the place together, it was by far the best meal of my life. After lunch, the physicist and his wife asked us to give them the Grandmothers' Empowerment and this we gladly did, all of us standing together with the family dog in a light drizzle in the garden.

On the way back to Riga, our hosts insisted that we stop at Laima's Spring to get some water. It turns out that Laima, an ancient goddess of the Baltic countries, is still revered in both Latvia and Lithuania. "Laima gave us this spring so people could take the water and be healed," our hosts said. And we were able to spot the small stream that flowed from the even smaller spring (one bubble of water, gurgling up from the earth), by the multicolored ribbons that were tied to all the trees there.

We carried empty bottles with us up to the streambed and while we waited for them to fill, we started singing. "Water, we love you," we sang to the water, and the Latvians joined in with us. And, no sooner did we sing the first line of that song than the spring sped up its production, going from one bubble to four! Kaspars' mouth flew open when he saw how the spring had responded to the song. Now it was *really* producing and he couldn't stop laughing and marveling as he pointed to the now excessively active spring.

It started to rain then, but we weren't about to leave an experience like this one for a little rain, so we stood together in the soft drizzle, singing one song about water after another. And as long as we sang to it, the spring continued its quadrupled bubbling. This surprising communication with nature thrilled us no end. We couldn't stop laughing and marveling at what was happening here. Nor could the spring stop producing! At last, we picked up our bottles, bowed and thanked the goddess, Laima, and as we turned to leave, the Latvians smiled and said, "We have songs for *everything* having to do with nature." And this time I believed them.

The next day we tore ourselves away from Latvia and drove on to the Gathering in Lithuania. A few of the Latvians would join us there later, so we'd see them again. And, though we didn't realize it at that time, as life unfolded, we would become deeply bonded with these people.

Four women came to the Gathering in the countryside outside Vilnius wearing their full Lithuanian costumes. And as these women sang, danced and glided across the floor in their long skirts and aprons, they helped weave the ancient songs and dances of their land into the work we'd gathered here to do. Together, all of us would work with the Ancestors of our family lines, the land of Lithuania, and the land of Northern Europe.

Before the Gathering began, we covered the walls of the hall where we were meeting with pictures of our ancestors and because more than a hundred of us had gathered here from different parts of the world, the power emanating from that hall was something to behold. We'd come together from America, the Netherlands, South Africa, Latvia and of course, Lithuania.

Lithuanian mothers, fathers, grandparents, and children had piled into cars and buses for this event in the countryside and now the room swelled with expectation. We clapped, stomped, danced, sang, laughed and cried together until joy and healing rocked that meeting hall, filling our hearts and pouring out over the land. At one point, the Lithuanians put we foreigners into the center of their circle and as they sang and danced around us, they called down blessings upon us. Grandmothers and little children were singing to us and blessing us with deep devotion. There was not a dry eye to be found. It was a moment that none of us will ever forget.

Miracles took place all throughout that weekend—miracles along with *so* much love. And all of it happened so naturally and so fast, one miracle after another, that we didn't have time even to remark on any of it…not until later.

When this Gathering in Lithuania was over, the Latvians who'd come with us to take part in it sat up singing and talking with the Americans, Dutch, South Africans and Lithuanians into the wee hours of the morning. And before we caught our flight on to England, we saw them once more. When it was time to board the flight for London, , who should show up in the Riga terminal but our new friends. There they stood in the middle of the boarding area, singing to us and loading us up with gifts, and when we were finally able to tear ourselves away from them, we carried the beauty and the power of their love with us onto the plane, onward to the Gathering in England.

The old Sufi song was thawing that famous British reserve

When we landed at Gatwick Airport, the beauty that is the English countryside rose up like a wave to greet us. Everything there was especially green—from the varied patterns of the fields to the hedges that lined the roads. And as we began our drive through the countryside, the villages we drove through were so charming that it felt like we'd entered a nursery rhyme. I knew I was overdoing it, but part of me kept expecting a Hobbit to show himself.

In addition to the charm of the countryside, we were touched by how warmly the English Net of Light team welcomed us. Some of them were new to the Grandmothers' message and weren't quite sure yet what this Net of Light business was about. But if they'd had little experience with the Grandmothers as yet, they loved and respected Deborah, the head of their team. And Deborah had had *a lot* of experience with the Grandmothers. So, everyone who'd come together for the Net of Light Gathering in England was game to learn. The Net of Light group leaders who'd traveled to the Gathering from across Europe and America to help introduce the Grandmothers and the Net of Light to the United Kingdom also added power and purpose to this Gathering.

And when it was over, the English and Irish came away impressed by the dedication of these European grandmothers.

We began in the main hall of the estate where we would meet throughout the weekend. We were singing and dancing "All I ask of you is forever to remember me as loving you," when I noticed what a heart-melting effect this song was having on this group. The ancient Sufi song was busy thawing that famous British reserve and as we danced from partner to partner while looking into each other's eyes, I watched people's attention move away from their busy minds and into their hearts. All over that room hearts were now opening and tears were falling, and, as the energy in the room moved into our hearts, we began to pass the Grandmothers' Empowerment on to each other. Then we cast the Net of Light for the world.

As the weekend went on, little by little, the One Love wove us all together. Those of us who'd traveled from America to this event in England were thrilled that although now we were gathered on what for us was the opposite side of 'the pond,' we were again feeling the familiar pull of the One Love. These people were not strangers to us, they were just new members of our family.

We also got right to work with the Ancestors of the Light—the ancestors of our family lines and the ancestors of the land of England. And we held this focus for the entire Gathering and also while traveling to the sacred sites of Stonehenge, Avebury, Glastonbury and others.

At the English gathering, we followed the Grandmothers' guidance, making it a point to also link ourselves with the gods of the Baltic countries. And it was this particular link that enabled us to make a strong connection between heaven and earth. The heaven-earth connection we formed here became quite palpable and when this occurred, more hearts in the meeting room began to thaw. As we sang, danced, prayed in that ancient hall, and performed ceremony, together we did some Big work. We chanted together and the One Love multiplied itself many times over and, just as it had in Latvia and then again in Lithuania, now it also lit up the countryside in England.

After the Net of Light Gathering in England was over, many women there stepped up to form groups and study circles throughout the United Kingdom. This quickly wove a network of lighted support throughout Scotland, Ireland, Wales and England. A forward momentum was developing now and, as we stood back and watched it come to life throughout Northern Europe, we couldn't help but marvel at the way the Grandmothers had brought everything about. Each point of light on that string of light that they had originally showed me was now glowing brightly. The Net of Light was now anchored in Latvia, Lithuania and in the United Kingdom.

"Live Across Time"

As the group of us that traveled together moved from Gathering to Gathering across Northern Europe, we became increasingly aware of the connection between heaven and earth that was being made around us and through us. There was something that now linked our individual circuits to the earth as well as to the Divine. And this was happening—all at the same time. We were able to stand back and witness it at the same moment that we participated in it.

We'd first felt the connection between heaven and earth in Latvia, both at the stone house and again at Laima's spring. At both places we'd witnessed magic and felt it moving through us. And this feeling was present again in Lithuania. There the bond between heaven and earth seemed to embed itself into the meeting hall with us. It was incontrovertibly there when the Lithuanians called down blessings on us. And it was there in the haunting songs of the land, in the dancing, in the singing, and the rituals we performed together—both the planned and unplanned ones.

The spirits of the land also rose up to meet us as soon as we landed at the airport in the United Kingdom. And they stayed with us there throughout the entire weekend. The ancestors, the ancient gods and the spirits of the land in Northern Europe were so present in everything we did together that they altered our sense of reality. And after almost two weeks of feeling what it was like to be in the midst of a growing bond between heaven and earth, when we arrived back home, I wanted to know what we could do to strengthen this connection *everywhere* in the world. As far as I was concerned, the anchoring of earth to heaven, of heaven to earth needed to become integral—everywhere. Every living thing deserved this magical connection.

The following month our traveling Net of Light group would fly to Australia for a Gathering at Uluru in the middle of the Australian Outback. And, just as we'd felt about the Gatherings in northern Europe, we also felt about Australia. Uluru, often called Ayers Rock, is the most sacred Aboriginal site in Australia and we wanted to accomplish the most good we could while we were gathered at this ancient and holy place.

So, with this goal in mind, a few weeks before we were to leave, I journeyed to the Grandmothers. But before I asked my question, I greeted my beloved teachers and then called on the old gods of Northern Europe as well as all forms of the Divine. Then I asked the Grandmothers, as well as the ancient gods, "What can we do to strengthen the connection between heaven and earth, not only in Northern Europe, but everywhere?"

No sooner did I get the words out, than, **"Yes!"** the gods of the northlands loudly chorused. The Grandmothers, who were standing right beside the gods, nodded their happy agreement. **"Now is the time to activate the connection to us and to the land,"** the ancient gods said. **"For time out of mind we have held this link and because we work intimately with the land, our connection to the earth will help you to also make the link."**

After they said this, there was a flurry of activity as more of the old gods, along with the elemental spirits of the earth rushed in to join us. **"Call on us,"** they cried together, **"call on us!"** and quickly I nodded 'yes.' There were so *many* of them! There must have been thousands present and as I looked at them, I took in a deep breath and bowed my head. Then I closed my eyes and turned my attention within myself. "Speak to me," I said to my heart, "speak to me and speak *for* me."

There was a long silence after that and then I heard myself talking to the beings who now surrounded me. "I don't know you," I said to these ancient ones who had gathered here, the gods as well as the spirits of nature, "but I want to know you." And, when I lifted my head and looked up at them, before me stood a goddess.

She had icicles coating her hair—that was the first thing I noticed about her. I could see her dark locks showing through the ice and also noticed that her cheeks were pink with cold. There were heavily muscled thunder beings standing beside her, and many small beings too—elemental spirits of fire, rock, earth, water and sky. Somehow, I knew who they all were. Dwarves were present as well, elves, and sky-beings that ride the winds. I'd never seen sky beings before and as I stood staring at them with my mouth open, the Grandmothers nodded encouragingly. **"Go on, go on,"** they said.

"All these beings who are gathered here are very much connected with the northlands of Europe and Asia," I explained to myself and to the Grandmothers as I continued to observe. "These particular spirits and gods are not much present in the Western Hemisphere," I said, "but they're all over the top of the Eastern Hemisphere." Somehow, I knew all this and as this information registered inside me, I understood that there are other spirits that are specifically present in the Western Hemisphere. Not these, but others.

Then my thoughts were interrupted by the sound of thunder, followed by loud shouting and singing as all the beings that had gathered together here began to call on the powers of the earth, of the rain, snow, sleet, winds, and of the heat of the sun. **"All in good measure,"** the Grandmothers affirmed and they stroked my arms to calm me. I had begun to shake and by stroking me, the Grandmothers were letting me know that this coming together of the spirits of nature would happen bit my bit and that it was nothing I needed to be afraid of.

"All of this will take place in perfect time," they said to me, and no sooner did they say this than I was assailed by an even greater cacophony of sound and movement. As the clatter and banging around me reached a crescendo, I watched as the beings who'd assembled before me shifted their stance, changed places and moved around. They seemed to be taking new positions now, holding places they hadn't held before. Then I noticed that they were standing at attention, standing in readiness. "In readiness for what?" I wondered….

"The worlds are coming together," they said, and I startled at their words. "What?" Then, as I watched, what looked like two very large plates began to slip together, sliding and bending slightly so they fit with each other. They weren't coming together in a violent way, but they were definitely doing it with force. Great power was present here and there was no holding it back. A tectonic shift of some kind was taking place right before my eyes.

Now there was more movement and more wild cries. My heart began to pound in my chest and my mouth grew dry as the screeching, howling, and trumpeting of animals echoed everywhere. Mammoths came pounding in then, massive beasts. Charging toward me at a dead run, they thundered their way through forests of trees that snapped and gave way before them. As they ran, their trunks were up and when they charged in front of me, I heard someone say, **"New ice age."** "I don't know what this means," I said to myself and to the Grandmothers, shaking my head to clear it, "but there are so many ancient animals gathered here—saber toothed tigers, mammoths, hairy horses, monstrous bears... These beasts are nothing I've ever seen before," I said. "These are creatures from long ago," I whispered, my voice filled with wonder.

Then suddenly all was silent. No sound, no movement at all. I held my breath, alert for what might happen next, but when I realized that I was running out of air, I gasped and said, "This is too much. This is simply too much. Way too much! Too much movement, too much change." I was really shaking now—my body quivering and twitching with tension and when I realized what a wreck I was, I quickly took in another breath and again I asked the question for this journey. "What can be done at this time?" I asked. "What can be done to strengthen the connection between heaven and earth?"

"Peace, peace, peace," I heard the Grandmothers singing. **"Peace in me..."** they sang. This was something we often sang at our Net of Light meetings and hearing it now was a great comfort. And, as the Grandmothers continued to sing, my body began to relax and settled down.

Watching me carefully out of the corners of their eyes, the Grandmothers spoke. **"Include these ancient animals when you work with the Net of Light,"** they said. **"Let them become part of this work. They too are Ancestors of the Light,"** they said, and "Yes," I nodded. "I understand, Grandmothers, and we will do this."

"Include the Ice Age and all ages on earth in the Net of Light," they said. **"Embrace all of what you call 'pre-history' in addition to history. Take a broader view now,"** they said; **"embrace the entire evolution of the earth. Don't look only at your own time and only at what you think of as 'history,'"** they said, **"but encompass the entire evolution of your planet.**

"Let these timeless connections with the old gods of the North, the elemental spirits, and all forms of life that have ever lived become part of the work you are doing. Don't pull away from the deep past because you don't understand it," they cautioned me. **"Include it!"** they said. **"The ancient past is NOT mythic. It is real. It's part of planet earth."**

I stopped still when I heard this and turned within myself. I would make this commitment. "I will do this," I declared to the Grandmothers and to myself. "I will embrace all beings." **"Make your reach larger,"** the Grandmothers nodded, and I thought of including the Anasazi, the prehistoric cavemen, and all life that has ever lived on earth. "I will include all of them with the Ancestors," I said to the Grandmothers. "They too are our ancestors."

"A Bigger and bigger reach," the Grandmothers said. **"Think big. Go big. From this point on be ALL-inclusive in the work you do. Go back to the stories of the first beings. Adam and Eve, Grandmother Spider Woman, all versions of the first beings taught by the various cultures of the world,"** they said, and so I vowed to do this too. I would think of Adam and Eve, of the Native American stories I've heard, think of the emersion stories, I would call up the stories of the Ramayana. I would do it. I would include everything and everyone.

"Let your feet sink DEEP into the earth now," the Grandmothers said, **"deep! Live across time,"** they commanded. Then, holding me with their eyes, they said, **"Live timelessly and embrace it all."** Now I caught a glimpse of Earth as She was before life emerged here and what I saw was a whirling mass, a spinning ball of fire. **"Yes!"** the Grandmothers cried. **"You see truly."** And as I observed this burning mass, I felt that fire within myself too and sensed its elemental power. **"Go there!"** the Grandmothers said. **"Work from this place too. This place will take you beyond all petty concerns. Go BIGGGGG!!!!!"** they chanted. Then they laughed and said, **"WE have spoken."**

"Keep your head up!"

What I'd seen on this journey had indeed taken me to new territory. Before this, for me, pre-history had only been a thought—and a vague one at that. Not part of my life…but now, well now that was different. However, I still had a hard time believing that all of this had really happened—the mammoths, the ancient gods of the Northlands and most of all, being told to link heaven and earth. It was a lot to wrap my head around and so, after a few days, I once again returned to the Grandmothers for a better understanding.

"Dear Grandmothers," I said as I stood before them. "I'm standing on new ground now, so please direct me as to how to proceed with this mission of linking heaven and earth.

"Heaven and earth are not, nor have they ever been, separated," they said. "It's only in the mind that they are separate. So, your job," they explained patiently, "is to move beyond the confines of your mind. The Baltic songs and dances are powerful in that they go beyond the mind. In some cases, people don't even know what they are singing about," they said, "but they feel the rightness and power in the songs anyway. And they are correct. The songs carry power," they nodded. "Those songs by-pass the strictures of the mind," they said. "This is a good place to start.

"Chanting and singing create different brain waves and a different energy field. Pursue this," the Grandmothers said, nodding emphatically at me. "Sing, and with the singing, incorporate dance movements to access this plane of energy, this plane which is non-material and therefore not part of the mind trap. Songs, chants and dances move beneath the snares of the mind. Go there!" they said. "Introduce more and more songs into our work and incorporate movement with them. We will guide you in this.

"Begin now to unify with the spirits of Uluru, the place where you will be traveling next," they said, and I looked up at them in surprise. "Begin now," they said again and I realized that we would be arriving at the sacred red heart of Australia—Uluru—soon, very soon. It was time to start preparing for *this* Gathering. "Okay, Grandmothers," I agreed, "I'll start right away."

"Drum and call the spirits of Uluru," they said, and so I quickly picked up the drum and began. And I kept up a steady beat until I saw long lines of aboriginal people converging across the Outback, walking toward Uluru. "They're coming together for this Gathering with us," I said, my voice filled with surprise. Then it came to me that we needed to send out a newsletter, asking people to unify with us as we prepared to work with the Net of Light in this most ancient holy place.

"We will be meeting there to link Uluru to the entire Fabric of Being," I wrote, "to link all power places on earth, and with everyone who works with the Net of Light." "We ask you to begin now to focus each day on this work," the Grandmothers said, "to drum and connect with the spirits of the land there. The Divine is with you," they said. "The Divine mandated this work and the Divine has engineered every part of it. The build-up for Uluru begins now."

I got chills when they said this but, "Yes, Grandmothers," I replied, "We'll begin now." Again, I asked them, "How can we help bring heaven and earth back into the One Love? **"Loving community,"** they fired back, **"loving communion. Build that,"** they said. **"Open your arms and hearts to one another. To all! We will guide you,"** they promised, **"to an ever-greater embrace.**

"Let go of judgment and simply love," they said. **"It's not your job to 'fix' things or 'figure out' what to do. We do that,"** they said. **"Your job is to stand in love with your hearts and arms open wide. When you do this, you make room for us to enter in, you make room for us to live and act through you. When you do this, your 'work' becomes our work; your life becomes our message. Keep it simple,"** they said, **"very simple. Choose love. Choose love every time. Say 'yes' to loving and then let everything else go.**

"The mind may judge this to be simplistic," they said, **"because the mind is ruled by the ego, but *it is not simplistic*. It is the wisest, most profound action you can take. When you are happy, love,"** the Grandmothers said. **"When you are sad, love. When in doubt, choose love. Always, and every moment choose love. Make that choice and the correct action will follow it, but first you must say 'yes' to love.**

"We are here now," the Grandmothers said to me, **"and we will never leave you."** I looked up at them when I heard this and I noticed how feminine they were, how beautiful and soft. I could feel them holding me in their arms and when I looked again, I saw that the face on one of them was my own face. "I am the Grandmothers and I am held by the Grandmothers!" I blurted out and for some reason this recognition made me cry.

Quickly they drew closer and moved me into a position where I was able to see more clearly. My head was up now and, in this higher, upright position I could see far out over the tops of buildings and the land before us. **"Far vision,"** they said to me, **"far vision. You get bogged down by the details of daily life—especially the dramatic ones,"** they laughed, **"and yet none of them have any lasting value. Keep to the Far Vision,"** they said, pointing fingers at me. **"Look only at what is real."** "Okay, Grandmothers," I said, "I will. I will. Lead on, Grandmothers."

"You have a job to do," they reminded me, **"your job is to hold this vision for yourself and others. Don't crumple and fold under the**

'weight' of daily problems, challenges and distractions, but hold to the far vision." "Okay," I said again, "I will," and now I saw that whatever problems came up with my family, disconnects with friends and neighbors, or disappointments and indecision in life—it was all nothing but a distraction from what they were calling the far vision. And again, I noticed that my head was up. UP.

"*Keep* your head up!" the Grandmothers said. "**Don't get pulled down by negativity, worry and the broadcasting of fear that's rife in the world today. These are only distractions. Arguing, competing, posturing, worrying, striving—nothing but distractions,**" they said, their heads shaking emphatically. "**Keep your head up and hold your eyes to the vista above the uproar. You are here on earth to do great things. You're not here for the daily dramas. If you keep returning your focus to your heart instead of letting it wander into the jumble in your mind, you will maintain what we are calling** *far-vision.*

"Most of those who listen to our messages are women," the Grandmothers said, "**women and a few men. This is because women are** *able* **to hear us while many men are not. Because you carry the energy of yin within yourselves,**" they said, speaking to women, "**your hearts are more open to truth and you're not as caught up in the yanking of the ego. Oh, you're not free of ego,**" they laughed, "**but you're not dragged along by it as much as those who are run by the energy of yang.**

"In parts of the world," they said, "**just because you are women, you're debased and abused. In other parts you're over-looked and diminished. The out-of-balance energy of yang that's running rampant in the world today doesn't understand yin,**" they said. "**It's out of balance with its own compliment and that makes it fear the steadiness of yin. And run-away yang energy tries to stifle women because women are reservoirs of yin. All of that is based in fear.**

"Few men or women know of the enormous power of yin that lies within a woman," the Grandmothers said. "**This hidden force is a potent weapon against lies, falsity and the bullying habits of out-of-balance yang. Yin holds steady…always it holds steady. It's not bullied, it's not fearful, and it never gives up on life. Yin IS. Yin is what you hold,**" they said, pointing to me. "**You are a subtle warrior.**

"Oh!" I whispered, "a subtle warrior! Wow! Those words…" Thinking of myself as a subtle warrior felt somehow right to me. For the most part I tended to be quiet and to operate under the radar. I, and everyone else who was involved with the Net of Light, tended to say little about ourselves, but we *did* a lot. Wherever we went, we held the Net of Light steady—for ourselves and for everyone else. "Subtle warrior," I said. "Yes," I decided, "I like that term."

"There has never been a time when Earth and Heaven were not joined together"

The next time I went to the Grandmothers, however, I was not so sanguine. For some reason I'd really begun to feel my age. At this point in life I was no longer young by any means; I was no longer even middle-aged. In fact, I'd begun to notice that I was now invisible to most of the population. I'd started taking medication, couldn't hear well any more, my body parts seemed to be taking turns breaking down, and sales people had begun to call me 'dear.' The latter kind of made me chuckle to myself but it was all a bit disconcerting.

"Grandmothers," I said, as I came before them, "for those like me who are moving into the winter season of life, there are certain doors we have to walk through. Scary doors," I admitted, "and there's no way around it, we have to walk through them. Loss of clout, diminishment of power, unreliable health, and all this while living in increasingly unstable times," I sighed deeply. "Sometimes as I go along, it feels like the road markers I used to count on to show me the way are either covered in weeds or have been bulldozed. Where's my home place now?" I asked them. "What can I count on?"

"**You are impatient,**" the Grandmothers replied. "I know I am," I answered, "and I'm sorry I'm like that, but I seem to be made that way." They laughed at me when I said this, and I laughed along with them. It was true and it *was* pretty funny. But as I was chuckling over the absurdity of it all, I noticed something strange. There was a slow rolling movement that seemed to be coming up from the ground underneath my feet. The movement was constant. It was making me feel unstable, hard to keep my balance and stand steady. Then it got stronger. It was coming in toward me now, heading in from several directions at the same time and converging where I was standing. "Is something rising up from the ground now?" I asked. "Is this about an awakening in the land? What *is* this?"

"The Gathering that's coming up in Australia is primarily for all the land on this planet," the Grandmothers said and I looked questioningly at them, wondering what this had to do with this feeling coming up from the earth. "Much will be changing soon and you're beginning to feel that change right now," they said. "When you gather together at Uluru, you'll weave new garments for the land. One garment will be specifically for Australia, and there will be others for all the countries on earth to wear. These will be garments of light," they said and they smiled at me as if what they'd just said was the most normal thing in the world.

I wasn't sure I understood what they were talking about but as I waited with them, I noticed that now, in addition to the rolling action of the earth, smoke was wafting up from the ground we were standing on. Fumes were rising from the earth and as I watched and waited to see what would happen next, I understood that it was the presence of the Net of Light that was making all this happen. The Net was drawing smoke and fumes out of the ground and as it did, it was lifting and magnetizing them to itself.

"Yes," the Grandmothers said, "this *is* happening. This is not your imagination. As we've told you many times before, it's time for the old poisons that have been stored in the earth to come to the surface now." I looked up at them with a question in my eyes, and they said, "Singing will do this. In Uluru, singing will help remove the poisons from the earth, so sing while you're there. Singing, chanting, prayer, laughter and music," they said. "All of these will magnify the power of love which will lift off the old fears, griefs, suffering, and anger. What you are seeing now,'" they said, pointing to the smoke that was continuing to rise from the earth, "is some of that poison.

"Angels will join in with you as you do the work at Uluru. They will sing with you," they said. "As your hearts open, the heavenly host will join in, and the songs you sing together will penetrate the earth itself, penetrate and lift the suffering that's been locked into the land. It will free it to go to God," they said, and as they spoke, their faces broke into radiant smiles. Then they lifted their arms high, spread their hands and cried, "It will rise into the light and go!

"Sing!" the Grandmothers commanded. "And then sing some more... and more. Let music do the work for you," they said; "as you sing, you will be lifted and the land will be lifted. Great Good will come from this!" they cried. "Great Good!

"All will go well at the Gathering at the great red rock," they said. "All will go very well. While you are at Uluru you will be working under the umbrella of song and within the Net of Light. We will be there with you," they promised, "and this Gathering will be a blessing for one and all.

"All over your planet the eternal spirits of earth are awakening now," the Grandmothers said. "In the northern and southern hemispheres, in the east as well as in the west. The sacred connections between Heaven and Earth that were forged long ago are making themselves known again. Awakening," they said. "This is the time of awakening.

"In May you saw the power of this connection in Europe," they said, "and soon you will see it at Uluru. Prepare yourselves for an infusion of force as power flows from Uluru into the Net of Light that is holding your planet steady. Your purpose in traveling to Uluru is to awaken this connection." Then twelve, intent Grandmothers looked me in the eyes and said, "We promise that the connection *will* take place.

"There has never been a time when earth and heaven were not joined together," the Grandmothers smiled, "part and parcel of the One Love that knows no separation. It is only the mind that assumes a separation between the so-called 'profane' and the 'sacred.' The ego mind created the myth of separation. However, this myth will dissolve soon, for in truth, all are one, have always been, and ever shall be one.

"When you travel to sacred places on your planet with the intention of linking them to the Net of Light, we support you," the Grandmothers said. "It is our will that the Net of Light be strengthened at this time. It must be strengthened to do its job of holding your planet steady.

"Alert others to the purpose of this mission so they too can participate in this linking and awakening. Each person who thinks of the Net of Light increases its power and helps it do its job of holding the earth during these times of change. The more power, the more blessings and the more good," they said. "Spread love," the Grandmothers said. "**Multiply goodness all over the face of this planet and stay connected with us in the Net of Light.**"

As soon as this journey was over, I sent out a notice, asking that others join us in the work that would soon take place at Uluru. From all corners of the world people responded to this call.

From horizon line to horizon line, stars coated the firmament.

The Grandmothers were right. The Gathering at Uluru did turn out to be a blessing, a blessing and a potent experience. Our group traveled by stages to the massive red rock that juts out of the desert, commanding the vast Outback. We flew from Los Angeles to Sydney, and after a few days in the city, took another flight into the Outback.

The air in the desert holds the clear light of that climate which makes it possible to see for vast distances. And, because there is little man-made light throughout the vast land of the Outback, the stars there are an unforgettable presence.

One morning around five o'clock, I felt such a longing to be alone with the stars at Uluru that I hiked out onto the land by myself. It was cold as I picked my way through the tough grasses in the dark but I found a bare place at last and lay down on the red dirt to get a look at the heavens. Millions of stars lined the bowl of the night sky, and that bowl cupped me from horizon line to horizon line. Stars were coating the firmament. Millions of glowing points of light—above me and to the sides. Twinkling stars, falling stars, and constellations I'd never before seen.

I watched as stars fell to earth and others seemed to sing and dance in the twinkling sky. The early morning air was crisp, and these lights in the sky were alive. As I lay on the ground, I cast the Net of Light and asked the ancient spirits of Uluru to pour power into the Net and strengthen it so it could comfort and heal a suffering world. And under that pre-dawn Australian sky, my connection to the stars strengthened so much that when I at last returned to America, I was able to bring the deep healing of Uluru with me.

Each day, we gathered around the great rock and did ceremony together. We sang and worked beside and underneath its red overhangs and at night we worked underneath the stars of the Southern Hemisphere. We sang with the rocks, the trees and grasses and anchored the Net of Light at this revered place, precious to the Aborigines, and now, precious also to us.

Our hearts opened to the land and the land opened to us. We opened also to one another and always to the Grandmothers, who had brought us together here to share in this work. And, in the end, each of us was aglow with happiness—so much happiness that several times strangers stopped us and asked if they could join our group. Of course, we said, "Yes!" We folded them in with us and when we finally left Uluru to start our trek back home, we were full of gratitude, full to overflowing.

CHAPTER FIVE

"Underneath the night sky, you will find and explore your friendship with the stars."

Several months after the Gathering in Australia, it was time to plan for the next Gathering, this one in California. This time we were being guided to Joshua Tree National Park in the Mojave Desert. I didn't understand why the Grandmothers were leading us to such a remote location—at least a two-hour drive from Los Angeles. This meant that people would need to fly in to L.A. and then either get a car or shuttle to Joshua Tree. So, before we started telling people about it, I needed the Grandmothers to let us know why we were meeting way out there.

"Grandmothers," I said as soon as I saw them, "this Gathering at Joshua Tree…. I don't know if people will want to go all the way out there, and yet it seems like the right thing to do. Why are we feeling such a pull to this location?"

"This Gathering feels different somehow," I continued, talking and thinking at the same time. "It seems like this one may have even more to do with the earth itself than with the people who attend it," I said, and as I continued to speak, I noticed that they weren't responding. "Grandmothers," I said then, "Uluru felt a bit like this too—like the work with the land was the most important thing. Will you please make the purpose of this Gathering at Joshua Tree clear?" I asked, and then, for some reason, I felt the need to repeat the whole thing all over again, word for word.

When I finished my second recitation, the Grandmothers nodded approval, and opening their arms, they showed me the wide, open spaces surrounding Joshua Tree. The first thing I noticed was that on the earth as well as in the atmosphere above the land, there was great luminosity. The air seemed to sparkle while a light desert wind carried a feeling of freedom over the land. As I felt the desert breeze against my skin, I was reminded of how the air had felt at Uluru, and as I breathed in the wide, open feeling of this place, my heart lifted. "This is why we're going to Joshua Tree," I murmured. "To get beyond the distractions of daily life, to go beyond our limitations and get to a place of clear vision."

Now I noticed that just like the Grandmothers, I, too, was standing with my arms outstretched and my palms facing upward. Slowly then I began to turn—rotating in a circle. The Grandmothers turned with me, and as we circled together, I noticed that the light was growing dimmer. The atmosphere had become dusky, and the colors were growing more and more indistinct. And then it was night. All was in darkness, and as we continued to turn like this with our arms upraised, I saw that we were rotating underneath the stars.

This went on for a while—a slow and measured turning under a night sky. Then, little by little the sky began to lighten and when it turned to day again, we still continued to rotate, but now we were doing it under the sun. As we kept on turning and turning, into the dark and into the light, the Grandmothers crooned, **"Receive. Receive from the earth. Receive from the star nations. Receive.** "Yes, Grandmothers," I whispered, mesmerized by the slow rhythm of our turning.

"Here, in this desert place, you will listen to the wind," they said, and I nodded my agreement. **"Here you will *be able* to listen to the wind,"** they said, giving me a long look. **"Here you will *be able* to feel us beating your heart, to feel us living you. Here you will *be able* to move beyond your mind,"** they said, and when I heard this, my breath caught in my throat. **"Here in this holy place, you will be able to do all of that,"** the Grandmothers said, **"and, as you move beyond your mind, you will open to a new level of clarity.**

"You are coming," they said, their heads slowly nodding up and down, and I looked up at them, not sure what they meant. **"You are coming, and you are *becoming*,"** they said. **"As you approach this place of purity in the desert, you will begin to shed. This is not a place of busyness and striving,"** they shook their heads. **"This is not a place of strife, nor is it a place of…."** They paused; searching for the right word, then shook their heads in defeat. There was no 'right' word for what they wanted to say. "**This is a place of clarity and freedom**," they said at last. "**It exists beyond the confines of human society.**"

I took in a BIG breath when I heard this, and after that there was only silence until at last, the Grandmothers spoke. "**You will step into freedom and great expansion at Joshua Tree. Those who will attend this Gathering are hungry for this**," they said, and they nodded to one another. "**This event will not be like the others**," they said. "**Begin now to work with nature, and start calling on the star nations. Under the night sky, you will find and explore your friendship with the stars**," they said, "**so begin now.**"

I had begun to work with the stars at the Gathering at Uluru, and after we got home from Australia, I often spent time in the evening at home with the stars. Even though we live in heavily populated Southern California, our home sits close enough to open land and the Pacific Ocean to often see the night sky full of stars. We don't see the numbers of them you see at Uluru or Joshua Tree, but we see them. And for me, the stars became a welcoming presence. For the first time in my life, these points of light were friends, and I often sat out in the garden with my new friends, talking to them, loving them and enjoying our connection.

"What humans have destroyed, humans must repair."

After a couple of months of working with the stars, one day the Grandmothers said to me, "**There are great rips and tears in the Net of Light. This is especially true in the Middle East, but the Net has also become weakened in the Northern Hemisphere—in Northern Europe and Russia. Wherever the template of light and love that holds the planet has been weakened**," they explained, "**terrorism, violence, and evil acts abound. These areas have been wounded**," they said, "**and so we are asking you to do some work there.**

"**The Net of Light itself is perfect**," they said, "**but because it interfaces with humanity, it can be torn by the acts of man.**" They had told me this before, but because of what was going on in the world now, their words went straight to my heart. "**This damage to the Net has occurred**," they said, looking very serious, "**and what humans have destroyed, *humans* must repair. This is the law**," they announced, their heads nodding as they regarded me fiercely. **"We are asking you to step forward now and strengthen the Net of Light that holds your planet. Many of you have been working in this way for a long time,"** they said. **"Please continue and ask others to help too. The Net of Light is needed now more than ever.**

"Some call it *Net of Light*, some *Cosmic Web*, or *Grid of Light*, *Sacred Template*, *Indra's Net*, and other names," they said, "but however it is called, it is the same construct. This is the Net of Light that will hold your planet steady during the times of change that are upon you. We are asking you to go forward and find your place on the radiant Net, and then hold, hold, hold light steady for yourselves and for everything that lives.

"You can pray for those who are suffering in your world, but you will do more good if while you pray, you broadcast light directly into the Net of Light. The Net holds everyone and everything that lives, so your prayers and the work you do with it will instantly reach everyone. When you water a tree," they said, **"you don't sprinkle water on each individual leaf. No!"** they declared. **"You water the roots of the tree which then send moisture to every branch, leaf, flower and fruit. It's the same with the Net of Light,"** they said. **"We especially ask you to magnify the power of the Net of Light for the Middle East,"** they said. **"This broadcasting of light will strengthen the entire Net and enable it to uplift everything and everyone in the Middle East. And everywhere on Earth.**

"Many times, we have told you that to begin this work, you can think of the Net of Light like a great fishing net that covers the earth from above and penetrates through all the land, air, and water. Somewhere on that radiant Net is a place that will feel right for you, so step forward and take that place. And, once you have, then let your heart pour love and light into the Net, which in turn will pour love and light back into your heart. Sit quietly, giving and receiving like this, and know that the more light you send out, the more will come back to you. That too," the Grandmothers said, **"is the law.**

"The Net of Light is lit by the radiance of the heart. It's your own heart that propels light through the gridlines of the Net and supports this planet. So, let your heart connect with the Net of Light and then rest in it, observing as love and light pour throughout the

Net and throughout your body. Rest," they said, "and feel what it's like to be held in the Net of Light.

"*Everything* is blessed by the touch of the Net, and as you focus the power of its radiance into the Middle East, it will begin to mend the tears there. This is blessing work," the Grandmothers said, "and we assure you that there is *nothing* more valuable you can do.

"As you work with the Net of Light, you yourself become a blessing," they said. "You bless and you are blessed—all at the same time," they smiled. "By thinking of the Net of Light, you automatically link yourself with the sacred and holy places on your planet, with the sacred beings who support life on earth, and with people of pure heart who seek the greatest good for everyone. Each time you think of the Net and let light flow from your heart, you do untold good. As we have said many times," they said, smiling into my eyes, "you become a walking blessing upon the earth."

"Terror is a foul disease and terrorists are sick with it, but you needn't become infected."

I sent that Grandmothers' message out in a newsletter so that others could also benefit from it, and afterward I heard from many people who were heartened by it. But the violence and acts of terror around the world didn't let up. So, again I went to the Grandmothers. "Please tell us about the terrorists who are menacing the world now, Grandmothers. They're causing so much grief," I shook my head in despair, "and we don't understand why they do what they do."

"At this point it's impossible for you to understand what's going on with the people who perform these acts," the Grandmothers said, "because you don't dwell in darkness the way they do. Terrorists live each day in fear and hate, and since this is not where you live, you can't understand why they do what they do."

"Grandmothers," I asked, "what *can* we do? How can we cope with this onslaught of evil?" "We think you're doing a pretty good job of it," they replied. "You're focusing on love and you're gravitating to expansion, not contraction. You're working together, pulling together, encouraging one another, and staying connected in love.

"Terror is a foul disease," they said, shaking their heads, "and terrorists are sick with it, but you needn't become infected." They held their eyes on me to be sure I understood what they meant, and I gulped, "Yes, Grandmothers." "There's always a certain amount of sickness on earth," they explained, "and sometimes a nasty disease will create an epidemic. Right now, there is an epidemic of cruelty and hate on your planet," they said, "and those who perform these murderous acts are infected by it. They've become twisted with hate, but you needn't allow them to infect you.

"Stay away from the sick areas of mass mind consciousness," they said, and I looked up at them, wondering what they meant. "Don't tolerate foul thoughts or foul behavior," they said. "Turn people who dwell in the dark away from your door and turn thoughts like that away as well. Keep your home, your mind, and heart clean, and when you venture out into the world, go to other clean, well-lighted places. Seek the company of loving people and life-affirming events.

"We ask you to also start praying for the diseased and damaged ones. Cast the Net of Light to the darkened places on earth—to the darkened places in the world outside and to the darkened places in the world inside you too. Open to the negative thoughts that have hidden themselves from you and let them now be lifted by the Net of Light," the Grandmothers said. "Let the intrinsic goodness of your heart rise up and expand. Trust in the purity of your own heart," they said. "This heart will light up the world.

"Keep your focus on the Net of Light," they reminded me. "And do this so the Net can bind you all together in love. We ask each of you to perform the job you've been given and to do it in small ways, in quiet, unnoticed ways. There's no need to call attention to yourself," they said. "Just be. You needn't speak about any of what we are telling you," they added. "In fact, you needn't *do* anything. Just quietly *be* the light that you are. Anchor and broadcast light. That's enough," they said. "That's what's needed now. Call on us each day," they nodded encouragingly, "and we will hold you steady.

"And here is something else," they said. "To move the energy on earth from terror to healing, hold all people as your brothers and sisters. This is especially important," they said. "Don't pull away from any group because of what they may have done. Don't even pull away from the perpetrators of evil crimes. Perpetrators are also your brothers and sisters. It may be difficult to think of them as the lost, frightened brothers and sisters that they are, but vilifying them will do no good," the Grandmothers said, shaking their heads. "**We ask you to remember that no matter how dark the deed, each person is a member of the human family. Love them from a distance,**" they said.

"**As you hold** *all* **beings in the Net of Light, the perpetrators and the would-be perpetrators of these hateful crimes will then also be lifted and filled with peace. Because the Net burns away negative states, it will automatically lift the fear and rage that fuel these horrific events.** *Hold all beings in the Net,*" they said. "**This,**" they said, "**is what to do with perpetrators of any kind.**

"**Although hysteria is mounting in the world today and fear is feeding,** *don't allow fear to feed on you.* **As evil as these terrorist actions are, they will eventually pass. We promise you that,**" they said, pausing while they sat up straighter. "*The Net of Light is the Fabric of Being of the Universe,*" they said, "**and it is no small thing to connect with the Fabric of Being of the Universe. The Net is the underpinning of creation; therefore, if ever you catch yourself falling into fear, call on the Net of Light!**

"**Call on it a thousand times a day,**" they said. "**Connect with one another through the Net, and as you do, welcome all the forms of the Divine you love. Call on Jesus, Allah, Buddha, Mary, Krishna, Lakshmi, the Grandmothers. Call! Each is a different form of the ONE, so when you call on one of them, they will all respond.**

"**Please don't try to go through these difficult times by yourself,**" the Grandmothers said." **Stay linked with us, linked with the Net of Light and with one another, and once you've done that, then relax and let light hold you.**"

"You opened a portal for the earth."

The Net of Light Gathering at Joshua Tree National Park was coming up soon. It would be our tenth Gathering in California, and similar to what had recently taken place in Belgium, again women and men would come together in ways few of us had seen before. Plus, this time with us would be a Native American singer.

We opened the Gathering in the early evening, singing and drumming with the singer, dancing while we took turns wearing the Ancestral Cloak. A group of men had come to this Gathering and that night, they walked the circumference of the retreat center, singing and drumming, to enclose we women in an energy field of protection. We were deeply touched that they would do this for us.

The next day would be a silent walk about in the desert of Joshua Tree. We would commune with the great rocks there and then gather in the open for a ceremony. That night we would work underneath the stars.

All Net of Light Gatherings are spiritually moving and physically beautiful and this one was no exception, but something happened this time that especially moved us, causing this Joshua Tree group of people to become very close to one another. I couldn't put my finger on exactly what had made this Gathering so memorable, but a few days after it was over, I journeyed to the Grandmothers for their wisdom. I knew they'd be able to tell me.

"Grandmothers," I asked, "what actually happened last weekend in Joshua Tree? Something is different now," I said and they gave me a cursory look. **"You opened a portal there for the earth,"** they responded, **"a portal between human beings and your planet."** I cocked my head when I heard this. "What do you mean, Grandmothers?"

They smiled sweetly and said, **"In the past there were many of these doorways on earth. In those days there was instant communication between the earth and its inhabitants, but when the doorways were closed, that stopped."** I started to ask what had happened to close the openings, but before I could get a word out, they said, **"But not any longer!**

"Doorways are opening again," they announced, **"and this one at Joshua Tree will stand open just as does the one at Uluru. There's no need to shutter and protect them any longer,"** they said. **"At this time communication** *needs* **to flow between humans and the elemental spirits of earth. When you convened at Joshua Tree,"** they said, **"you did the work of opening the portal not only there, but at hundreds of other places on earth."**

"Hundreds?" I questioned. I was having a hard time believing what I was hearing. **"Yes,"** they nodded. **"The Net of Light multiplied the work we did together in the desert. Magnified it many times over. That day multiple openings took place all over the planet.**

"That's why you're so tired now," they explained. **"You performed the task we set out for you, and it was a big one. You did it, and** it's done," they said and brushed their hands together for emphasis. **"Complete.**

"So, rest now until we return to present you with the next level of work. Sleep and let us cradle and blanket you in love." And reaching out their arms to me, **"Rest,"** they said. **"We're wrapping you tight."** I let them hold me like that. Actually, I was too stunned to do anything else. Then I took them at their word and went directly to bed—staying there for most of the day.

"We're not what you'd call an 'organization'; we're more like an organism."

Several days after receiving this message I sat myself down at the computer. I was aware that there was something working its way into my consciousness. It had to do with what had taken place at Joshua Tree.

For quite a while I'd noticed that whether we were at a large Net of Light Gathering or a smaller monthly meeting, the thoughts, feelings, and actions of everyone present seemed to be meshing. This sense of coming together as one had also taken place at Joshua Tree. What was happening in meetings now was different than it had been twenty years ago when the Grandmothers had first appeared. Now we rarely felt the static energy of one person pushing against another. Power struggles that used to pop up fairly often had faded and almost disappeared. And as I thought about all this, I realized that this change had happened so gradually that I hadn't really noticed it. But I was noticing now.

These days we seemed to be so in sync with one another that we often 'finished each other's sentences.' And, whenever we met, a *theme* for our meeting quickly came to the fore. Now I did very little in the way of conscious planning for our meetings, but in spite of this or maybe because of it, each time we came together, we ended up center-ing on a particular theme—each time. And I began to hear from other Net of Light group leaders who were experiencing the same thing.

At the Joshua Tree Gathering I'd finally spoken about it. "We're not what you'd call an 'organization,'" I said; "we're more like an organ-ism." When I said this, everyone nodded and laughed because they had noticed it too. And at a recent Net of Light meeting in Laguna Beach, the Grandmothers played with us to prove it.

We were working with the Grandmothers' three books at the time when our circle devolved into something we laughingly named 'Grandmothers' Roulette.' We were passing their books around the circle and each of us would read a paragraph or two from wherever her eye happened to fall. People then shared their responses to what had just been read and group discussions ensued. These might be long or short, but our goal was to be entirely open to the Grandmothers' guidance…and then explore whatever responses came to mind.

We found that when a reading brought up an issue for someone, the next randomly picked reading would often also center on that issue. Center on it exactly. And this happened over and over again. For instance, when Jo mentioned that she'd used the Ho'opono pono prayer as a response for the survivors of the latest terrorist atrocity, we plunged into this beautiful Hawaiian forgiveness prayer and chanted it together. And when we went on to the next reading from one of the Grandmothers' books, it turned out to be about *the power of forgiveness.*

We spent an hour together, playing this game, and over and over again we were astounded by one serendipitous response after another. Unbeknownst to us, we were weaving something, and at the same time that 'something' appeared to be weaving us. The Grandmothers were playing with us and we, with them. There were a lot of tears that day as well as a great deal of joy, and much passing of the tissue box. This way of 'working,' we decided, was for us.

Stories of Men, Women, and Forgiveness

The Gathering at Joshua Tree had been beautiful, a real success. And the next thing coming up was the Gathering in Belgium. A group of us would be traveling there, just as we'd all gone together to Australia, Latvia, Lithuania and England. And because the Grandmothers had been giving us so much information on how to effectively work with the Net of Light during these perilous times, I assumed that this would be the focus for the Belgium Gathering too. But as it turned out, it was *a* focus, but not *the* main event.

We would hold this Gathering in a large sports complex outside Antwerp that had been chosen for its easy accessibility. We'd set Friday evening aside for new people who weren't yet working with the Grandmothers, and though these people wouldn't attend the whole Gathering, they would be able to get a taste of the Grandmothers' work.

About a hundred people came to the Friday night meeting, and after we'd shared the Grandmothers' message of returning balance to earth and creating harmony between women and men, a young man stood up to speak. "I'm standing here," he said, "asking women to forgive men for the terrible things men have done to you." And as he spoke those words, you could have heard a pin drop.

"I have done those things too," he continued, "and now that I see you women here and understand what I've done to you, I want you to know I will never do those things again." Shaking with emotion, the young man bravely spoke on, and as the women in the room listened to him, tears poured down their faces. Many of them murmured words of forgiveness to him.

Then a woman stood up. "I would like to ask forgiveness from the men," she said, and everyone looked at her in surprise. "I would like to ask forgiveness from the men for the way we have failed to understand them. Men give to the world," she said, "and often we don't understand that. We want men to give to us," she said. "We want them to give at home and so we don't value what they are giving to the world. Men are supposed to give to the world," she said, "and so I ask the men here to please forgive us." Again tears fell as women nodded their agreement and men smiled.

Wordless now, we all simply looked at each other. It felt like a miracle had just taken place, and it was only Friday evening! We were feeling like family, and the Gathering hadn't really started yet.

The rest of the weekend was just as full-hearted, although most of it wasn't quite as dramatic. We worked with the Net of Light, casting it for the world, and we worked with our ancestors as well as with our individual selves. We danced and sang and shared deeply with one another. On Sunday morning a few of the men began to ceremonially move through the large crowd of women at the Gathering, looking into their eyes while singing, *"All we ask of you is forever to remember us as loving you."*

All eyes were on these men as once again this much beloved Sufi song worked its magic. The women throughout the hall were being deeply affected by the men's singing when suddenly a woman dropped to her knees and began to howl. Seeing these men expressing their love in this intimate way had plunged her into the pain of her past, and now she began to keen for every woman who had ever suffered at the hands of a man. Caught up in a current of grief, she couldn't stop keening, and when one of the men realized that she couldn't help herself, he dropped to his knees in front of her. She clung to him, but she still wasn't able to stop howling. By now most of us were crying along with her. We could feel the depth of her pain but didn't know how to comfort her.

Then the man who'd been holding her began to slowly drop down to the floor in front of her until at last, his head was lying at her feet. He bowed there before her and made himself completely vulnerable. Later, he told us that when he dropped to his knees, he felt terrible shame and guilt for all the crimes men have perpetrated on women. He realized then that he had to go farther down, to really abase himself before her… and so he did.

When she saw the totality of his remorse, saw how deeply sorry he was for all she had suffered, she stretched out her arms to him. Then she covered him with her body, and as she held him and rocked him, her cries began to subside, and all of us felt the change taking place inside her. A collective sigh moved through the room, and as we silently gazed at one another, we understood that what we had just witnessed was the healing power of love. In our hearts we too then bowed to this woman and man, full of gratitude to them for giving us an opportunity to share in such a healing moment. We knew that no one in this room would ever be the same again, and I don't think any of us have been.

After we returned home, I thought back on this Gathering in Belgium, and it dawned on me that something big is happening now between men and women. The morning before the last day of that Gathering, a group of us were sitting around the breakfast table, talking with a musician who's been a part of the Net of Light work for a long time. Sharing with us from his heart, he said, "In my life I've often felt confused by women." And when we probed to find out what he meant by this, he said, "I have often stuttered and sweated around women because of their great *beauty*. It's their inner beauty that affects me like this," he said. "It overwhelms me."

As I listened to this exquisitely sensitive man, I understood that he 'gets' the essence of a woman at her best. How women are naturally attuned to one another, to the natural world, and to their own hearts.

The women he was talking about live with their hearts open, and the beauty of this open heart is what smites him.

Then he said, "For me, it's not like that with men. I never have such a feeling with men," and from the way he said it, I could see that this is true for him. He is a rare man—not threatened by women or greedy to possess them, but a man who admires and understands the nature of a woman who is alive at her core.

"A hive is forming now, a golden comb, within which you will be able to live, move, and connect with one another."

After I'd been home from the Belgium Gathering for a couple of weeks, I had a very unusual experience. While lying half-asleep in the middle of the night, I woke, seeing and feeling the Net of Light like liquid honey. The Net was making a viscous connection throughout the whole earth, and I was watching and feeling it as it happened. There was a lot of movement within the Net—movement I'd never seen or experienced before. And the direction of the movement was downward, as if together the stars and the angelic kingdom were releasing a golden liquid into the Net of Light. The thick downpouring of gold flowed over the planet, making it possible for everything on earth to connect with everything else. The molten flow was bonding different forms of life together, and as I watched this take place, I felt a corresponding sense of comfort, a cozy feeling inside myself. Then I heard a great humming sound that kept thrumming and humming until I was enfolded in it. I was being fanned by millions of bees! Cocooned in their delicate wings. I LOVED the feeling of being covered like this and was reveling in being at one with this golden movement. So, that afternoon I took a journey to the Grandmothers to ask what all this meant.

As soon as I asked them, they responded, **"This was not your imagination. A hive *is* forming now, a golden comb, within which you will be able to live, move, and connect with one another. Believe it or not, this is real,"** they said," **but to actually experience this golden substance, you must sit quietly and think of opening to its downward flow. Molten light, liquid gold,"** they said. **"Feel it!"** they commanded, and I did.

"The body is a good teacher," they reminded me, "so let your body be the first to experience this. And as the body opens to this honey-light, it will teach the mind how to also receive it. The heart doesn't need to be taught," they said; "it already *knows* the truth.

"As soon as you open to receive this downpour, begin to breathe out slowly. This will allow the spaces within you to relax and fill with goodness. Golden goodness," they said, and I laughed.

"You've never imagined anything like this, have you?" they smiled. "You never thought you could accept this much good, did you? Goodness flowing into every part of you," they said, "to over-flowing. Let yourself receive, and once you have, then open to take in even more of it. Your capacity to store goodness is growing. You're going to become a vessel of good," they said, "*all good.*

"Each time you breathe out, more space opens up inside you," they explained, gesturing expansively, "and this allows light to rush in and fill you to over-flowing. As *you* receive this good, know that *everyone else* is receiving it, too, right along with you," they said, their smiles broadening at the thought. "When you say 'yes!' to this inflow, your 'yes!' affects everything that lives. We've told you this many times," they said, "but we'll say it again. '*You cannot help yourself without helping everyone else.*' So, let yourself receive like this, and then let yourself receive again. Why not?" they asked me. "Why wouldn't you?

"It's time for you to fully become what you've always been," they said. "Time for you to step out of the closet, so to speak, and to admit who you are. You are a radiant being of light," the Grandmothers said, and they showered me with a look of such love that I choked up. "You are goodness itself. You are golden. Accept your birthright," they said. "Every time you think of this downpour of golden goodness, you'll receive more of it. You'll be filled with happiness, and the world will also be filled with happiness. Play your part!" the Grandmothers cried. "Stand and receive! Claim your birthright so that the world can also claim its birthright."

CHAPTER SIX

"You underestimate yourself."

The next time I went to the Grandmothers, as soon as they laid eyes on me, they said, **"We want to remind you of something—and you** *need* **reminding."** "Yes, Grandmothers?" I responded, "But inside myself, I groaned, "Uh oh. What do I need reminding of? What's coming now?"

"You still tend to think of yourself as a separate person," they said, and I looked up at them in surprise. "Still?" I said, and they stared back at me. "Well, uh yes!" I finally agreed, taken off guard by their steady stares. "I'd hoped I'd gotten beyond that way of relating to myself," I said to them, "but you're right. I still get stuck in that way of thinking." **"We know! We know!"** they laughed. **"But this separate view you have of yourself is wrong! Wrong, wrong, wrong!"** they said, waving their hands as if to chase it away. **"And it's *this* view of yourself that causes your misery."** They shook their heads. **"You're more than a separate person,"** they said, **"*much* more.**

"When we first showed you the Net of Light, you thought of it as a way to connect with others and a tool to lift suffering." "Yes, Grandmothers," I said, "that's right." **"You thought we were giving you the Net of Light to 'help' the earth."** I nodded to them in agreement, and with a twinkle in their eyes, they said, **"Well, listen now.**

"*The Net of Light is more than you think it is*. It's the Fabric of Being, and as such, it upholds and weaves together everything in the Universe. And it's able to do this," they smiled, **"because *it is love*. This is also what YOU are,"** they said, and I looked at them expectantly.

"When you think that you're just a speck on the earth, one among millions, you underestimate yourself. Of course, on the physical

level you *are* a speck," they said, "**but in reality, you're one with the Net of Light, one with the Fabric of Being of the Universe.**" Now my head began to spin. They'd told me this before, but they were speaking today with such intensity that the real meaning of it was too much for me to take in. When they saw that I was feeling overwhelmed, they drew me close to themselves. Holding me tight against their breasts, they wrapped their arms round me, and when they did this, the tension that had so quickly built up inside me began to let go.

"**You're at one with us,**" they explained to me. "**You're *not* separate. See!**" they said, "**Right now you're allowing yourself to melt into our embrace; you're letting yourself become one with us. Let us hold you like this,**" they whispered as they rocked me back and forth. "**Relax and breathe with us. You are our own,**" they sang, "**our very own. You're one with the Divine. Your heart is beating with our hearts. Feel it,**" they said, and then they rocked me some more.

Tears began to well up in my eyes, spilled over and started running down my cheeks. "I feel so relaxed here with them, so comforted, so safe," I thought as I allowed myself to sink further into their embrace. I was feeling all these things as they held me close like that, and then I became aware that something deep inside me was starting to melt. What was melting?

"**You can never be alone,**" the Grandmothers assured me, responding to my question. "**You're as much a part of the river of love that flows through life as we are. *The Net of Light is what forms the underlying pattern for life everywhere,*****"** they said, and I noticed that they were watching me to see if I understood what they were getting at.

"*The Net of Light exists everywhere. It exists in everything.* **The Net of Light cradles and connects all that is,**" they said. "**It's the light and love of the Net that's flowing through you now just as it's flowing through us. How can a drop of water in a river hold itself separate from the other drops?**" they asked, watching me carefully. "**It can't,**" they answered. "**Nor can you.**

"**This flowing stream of life *is* who you are,**" they said, patting me gently and then enfolding me again. "**You are one with all that is. You're divine,**" they declared, their faces lit by smiles. "**Your body, your personality and your mind—these are nothing but manifestations of that flow. Manifestations that occur for a short period of time,**" they said, their heads tilted wistfully. "**And whenever you let** go of that cramped sense of self you've become so attached to and instead allow yourself to simply go with life's flow, life can carry you farther and farther.

"The power of this ever-flowing Light/Love is so great, it can't be measured," the Grandmothers said. "Nor can the power of your *being* be measured. You are not a separate someone," they said. "Let that old thought melt away now. Do you see what we're getting at when we tell you that you underestimate yourself? Do you understand who you ARE?"

"Yes, Grandmothers," I said. "I hear what you're saying, and I understand. At least I think I do." I looked at them questioningly, and seeing my look, they responded. "Unhappiness arises only when you think of yourself as a separate, limited person," they said, peering into my eyes to be sure I was with them. "It's time to let go of that old lie now," they smiled, and spreading their hands wide, they said, "Open to the Net. We ask you to do this because each time you do, you automatically lift yourself and lift the world." Then they laughed and said, "You will never, ever be unhappy in the Net of Light!"

I thought about this—that once I really began to see myself as part of the Net of Light, I would no longer think of myself as separate from God. I knew the Grandmothers were right about this, and I could already feel inklings of this new orientation to life slowly, slowly developing in me. The Net of Light was melting my sense of separation from the Source. I'd noticed that even when I tried to pray in the old ways I'd been taught, tried to beseech God or the Grandmothers as if they were 'out there' somewhere, I couldn't do it. I'd been taught to pray like that, taught to relate to God as if the Divine were apart from me, but it no longer worked. Now I found it hard, even impossible, to pray to the Divine in order to feel connected with it. Now when I wanted to really feel connected, I had to drop into my own heart, sit there quietly and wait for God/the Grandmothers/the Divine. The sense of myself as a separate person, something I'd carried around with me all my life, was beginning to melt away.

"Let the earth love you back."

Over time I came to understand just how relentless the Grandmothers are. They NEVER give up, and time after time, from being on the receiving end of their tenacity, I came to understand that they never will. Over and over again they've shown me my connection to the Net of Light. Done it one way and then another, determined that I'd at last comprehend my part in the great Oneness of life.

Since the Grandmothers first appeared that day when I walked the dog beside the beach, I've come to understand that what I used to think of as *my life* doesn't belong to *me* after all. The Grandmothers say that life is sometimes an adventure but is always a series of lessons we've come here to master. So, in lesson after lesson with these wise teachers, I've found that I'm not really here to have *my* way at all. Basically, I'm a student—here to learn.

I'm on this ride with the Grandmothers, and actually whether or not I or anybody else recognizes it, we're *all* on this ride. I've learned not to get too attached to my agenda because I keep finding that it's not actually *my* agenda after all; it's *our* agenda.

I usually start my day with an idea of what I'll be doing, but I'm always aware that whatever I have in mind for the day can and will change at any moment. So, I move forward with whatever my plan for the day is until the Grandmothers drop the next teaching on me. I can't say that I ever know what's coming next or when it's coming, but strange as it may seem, I've grown to kind of like it this way. It's an adventure for me. And it's not that all these lessons from the Grandmothers are enjoyable, but they all seem to be necessary, even liberating.

At some point the goal setting and scrambling for a desired result that I used to engage in simply stopped working. When the Grandmothers first said to me, **"You're not the 'doer'; you're the 'be-er,'"** I had no idea what they meant. But they've been working on me for over twenty years now, so this lesson is finally sinking in.

Last week I spent a lot of time in my garden pulling weeds, planting, digging, and cutting back branches, and one hot day when I'd been hard at it for a while, by mid-afternoon I was tired. When I came inside, I dropped my muddy gloves and shoes at the door and flopped down on the couch. And I remember, that when I exhaled and folded myself onto the cushions, I had the strangest feeling that something exciting was about to happen to me. So, I snuggled back against the pillows and sort of waited to see what it might be.

From the horizontal position I'd gotten myself into, I had a good view of the garden, and, as I gazed out the front windows at all the green out there, suddenly a rush of love came pouring into the house, flooding in from the plants in the garden and pouring down from the hillside behind the house. Then something wonderful began to wash over me, flooding into my body. Happiness, a feeling of lightness, and joy came coursing through me. Grace. It felt like I was being bathed in a cascade of grace. Grace and love were flooding the room, and as they did, I could feel them actively seeking me out. And when I became aware of that, I lay absolutely still, waiting in anticipation.

"Oh, my God!" I finally whispered as the cascade of love mounted inside and all around me. "The garden loves me!" I cried. "It loves me!" Wave after wave of love was rushing in now, and I lay there on the couch, amazed by it, so amazed that I almost forgot to breathe. "Nature loves me!" I exhaled at last, and now the tears started. "*All* of nature!" I cried, hardly able to believe what was happening. But I was being flooded, absolutely flooded with love. Feeling after glorious feeling poured over and through me, and it kept on coming for a long time.

"It's only a feeling," I told myself at last, my mind trying to minimize my experience. But my heart would have none of that. "But what a feeling!" I exclaimed. Although what was happening to me now was nothing that I could actually explain to myself, *I knew* without a doubt that something BIG had just moved between nature and me.

"How could something like this happen? How is this sort of thing possible?" I whispered to myself. And the rest of the afternoon I went around in a kind of daze—this strange, sweet secret locked in my heart. And when I went to bed that night, I marveled some more at what had happened there on the couch, cried a few more tears of joy, and then cuddled up with joy for the night.

When I woke the next morning, I felt I just *had* to understand what had taken place between nature and me. I had to know. This was something that couldn't wait, so I went to the Grandmothers. I felt sure they could tell me.

"There is a goodness rising now," the Grandmothers said after I told them what had happened the day before. **"A deep-down goodness. It's right there under your feet, and it's all about you,"** they said, spreading their hands wide for emphasis. **"You're actually enfolded in this goodness,"** they explained, and I looked up at them in surprise. **"In fact,"** they said, **"you're so enfolded in it that wherever you go, it goes with you. You're living and moving in a matrix of good."**

"Really, Grandmothers?" I asked. "Is this really what this was about?" Their answer had surprised me, but I was happily surprised. They explained a bit more about this rising tide of goodness, and the more I listened to them, the more I felt its presence. "That must have been what happened to me yesterday, Grandmothers," I said at last. "I must have tapped into that rising tide you're describing. There *is* something inside me now, Grandmothers," I said. "I can feel it floating around in there, right in the center of my body, and whatever it is, it's really supporting me. Filling me with such a sense of contentment," I said. "Something did rise up yesterday, and now it's permeating all of me. And…," I paused as I thought more about it, "you're right. The only world that fits this feeling is *goodness*."

I stopped talking then and just stared at them. Amazed. **"Did you think all the love you've been sending to the earth for so many years would not come back to you?"** they asked me. **"Did you think you were the only one doing the giving? That giving only flowed in one direction—from you to Mother Earth?"** they asked, and I felt my body twitch, startled by this question. I also noticed that my hand had come up and was now covering my open mouth. I was holding my breath.

"What we're telling you is true," they said, smiling at my reaction. **"Don't doubt us and don't doubt yourself,"** they said, and now they eyed me with compassion. **"Remember,"** they said, **"that what you think of as 'yourself' is in fact Ourselves. There is no difference between you and us,"** they said, shaking their heads. **"The only time there's a difference is when your mind draws you into doubt. Then your mind flies east, west, north and south and confuses you. So, relax,"** the Grandmothers gestured slowly with their hands to settle me down, **"and let us lead you. We will guide you—always,"** they said, and I noticed that they were again regarding me the way a patient hen regards her chick.

"There's no detail so small that we won't cover it and then direct you," they promised. **"You are we and we are thee. We are the same,"** they said, and now I couldn't take my eyes off these majestic, great-hearted women. They were pouring so much love onto me. And the things they were saying! Their words once again made my eyes spill over with tears.

"Lovely one," they said at last, and they gazed at me with so much affection that I really choked up. **"Receive what Mother Earth is giv-**

ing you. There is a *TWO-WAY FLOW* OF LOVE taking place," they said, **"and you are part of it. You are giving and She is giving. It's like breathing,"** they explained. **"You can't live only by exhaling. You have to inhale, too,"** they said, **"so take it in. Start inhaling all this goodness. Receive it,"** they said. **"Let the earth love you back."** And seeing how dumbstruck I was, they repeated, **"Let the earth love you back."**

After this session I went straight to bed. My poor body was thrumming and humming with joyful, but heretofore unknown, feelings, and I lay there under the covers, vibrating—and then vibrating some more. When my body finally calmed down and relaxed, I took a long nap. And when I got up, it was with a decision to take life more slowly—at least for a while. Slow had never been my style, but at this point, slow was all I had in me. The experience with Mother Earth and this journey to the Grandmothers had given me a lot to think about. I knew I'd be absorbing it for a long time.

I was beyond thrilled by what I'd discovered in this encounter with Mother Nature. The earth was alive, truly alive. A living Being—capable of giving love and compassion. We humans love the earth, and the earth loves us back! "She loves us! She loves ….me!" I kept marveling at this truth. This part of the relationship continued to move me, and as I was transcribing this lesson, I felt that rush of love all over again.

"The BIG LIFT"

After this experience, at least a month went by before I went back to the Grandmothers. It was unusual for me to stay away this long, but I was so full from what I'd learned that there was no more room for anything else in me. "I'm digesting," I told myself.

The next time I went to them, as soon as I started talking, I felt a warm feeling in the center of my body, and with the warmth came a sense of happy expansion. Then, as I relaxed and allowed myself to widen into it, I noticed that someone or something was present and was flooding me with light. Pink, gold, blue, and white lights were dancing in the air before me. They were weaving patterns in the air, and the patterns they were making were what was lifting me up. Whoever or whatever this energy was, it began to wrap me in these lovely colors, as upward and upward I rose, and when at last I got over my surprise at what was happening to me, I looked around and saw that I wasn't alone. Everyone I knew was rising right along with me! We were all part of this upward movement.

Then the Grandmothers spoke. **"At this time, while the energy on earth is changing, those of you who stay connected to the Source will sense a lifting like this. You'll experience a rising and an expansion, and as you lift up, you'll draw thousands with you.**

"Staying connected to the Source during these difficult times you're living in will create a higher and higher vibration for you," they explained, **"and this vibration will form an updraft, one that's able to lift huge amounts of energy. Wherever there is *high* energy like this,"** they explained, **"the updraft it creates causes elevation.**

"At this time many people have made a commitment to keep themselves tuned to the Divine, *no matter what!*" they said. **"More and more of you are doing this now, and the decision you've made is enabling you to hold your vibration high.**

"Here's how it works," they explained. **"Everything is energy. *You* are energy; *we* are energy; *everyone* is energy. And,"** they said, **"when people call on us or any form of the Divine, energetically they automatically connect to the Net of Light that supports life everywhere.**

"Because the Net of Light is what it is," they explained, **"it lifts those who call on it, and at the same time, lifts everyone with whom they're linked. It's the LOVE,"** they shrugged, **"and this happens automatically. *Your* connection to the Source,"** the Grandmothers explained, **"also allows those who are linked with you to benefit from the Source. This divine connection is potent,"** they said, giving me a meaningful look, **"and the growing reach of the Net of Light is now enabling hordes of people to lift up. Animals too,"** they said. **"All forms of energy are rising now—rising together and expanding. Do you see how important it is for you to stay connected to this Source of light?**

"This upward motion we're talking about includes low frequency energy as well as high frequency energy," the Grandmothers explained. **"What you think of as low or negative energy is also rising—surfacing from the depths,"** they laughed. **"And as this heavy energy comes to the surface, you often see violence, hate, and fear popping up all over the world. But don't worry about that,"** the Grandmothers said, putting their arms around me to reassure me.

"Even these difficult forms of energy will be affected by the updraft. It's true that these energies are rising from a lower place, but like everything else, they too are rising."

As I gazed at the Grandmothers, I felt so much gratitude for them. Grateful to them for helping us understand why our world is in such a mess and grateful to know how we can help. "Staying tuned is the key," I muttered to myself, "staying tuned to the Source." And as I thought about this, again I felt that warmth inside me, something greater than my small self, moving me upward. Lifting me, lifting others, lifting everything.

"*Nothing* is a mistake," I whispered to myself. "*Nothing* is wasted. And each good thought, each happy moment, every bit of loving service—all of it contributes to this elevation that I'm seeing now. Energy is rising all over the globe. Of course, only a few of us are aware of it yet," I said, "and though we'll probably never see it reported in the news, this inexorable upward movement *is* taking place. Present everywhere, at every moment. *The BIG LIFT.*"

Send in the Spiritual Marines.

Around this time, I received an email asking for prayers for young children suffering from heart problems. The letter included pictures of the kids—some of them just babies. So, I prayed for them, asking that their fears be taken away, that they feel themselves held in love. I thought of their families, and as my heart turned over, I saw and felt the Net of Light lifting them too. The Net responded immediately to my call, and as soon as it embraced them, the babies as well as their families relaxed.

How real this prayer was! I could feel it in my body, and when the Net of Light lifted all of them, my eyes flooded with tears. I realized then that without any real effort on my part, a loving thought (this prayer) had simply flown out and instantly produced a loving response. It was so simple, so effortless…and so REAL!

As I thought it over, it came to me that the Divine, (God, Jesus, Allah, the Grandmothers, the Net of Light—whatever name you call it) is energy, and so it readily responds to thought. "The Divine *is* energy!" I thought as I remembered a law of energy. *Thought directs energy.* "The Divine *is* energy, so of course it responds to thought," I said to myself.

And when I'd brought to mind those babies, I automatically linked the light in my own heart with the Net of Light, which created the movement to speed light to them. The impetus of 'my' love was all that was needed to move the Great Love forward.

We're all part of the Net of Light, but most of the time we're asleep to that fact. We spend our days 'drugged' by the material world, believing that we're only these limited, physical bodies, these 'flawed' personalities, and, of course, the world confirms this.

But we're part of the Divine. That's why I felt it in my body when the Net of Light took hold of those babies. Every time we send out a thought of love, great good takes place. Each moment of thoughtful blessing (which is what prayer for another person is) automatically sends in the 'spiritual marines.' And this is something we can do every day, something we can do every minute.

As I thought this over again, I heard the Grandmothers say, **"You long to serve; you long to feel that your life has purpose. And this is correct, as service will lead you to connect with the purpose of your life. Praying for these sick children *is* service,"** they said. **"It's an opportunity that was given to you, and we thank you for taking it.**

"Come together in the 'community of the good,'" they continued, and gesturing broadly, they opened their arms wide to indicate the size of this community. **"Go where love is practiced, wherever love is lauded and lived. Whenever you can, spend your time with open-hearted people. Let love live in you and pour forth from you. Let your head, heart and hands move into active service. Give to those in the family of life who need this love. Give to people, to animals, to the waters, and to the earth Herself. Let kindness be your first response,"** they said, looking at me, their eyes full of love. **"Let goodness and generosity fill your heart. You were born for greatness,"** the Grandmothers said. **"Loving all and serving all IS greatness.**

"You've outgrown 'filling up' your time with activity."

We attended a dinner party the other night, and though I liked the people we were with and the conversation was lively and funny, the evening didn't leave me with a warm, expanded feeling like I'd hoped it would. Afterward, I realized that I often bemoan the loss of close friends, the kind we had at an earlier time in our lives and don't experience much now. I miss sitting around a table with people like that, people we're really bonded to. I especially miss the love. So, at a loss as to what to do about it, I went to the Grandmothers. "Grandmothers," I said, "please speak to me about this loss I feel. It weighs on me."

"What do you want?" the Grandmothers asked me abruptly. **"God or friends?"** "Well, God," I replied, their response sobering me, "but can't we have friends along the way too? God is the main (the only event, really)," I said, "but it sure does get lonely down here on earth."

The Grandmothers laughed and laughed when I said this. "Maybe they think what I'm saying is ridiculous," I thought, "but I still remember my earlier friendships, as with Mahri, for instance, and things were different then." I was about to say this to them when they spoke again. **"Those friendships *were* different,"** they confirmed. **"They were friendships that were centered on God. They weren't just chit-chat. Last night,"** they added, **"was basically chit-chat. That's why it left no lasting good feeling in you.**

"You've outgrown that way of being," they said, **"outgrown 'filling up' your time with activity. You were born for us, not for vacuous entertainment. Politics, social observations, gossip…. What do they do for you?"** they asked, riveting me with a look.

"Uh, not much, Grandmothers," I grudgingly replied, realizing that they had a point. "But I like people," I said, "and I feel warmly toward them. I *really* like them," I said again, "and I *do* get lonely." **"We know,"** they said, **"but this life is a one seat sofa. One seat,"** they said. **"It's not a house party. Your most important relationship is with the Divine, so keep your mind and thoughts there. Don't be distracted by all the passing shows,"** they said. **"Be pleasant to everyone. Love them, but to fill your heart, turn to us, turn only to the Divine.**

"You can go to all the parties and dinners you want, but *only God is truly here for you*," they said. **"No other. Remember that. The rest just comes and goes,"** they said, and I watched as a blanket of fog blew in and then blew out again. **"That stuff isn't real,"** they said to me. "Remember…."

"Return Mother Earth and her people to their original design."

I kept remembering the Grandmothers saying that life was not a house party and that my primary relationship on earth now was with them. "Why," I asked myself, "is this so hard for me to remember? I know it's true, so why don't I just accept it? Why am I always wanting something else? Ugh," I groaned. "I'm sick of this issue. Give me some work to do, Grandmothers. Give this mind of mine something to do."

Then I recalled that I *did* have something to do. There was a Net of Light Gathering coming up again at Uluru in the middle of the Australian Outback. And to support the work at Uluru, the Grandmothers had asked us to hold several Net of Light Gatherings in different parts of the world. These would all take place around the same time and the power that would ensue from this multiplied work would solidify a connection between the earth and her people. **"Do it now!"** the Grandmothers had said when they'd laid this work out for us.

"Return Mother Earth and her people to their original design," the Grandmothers had said. **"Return them to the sacred connection they share. Now is the time for this. Let there be no more separation between earth and her people. These connections will strengthen the Net of Light so it can better do its job of holding the earth steady during these turbulent times."**

We would work again at Uluru. Two years earlier we had gone there, and now again we would ask this ancient site to support the Net of Light as it holds the earth steady. Because Uluru is one of the great power places on earth, this site in the Australian Outback would hold the center point for the work of all the other groups also. We'd hold the Uluru Gathering from July 20 to 26, and people would be traveling to this isolated place from all over the globe.

And while we held ceremony at Uluru, other Net of Light Gatherings would take place all over the earth. Europe, the United States, Canada, South America, New Zealand, Asia, and Africa would all tie in together. Each place would support the others, so the entire planet would be blanketed by and deeply anchored in the Net of Light. This was our purpose. Together we would magnify the power of the Net throughout the planet—to bless life and hold the earth steady.

We posted the places, dates, and times of each Gathering on the

Grandmothers' website and asked those who couldn't get to one of these events to link up from wherever they were. "Please connect with the Net of Light, with Uluru, and with all the sacred sites on earth at the end of July," we asked, "as well as with the extra Gatherings that will take place across the globe. Simply call on the Grandmothers and the Net of Light, and once you have, then ask for the light to flow. And…if you decide to amplify the power of this connection by holding a small gathering in your area, let us know." By the time July 20 rolled around, there were twenty-two gatherings scheduled around the world, each one harmonizing with the Mother Meeting in Uluru.

When it was over, the Grandmothers were pleased by the way people had responded to their call to solidify the connection between the earth and Her people. And shortly after this multi-layered July Gathering was over, they spoke about it.

"**Thank you for making this sacred connection,**" they said to everyone. "**Light *is* and Love *is*. The Net of Light is real, but until someone says, 'yes' to it, it cannot fully anchor. Before it anchors, it's like a cloud floating through the atmosphere,**" they explained. "**It's there,**" the Grandmothers said. "**It's there, but until you make the decision to embrace it and make a home for it, it can't truly align with you. It's your decision to open to love and light, your decision to say 'yes' to the Net of Light that gives it a home,**" they said. "**And it's your decision to open to the potency of the Net of Light that amplifies its power for everyone on earth.**

"**Become this earth anchor now,**" they said. "**Become a home place for light and love. Say 'yes' to the Net of Light. Anchor now,**" they said as each Grandmother pounded her fist into her other hand. "**Anchor deep. Once you make this decision to be an anchor point for the Net of Light, your life will change,**" they said. "**You will become the person of power you were born to be. No more skating along on the surface of life,**" they laughed, shaking their heads, "**no more 'yes butting,' and no more indecision. Once you become this earth anchor, you will be purposeful and complete.**

"**Feel this anchoring taking place deep in the center of your body,**" they said. "**Feel it now. Feel light flowing downward through your mid-section and dropping into the earth. You *are* a home place—a holding tank for the energy of yin. Wherever you go,**" they said, nodding their approval, **"your presence will amplify the power of the Net of Light. You were born for greatness!"** they declared. **"And we assure you that this is not just a saying.** *It is the truth.* **You** *were* **born for greatness. So,"** they added, **"go slow and go deep as you begin. You will not be doing this work alone. At every moment you will find us with you and within you.**

"You are in your right place at the right time," the Grandmothers assured me, **"and everything is happening exactly as it should. No matter how the world may appear to be, we promise you that greater goodness, greater power and light will come forth from these dark times that you're living in than you can possibly imagine. So, drop anchor now,"** they said, **"and broadcast light."**

CHAPTER SEVEN

"You signed up because you wanted to serve the light."

It was now autumn, and we were heading into the run up for the U.S. presidential election. Life in our country had never felt meaner. It was a political firestorm, and because I'd never seen anything like *this* heat, to understand what was *really* going on, I went to the Grandmothers. "Help!" I cried. "It feels like cruelty is taking over the world and everything is being torn to pieces. I don't understand this. How can we help? What can we do? What can any of us do?"

"**The world is challenging you,**" the Grandmothers said, shaking their heads, "**and life is so confusing that sometimes you're overwhelmed by its craziness.**" "Yes," I said. "That's exactly it. Everything does seem crazy."

"**This is the Kali Yuga, after all,**" they reminded me. "**Don't forget that. You're living in the depth of negativity that was foretold thousands of years ago. You're right in the midst of it.**" "The Kali Yuga!" I gasped as I recalled the age of destruction the Hindu Vedas had spoken of more than seven thousand years earlier. This truly *is* it, isn't it?" I asked. "This *must* be it."

"**You're living in difficult times,**" the Grandmothers said, "**and.... you signed up for them. You signed up because you wanted to serve the light,**" they said, giving me a knowing look. "**You wanted to perform work of great value. The fact that you're alive at this moment is no accident.** *You were called to earth to hold light steady in an unsteady world.* **You were called and you answered the call. And...,**" they paused, giving me a look of compassionate understanding, "**once** you responded to that call, there was nothing more for you as an individual to do.

"As soon as you said 'Yes' to us, you became an instrument for light. So now, at every moment, light and love are flooding through you. Unfortunately," they said, "sometimes you become so distracted by all the dramas taking place around you that you lose awareness of it. But the truth is, you are channeling light—you are *always* channeling light. Even when you feel tired, discouraged, and lost, you aren't really," they said, nodding wisely. "As soon as you answered *'Yes'* to us, we stepped in to fill you, to guide and direct you. So," they eyed me, as they spoke, "you can't be lost. You're never alone. Never!" they declared. "We're as close to you as breath.

"Remember this now," they said. "Remember this during these challenging times. Let us hold and enfold you, rock and cradle you. We will drive with you, cook with you, work with you, and live with you twenty-four hours a day. There is no separation between you and us," they said. "Separation is an illusion." Then these regal Grandmothers drew themselves up to their full height and declared, "You are one with the Divine. Rest in our embrace and let us take care of everything. We will nudge you forward. You can count on us. Simply ask for our guidance and then move in the direction we point out.

"Lean on us," they said. "Give us your worries and instead of fretting about one thing and another, enjoy your time with us. Enjoy your time with one another too. Each of you is a precious flower in our garden," they said as they gazed fondly at me. "*Bloom as you were created to bloom.* "Let yourself be, and be yourself. There's nothing wrong with you. We love you exactly as you are.

"Begin today to love yourself, and to love one another too," they said, "the same way we love you. As you let go of all the things you think you *should* do and be, and instead allow us to do those 'hard' things, you'll find yourself enjoying life more. *It's time for you to be happy.* You are greatly loved," they said, their eyes soft. "Really. You have no idea of how greatly!"

For years I'd had a sense, an inner knowing really, that I'd chosen to be born at this time. I knew it wasn't an accident that I happened to be alive now. All my life I'd wanted to serve and had worked in various helping professions, so in some way this work with the Grandmothers was the next chapter in an on-going saga. But...I never expected to be living through times *this* ugly. Or *this* critical.

"Oh well," I said to myself. "Too bad, so sad, Sharon. Just get on with it! As long as you're here, you want to be fully here. So, let the learning continue!" And with this in mind, a few days later I returned to the Grandmothers.

"Take the time now to be with us."

As soon as I stepped before them, the Grandmothers took a long look at me and said, **"The next step you take will be with us, with Bear, and the compassionate animal spirits. Take the time now to *be* with us,"** they said, and "Yes," I answered, nodding to them and to Bear, who was standing with them, "that's what I want too."

"Put your focus on your relationship with *us,*" they said, zeroing their considerable energy in on me. The impact of their gaze hit me hard, and quickly I aligned myself with them, calling every part of myself to come to *this* moment. Now was no time to space out, no time to allow my attention to fragment. Something big, something important was about to take place. I knew it.

"You are near and dear, Grandmothers," I confessed to them; "you are near and dear, Bear," I said to my beloved Bear. "You are comforting," I said to all of them; "you are home, you are safe and you fill me up." And as the words kept coming out my mouth, I felt my closeness to the Grandmothers and even more, to Bear. The upwelling of love so overwhelmed me then that I started to sob, even to shake with sobs.

"Umgh!" Bear responded, his growl soft, and reaching out a great paw, he drew me to himself. Wrapping those paws around me, he held me close to his chest, covering me with his fur, and when I felt that bristly softness against my skin, I cried even more. "I'm so sorry, Bear," I said. "I'm so stubborn. I cling to being in a hurry all the time, to being independent, to being whatever it is I think I'm being—oh, I'm so sorry for keeping myself busy and staying away from you for so long. Being with you is just right for me," I said, "and I've missed you so."

"Umghph," he groaned, patting me as if to say, "Hush, hush now." I folded myself into his arms then, whimpering as the old, hardened edges of my 'self' began to melt away. I was softening; I was letting go. "I'm with Bear," I said to myself. "I'm his."

"Rest," he rumbled in my ear, "**just rest. There's nothing to do yet. More is coming. Don't worry about that. More is coming,**" he said, "**but for now, just rest.**" I kept on crying. It was all I could do. It was like I'd finally 'come home,' and I was so relieved to be at 'home' with him that all I could do was whimper, "I'm not alone anymore. I'm not alone. I know this world with Bear and the Grandmothers," I said to myself. "This is *my* world, and I'm so glad to be here."

"**Wait, wait, wait,**" they chorused—the Grandmothers, Bear and the Holy Man. "**Wait, wait, wait.**" "Okay," I agreed, sighing happily, "I will," and then I snuggled deeper into Bear's arms. "There's nothing I have to do now," I told myself. "They're taking care of everything. And they'll keep right on doing that," I sighed in contentment, "so all I have to do is rest and wait. Rest and wait. Thank God," I mumbled, and that's the last thing I remembered.

"Outside Time"

Three weeks later, in the wee hours of the morning, I started up, wide-awake. Wadding the covers around me, I huddled in bed, wondering what had happened to wake me up like this. But it was Bear. He'd come in a dream, and as usual, he'd scared me wide-awake. "Okay, okay," I said as I took in a few breaths, "I understand what this is about. You scare me so I'll wake up and remember a dream. And you did it again! But I'll journey to you in the morning," I said to him and to myself, and then I rolled over and went back to sleep.

"Bear," I said the next morning as I prepared myself to journey. "You came in a dream last night. Actually, the raccoons came first," I said, remembering that two raccoons had been stomping around on the roof before I went to bed. "Then I dreamed of you," I said, recalling more of the dream now. "There were also two of you!" I cried, surprised as I recalled this part. "There were two of you in the dream too. Two raccoons, and then two Bears?" What did that mean? I wondered.

I thought about it for a while but didn't see the connection. "There's something here, but I don't know what it is," I said at last. "Well, anyway, whatever it means, I'm going to come to you now, and…," I hesitated, "I'm going to come in the old way." For some reason, today I felt the need to take the long route to the lower world—not to use the

Grandmothers' Circle of Stones, but to journey to Bear in the way I'd first been taught.

So, I turned my focus within myself and asked for my *sipapu*, my opening into the lower world. And as soon as I saw it, in I dove and barreled down through Mother Earth until at last, I reached the lower world. Once there, I plunged into the now familiar river where my canoe was riding high in the water, waiting for me. I climbed in and paddled until I felt the canoe ride up onto the now familiar bank.

When I climbed out onto the sand, I took a step forward to call to Bear, but he was already there—towering before me. "Oh, Bear!" I cried. "I'm so grateful to see you!" my voice choked with emotion. Every time I saw him, my heart swelled in my chest just like it was doing now, and tears began to pour. It happened every time. "So much emotion!" I said, "every time I see you! I'm so grateful to you, Bear," I whispered, and before I knew it, I was down on my knees before him.

"Bear!" I cried, "you always come! These days I don't journey to you that often, not like I used to, and yet you still come. Always! You're so faithful! And this moves me so much," I continued, speaking through my tears. Then for some reason, the thought of the upcoming Net of Light Gathering in Ohio popped into my mind. "Is this why you're showing up now?" I asked him. "Is there something you want to teach me about the Gathering in Ohio? Because if there is," I said, "I want to learn it."

Bear leaned his great head in close to me then, and I noticed that he wore a thoughtful look. I could also see that he was happy that I wanted to learn from him. Somehow this pleased him. He growled deep in his throat, breathed on me and placed his paws on the top of my head. Then slowly he ran them down to my shoulders and holding his paws there, he leaned into me and looked into my eyes. Then he pulled me close to him, so close that we were looking into each other's eyes. And when he did that, I couldn't help but notice that standing on his back legs like this, Bear was *far* taller than I.

For a moment his great size scared me, but when he saw that, he quickly opened his paws, took me in, and, rumbling low in his chest, softly drew me to himself. "Ohhhh!" I exhaled as I felt his warm fur, then I collapsed into his massive embrace. "This is a kind of mergence," I marveled as I noticed the way my body seemed to melt into his. "I'm becoming one with Bear." And when I spoke these words, I heard how quiet my voice sounded. Then I became aware of a deep droning noise that seemed to be coming from somewhere around me. "What's making that noise?" I asked, but the droning went on and on until I realized it was *me* making this sound. It was coming from me!

I was *growling*! "This is *my* growl," I said, amazed at what I was hearing. And then Bear began to growl, too, right along with me. We droned on together for a few minutes, and then the drone melded and became one sound—my growl and his growl. It was my breath and his breath. "Oh!" I gasped, "This *is* union with Bear. I'm becoming one with him."

"W-o-w," I whispered, drawing the word out. "I don't remember feeling anything like this before." Then I noticed my body, noticed that it didn't feel like me. "What was this?" I wondered, and then I saw that it *wasn't* my body after all! It was *his*! "I'm walking the way Bear walks," I said as I observed myself almost rolling along the pathway, my gait slow and rhythmic. "And now I'm down on all fours too—just like he is," I thought as I observed the two of us. I shook my head in disbelief.

"Bear's not separate from me anymore," I said, my voice full of wonder. "Not separate at all! *I'm him!*" I cried. Then I watched as 'Bear' looked over his shoulder at me, and when I saw this, I realized it was actually 'me' who was looking over my shoulder at this other 'me.' "It's me in his body," I squeaked, "and I…. and… I mean, we're walking." I could feel the rhythm of that walk again—a heavy, easy, rolling movement. This movement was something new for me, a movement I'd never felt before. Right now, *I was Bear*, and as this lumbering body that was now mine swung down a sun-dappled trail in the woods, an old song started playing in my head, *The Banks of the Ohio*:

"I asked my love to take a walk, to take a walk, just a little walk.
Down beside where the waters flow. Down by the banks of the Ohio."

I sang on, and then, in my Bear body, placidly I plopped myself down on the riverbank, and as I did, I noticed that I was sitting Indian style. Legs crossed, I continued to sit like that, watching the water of the river flowing downstream and studying the boats on the river. They were old-fashioned ones, keelboats, and they were being piloted by a variety of rough-looking characters. I sat there and watched these men for quite a while, and as I watched them work, I realized that there weren't that many boats in the water—only a few.

That was when I realized that what I was seeing must be coming from another time. It had to be. This wasn't the sort of commerce you would see on a river today, and as I observed the scene before me, into my mind flew an awareness of that particular period in history. There was a rawness, a roughness present in the scene, and I noticed now that it was unsettling me. The men who were floating the boats down river were pushing and shoving at each other as they worked, literally throwing their weight around.

I'd seen this sort of male behavior before, so I was surprised that it was disturbing me now. But then I heard myself say, "There's a roughness here, and that same roughness is also evident in our present time." And when I said that, Bear let out a long **"Wahhhh"** sound, growling low in his throat. Then he placed a reassuring paw on my back to settle me down, and when I felt his touch, I realized that now *I* was no longer Bear. No. Now I was *with* Bear. Once again there were two of us, and when I became aware of that, I relaxed.

"Oh, yeah," I said to myself, "this is *way* better. I feel like myself again." And shaking my head, I had to chuckle at my response. "It's a lot easier for me to *see* Bear and be *with* Bear than it is for me to *be* Bear," I admitted. Becoming Bear had shot me out of my comfort zone, and now Bear, in his compassion, had moved me right back into it. "I guess my mind's not free enough yet for that mergence business," I muttered while Bear nodded his head impassively.

A few minutes went by as we simply sat quietly together, and then I asked him, "Bear, what am I to learn here on this journey? You came in my dream," I reminded him. "You scared me awake, and now what do you want me to learn?"

Bear didn't say anything, but now I became aware that the men in the keelboats were standing with long poles in their hands, using them to propel the boats along. Each time they leaned on their poles, they made a connection with the river bottom and as I watched them work, I could feel the power of connection they felt as they moved those boats down river. The next time a man pushed off, I heard Bear crooning **"d e e p"** in his big voice. And when I heard that, I saw myself standing deep in the river, my legs spread in a powerful stance. I was in the water up to my hips, and as I stood in the river, I could feel that I was not only anchored in the water but also anchored to the earth Herself. Like those poles the men were working with, I too was anchored deep.

The feeling of being anchored like this lasted only a moment, and then my awareness moved to the water rushing furiously around me. And though it was running loud and fast, this wild river didn't frighten me. Not at all. I was too steady for that. I couldn't help but notice, however, that there was a lot of disturbance in the water—eddies and swirling currents everywhere. And after I'd watched for a few minutes, my mind moved back to the up-coming Gathering in Ohio. "Will there be disturbances like this at the Gathering?" I wondered. "Is this why I'm being shown this roiling water?"

Then I remembered that the first time I asked the Grandmothers about the Gathering in Ohio, they'd surprised me by making what felt like a pronouncement. **"Let a great reconciliation take place within the center of the United States,"** they'd declared. **"An Ancestral, racial, and cultural healing to free the past, the present, and the future. You have suffered long enough from separating one group of people from another,"** they said, **"and today we call you to the One Love. Join your hearts with ours as together we reach throughout the Net of Light to speed this** *great reconciliation.*" When they'd made this declaration, I'd known that something important was going to happen at the Ohio Gathering. And now as I watched the waters of the river, their pronouncement rang again in my mind.

So much was moving in the water as well as in my thoughts that when at last I brought my attention back to myself, I couldn't tell at first whether I was Bear again or I whether I was just sitting with Bear. "Maybe both are true," I finally decided. It didn't seem to matter to me now whether there were two of us, or only one. What mattered to me was how *calm* I was. After all the switching around from being me to being Bear to being me again, I was amazed by my relaxed attitude. As I continued to sit on the bank, watching all the comings and the goings on the river, I noticed that I was steady as a rock.

"It's interesting that I can see all this activity, all this drama and movement on the river," I mused, "but nothing can see me. I'm sitting here but these people on the river don't know I'm here," I thought. "I'm an observer, someone who sits behind the scenes and watches. It feels like it did earlier when I was able to both see Bear and be Bear—all at the same time. I'm just an observer," I repeated, and, for a moment that thought made me just a tiny bit dizzy. But that feeling didn't last long, and quickly I returned to the rock steady state inside me. And from that anchored place deep within myself, I continued to watch the flow.

Finally, I took in a breath, cocked my head, and asked, "What's really going on here? What am I here to learn, Bear?" As I turned to him, I began, "You came to me. What did…?" but he interrupted before I could continue. **"Anchor yourself,"** he said, and with those words, I again felt myself merging with him.

Now I was *really* big. *Massive.* I was B E A R. "Nobody can topple *this* Bear," I said as I felt the enormous power of myself. "I'm anchored." And then off in the distance, someone spoke. *"Outside time,"* a voice said.

"Oh!" I exhaled as recognition came flooding into me. "Bear exists outside of time," I said, "and who I truly am is also outside of time. It doesn't matter if I appear to be Bear or if I appear to be me. I'm actually behind the scenes somewhere, outside of time." Understanding was coming at last.

"I get it," I said then. "I'm only going to Ohio to perform my part in a play. It's an important part," I said, "and it's an important production, but it's only a drama. I'll play my part, perform my role in this particular play, but *what* I am is NOT an actor in the play. *What I am* is actually *outside time*. I exist beyond all the roles I've ever been given, beyond all the dramas that have ever occurred and ever will occur. And this same thing is true for everyone. The play is just a play," I realized as I shrugged my shoulders in relief. What a lovely feeling of freedom this was giving me!

Now I began to look back at all the preparations I'd made for this Gathering in Ohio and to glimpse the further preparations I would need to make. I looked, and it all looked good to me. It *was* good, but the quality of being anchored beyond time and space was what really mattered. Being able to observe the drama of the play rather than be identified with it and caught in the drama. "That's where the power is," I said and Bear nodded his head in agreement. **"Yes!"** he boomed, **"yes!"**

"Bear," I said, "please help me to look at everything in life this way. Help me stay 'outside time'—to observe and live *only* from that place," I said. "Help me stay out of the dramas and pulls of the moment." Bear laughed then, chuckling at my use of the word *only.* **"There is a time** for drama," he said. **"Lighthearted drama is good. That's part of the play. You can *enjoy* the play."** "Okay," I replied, and thinking it over, I nodded in agreement. "I think I understand what you're telling me here," I said, and when I looked at him, he appeared to be smiling. **"*Play* your part,"** he said, and I heard the emphasis he put on the word 'play.' Bear wanted me to enjoy my role in this drama in Ohio and not worry about a thing. "Okay!" I smiled, as I turned to him, "I will."

I looked back at him then and asked, "Bear, is there anything else?" And no sooner did I ask than once again, I felt myself as him, felt the mass of my Bear self. My human self once again had moved into the greatness of this Bear Being. "Thank you, Bear," I bowed, growling to him with a deep, long *hummmm*. We folded our paws together then, and standing head-to-head, we locked our eyes. "You are precious to me, Bear," I said, "so precious. You are magnificent," and when we hugged, I felt that merging sensation once again.

I closed my eyes and rested in his arms for a moment, and the next thing I knew, I was leaving him. I was leaving him, but I wasn't *really* leaving. "I can't leave him anymore," I said to myself, "because I *am* him." And as I spoke those words, I began to morph back into my human form.

"In and out, in and out," I laughed. "I'm Bear. I'm me. I'm Bear. I'm me," and for some reason, this moving from one identity to the other tickled me. I was giggling as I piled myself into the canoe and pushed off onto the river. "What the heck?" I said. "This 'play' business is kind of fun."

I looked around then and saw the *sipapu* waiting for me, so I began my journey back up through Mother Earth, climbing and climbing until finally I emerged in my front garden. Then I looked around at the garden I love, walked into the house, climbed the stairs, lay down on the bed and said "thank you" to my dear teacher. "Thank you, Bear, thank you."

During the Gathering in Ohio, I was surprised when I had to go through a few minor health challenges there. But because of Bear's advice to stay *outside time,* I was easily able to handle them and still keep my focus on the Gathering. Several times during the weekend, we magnified the power of the Net of Light throughout the Heartland, anchoring it deep within the land there. We also worked with the original peoples of the Midwest to heal the racial and cultural divides that had become imbedded in the land.

Calling on the Ancestors of the Light, we performed deep forgiveness work on the historic rifts between the early European settlers and the original peoples of that area. Reverently, we called out the names of the tribes of Ohio and spoke the Ho'oponopono prayer for forgiveness to them. We also worked to heal theschisms between people of different races and cultures who had moved to this part of the country, harmonizing the connection between established groups and new immigrants.

Over that weekend, together we shared from our hearts and experienced repeatedly the blessing power of forgiveness. All of us were deeply moved by our time together, and when this Gathering was over, several women stepped forward, asking to become Beacons on the Net of Light, to anchor the Net in their towns and cities, to call groups together and practice living the Grandmothers' message. New study groups would come together now to read and discuss the Grandmothers' books and spread their work throughout the Midwest and Southeast. We had truly bonded with one another and decided to meet again the following year.

"The history of the Old and New World differs."

By this time, all of us had been working together with the Ancestors for a few years, focusing on healing the pain of the past. We'd done ancestral work together in California, Alabama, Australia, New Zealand, all over Europe—and now in the Midwestern United States as well. And each time we connected with the Ancestors of the Light and dove in together to heal the pain of the past, no matter where we were, tears fell, magic happened, and loved filled the room.

Over the years that we'd done this work, we'd learned many things. One was that wherever one tribe, clan or nation had invaded another, there were wounds to be healed. So, each time we held a Net of Light Gathering, we did ancestral healing to mend these racial, national and cultural divides wherever we found them. And as we worked, we began to notice that what was needed in Europe was different from what was needed in America, New Zealand and Australia.

Europe, part of what we consider the Old World, is a place where cultural divides began long ago. Divisions in Europe are also multi-layered because every time a country was invaded, a new divide took place. And because there were layers upon layers of invasions and cross-invasions, not to mention vast numbers of wars, there was a lot of ancestral healing waiting to be done in Europe.

In the countries of the New World, violent clashes between cultures didn't occur until relatively recently. As far as we know, the indigenous cultures of the New World were fairly stable until foreign invaders showed up three or four hundred years ago. Tribes had warred with each other, but when European colonists showed up and waged war on native peoples' way of life, they were not only destroying them as individuals but also were attempting to destroy their entire culture.

As the Grandmothers' teachings of the Net of Light spread over the world, we found that the healing work needed in Europe was the most challenging, nd the religious history of Europe contributed to that. Before the Roman Empire and the spread of Christianity that followed it, man's spiritual bond with Mother Earth had been strong—as strong in Europe as it was in all parts of the world. But as Rome and then the Roman Catholic church came to dominate Europe, the deep connection that humans and earth had shared for time out of mind became threatened.

So-called 'pagan ways' were always frowned upon by the patriarchal structures of Rome, but when the Roman Catholic church took over as the official head of Rome, these old religious ways were vilified. After millennia of humans living in co-operation with nature, suddenly with the arrival of the church, the spirits of the earth were labeled as evil. When this occurred, even the traditional healers of that time—those who worked with plants, herbs and growing things—were at risk for their lives. The Dark Ages, the Inquisition, and the witch trials quickly followed, showing us patriarchy at its worst.

While the movement away from harmony with the earth was taking place in Europe, in the New World, indigenous peoples were still living as they always had. Their cultures continued to be nature based—their songs, ceremonies and beliefs testifying to their bond with Mother Earth. However, when European colonists arrived in the New World, they attempted to destroy this way of life and erase these indigenous cultures.

Because of the way the history of the Old and New World differs, we found it much easier to connect with the elemental power of the land in the New World than in the Old. Europeans have been 'cut off' from Mother Earth for far longer than have the inhabitants of the New World. So, in spite of the genocide and persecution of the indigenous peoples in the New World, here the ancient bond between human beings and the earth still exists.

Today many Europeans are working hard to reconnect with their land; however, in certain countries this is easier to do than it is in others. For example, in both Lithuania and Latvia where Christianity arrived late and where people were often 'converted' at sword point, a connection to the land as well as to the old gods of nature still exists. This makes it relatively easy for these people to work with the Net of Light and be open to the love of the Grandmothers. But in many other countries of Europe, the link to the land is quite faint and people have to work hard to re-establish a connection with Mother Earth.

Ancestral work is helping revitalize the ancient connection to the land in Europe and elsewhere. Each time people participate in ancestral healing, wounds from the old cultural divisions that permeated the continent of Europe begin to heal. And now, there are Net of Light groups all over Europe that meet regularly to anchor the Net of Light in the land there, re-sanctifying both the land and the human connection to it.

Around the time I was putting this part of the book together, I received a note from Marian, a Net of Light Beacon in Ireland, who'd just returned from a spiritual workshop in Dublin. Her letter speaks to some of the healing work that's taking place now in Europe.

She wrote:

"I am constantly referring to the Grandmothers' messages in *Our Love Is Our Power* (the Grandmothers' second book), so when one of the presenters at the spiritual event last weekend mentioned the beautiful energy of the Grandmothers, I felt she was speaking my language.

"Right after that, one of the participants began to go through some deep work of her own and I sat there while she was going through her own personal horrors. I was holding space for her with everyone else at the workshop as the leaders talked to her. Then one of the leaders said, 'Will Grandmother please stand up?' and I nearly froze in shock. 'Come here,' she said to me, and I can't remember her words exactly but basically I was to help care for this lady. I think the idea was that the Irish grandmother (me) was to help the lady who'd just returned to Ireland to work on her issues with this country.

"So, I took my blanket and gently, and with as much care and reverence as I could, wrapped it around her on the floor. I happened to be wearing the shawl I'd been given when I received the Grandmothers' Empowerment, so I placed one hand with a piece of that shawl on her head and one hand over her heart and oh boy did I call on the Grandmothers!

"When I felt her beginning to release her fear, I gently removed my hands, straightened up, and channeled the energy of love to her. I felt this beautiful energy and then someone with a lovely voice started to sing 'O how we love you,' (the Grandmothers' song), and everyone joined in. You can imagine what it was like! I then took my shawl and wrapped it gently around the lady's head and shoulders.

"Then, as the leader was checking in with people, suddenly the girl beside me tried to talk but couldn't and became frozen—rigid in fear. The leader came to her and worked with her and the next thing I knew, she had taken my hands and had me holding her. Again, the Grandmothers came in. I'm telling you all this just to paint the picture of how it went. I only realized this morning that while this was happening in Ireland all of you were meeting in Ohio.

"Bless you all."

"These are not 'Good' times. These are 'Great' times, 'Godly' times."

The world of the Grandmothers and the Net of Light was challenging, uplifting, and always fascinating to me. However, I was discovering that the day-to-day world in America was also challenging, but NOT uplifting. And as politics in America got uglier and uglier, and Americans began to act in ways I no longer recognized, I found myself struggling to stand steady—emotionally and spiritually.

"We are watching you," the Grandmothers said one day. I had just arrived at their circle and was about to ask them a question when they said, **"We're watching as you struggle to find a safe harbor for yourself. You are seeking stability in the world around you, and you're trying to do this as the storms and disappointments of the times**

you're living in rage around you. Nations are quaking now," they said; "the very land under your feet is quaking, and many of your hallowed institutions are falling. It's difficult to find steady ground now," they said as they stood back and appraised me. "We understand what it's like for you at this time on earth," they nodded, "and so we've come to uphold you."

I gulped when I heard this. The Grandmothers had read me right, and now I stared at them, holding my breath, tears welling in my eyes. "What is taking place in your world at this time is not a terrible mistake," they said, and I gulped again. "It seems like a mistake to me, Grandmothers," I said, my voice wobbly. "The present upheaval in society must occur," they assured me as they continued to eye me with calm, steady looks. "No good will come from blaming others for the ills you see around you now. After all, which of you is blameless?" they asked, piercing me with their gaze.

"This is The Great Shift that was foretold long ago," they said, "and now it has come. You are living through it, and you have a part to play in this shift. Whenever you link with us or with any form of the Divine you love, you are able to hold steady, even while all about you is collapsing. At this point in time, it's impossible to find stability in the outer world," they shook their heads, "so don't waste your time looking for it.

"And don't respond to all this upheaval by falling into despair. Don't hide yourself away; instead, gather with those who, like you, are also seeking the highest good. Call on us, hold to the Net of Light, and come together to study our books and messages. You will find what you need there," they said.

"You have taken birth at this time in history," they said, holding me with a steady gaze. "You made this choice purposefully, and what is occurring on earth now *is no accident*. You were born for great things. Quiet your mind," they said, nodding slowly to calm me, "and turn within yourself to the presence that has never left you and never will. Stay in this place of inner silence," they said, "and from here we will guide you."

Over and over again I re-read this message from them. I needed it and knew I would need to hear it many more times. In November we would hold the U.S. presidential election, and with all the political storms and dramas raging, I would need to call up every bit of steadiness I could muster.

"Go slow."

Just before the election, Roger and I would leave for a trip to Japan. Roger had been there during the Vietnam War, but this was a country I'd never visited. So, before we left, I asked the Grandmothers about what possible 'work' I could do while we were there. We'd be traveling with a small group, journeying together through the countryside, following the old Samurai trail through the mountains, small villages and towns. We would use public transportation, stay in traditional inns, wear kimonos and eat only Japanese food. Our goal was to get a 'real' experience of Japan, and though all of this sounded enticing to me, I also wanted to do whatever work I could while on this trip. So, I went to the Grandmothers, hoping to get my marching orders.

"**There's something in the land in Japan that's important for you to understand,**" they said, and the phrase that came to me when they said this was 'anchor in.' Then they began to speak, not only of this trip but of life in general. "**Do not skim and skitter over the surface of life,**" they said, "**but send down your anchor and connect to the depths. Unless you drop anchor,**" they said, eyeing me from under their raised brows, "**you will end up living a superficial life. You will just bob along, and, distracted by the ever-changing activity in the world, you will forget why you were born. Don't do that,**" they said, shaking their heads. "**Don't waste your life looking for entertainment.**" "I won't, Grandmothers," I promised, looking hard at them and wondering why they were telling me this now. "I don't want to waste my life," I said, and now I really studied them.

"**Go slow and go deep. You need to connect to Mother Earth—now. Do not put this off,**" they said, and they gave me a fierce look. "**You need Her and She needs you. NOW!**" they ordered. "Okay, Grandmothers," I said, "Okay. I agree, and it sounds like this is REALLY important."

"**Turn your awareness within yourself,**" they said, "**and think of your connection to the Net of Light, and to us, the Grandmothers. Then call your Mother,**" and I looked up at them in surprise. What did they mean? "**She is waiting to hear from you,**" they said. "**She won't** force Herself on you or interfere in your life," they shook their heads. "No. She won't do that.

"*You must reach out to Her,*" they said with feeling. "**The first move must come from you. And then you must wait on Her.**" Now I understood that they were referring to Mother Earth. They were telling me that I needed to initiate contact with Her. "**Again, we tell you,**" they fixed me with a look, "**She is waiting. Make a conscious effort to connect with Her. Sing to Her,**" they said, "**speak to Her, light a candle for Her. Go out of your way to offer something beautiful to Her. Go slow,**" they said again.

Now I understood that I was to seek contact with Mother Earth. And this connection with Her had something to do with why Roger and I were going to Japan. "Okay, Grandmothers," I said, "I'll do it. I'll look for ways to connect with Her on this trip."

Learning in Japan

On our first day in Tokyo, Roger and I spent several hours wandering through a forested park near our hotel. The park was right in the center of this intensely populated city, but even so, it was so vast, so heavily treed, so filled with statues, bridges, and pagodas that it seemed a world unto itself. Here we came upon hundreds of sculptures of babies and children, all of them wrapped in red scarves, as well as shrine after shrine of Buddha-like figures—some small, some massive. Candles glowed everywhere as people quietly walked among the shrines of the park. It was its own world.

In a few minutes we were scheduled to take a tour of the city, so while Roger waited for the tour bus at the edge of the park, I came upon an out-of-the-way shrine just inside the park's border. Hidden away, down a small pathway stood an old shed with a dark Buddha-like figure, an altar with flowers on it and, resting at the base, a bucket and rags. Clearly someone was looking after this shrine.

Standing quietly before this Buddha-like figure, I bowed my head and began to talk to him. I had determined to focus on healing and communicating with Mother Earth throughout Japan and here was an opportunity to do that. And although this place was somber and somewhat spooky, I was thrilled to have found it, to have found a quiet place like this and to have it all to myself.

Quickly, I told this god of the forest about the Net of Light and of the great need for light on earth now. I was aware that the bus might show up at any moment, so I hurried to explain it all to him as fast as I could. I asked him to please help anchor and spread the work of the Net of Light, assuming that he must be a form of Lord Buddha. He certainly looked like him. And remembering Buddha's great compassion, I asked him to feed light into the Net of Light so it could support the earth. As I continued to stand before the god-like figure of the forest, I quickly shared all of this, hurrying to get it out before the bus arrived. The Grandmothers had urged me to connect with Mother Earth, and I had discovered this shrine in the heart of Tokyo, a good place to start.

That night I began to get sick …really sick … and immediately I knew that it had to do with the god figure in the forest. I didn't know why, but I was convinced that there was a connection. Bronchitis and extreme fatigue set in fast, and two days later after a freezing afternoon in the mountains with the snow monkeys, I had to step off the pathway in the forest to throw up.

We would spend that night in a rustic inn in the mountains. It was a lovely spot, and as the snow started to fall, it became even more beautiful—and cold. But I had to skip the elaborate Japanese dinner that night and forego the hot baths at the spa because now all I wanted was my bed.

The next morning our group left us in this charming mountain town. They had a schedule to keep, and I was too sick to go with them. Hopefully, we would rejoin them later that day. Roger had all our travel directions—for the train and bus connections we'd need to find our way. Now everything fell on his shoulders, because I was of no use whatsoever.

When the group left us that morning, Roger and I put on our warmest clothes and walked out into the snow to find a doctor. In this out-of-the-way country place, no one spoke English, but fortunately, we were still able to find a doctor. She was kind and patient—a great gift to us as we had to communicate with her in sign language. She gave me medicine, charged us very little for her treatment, and let us know that in a few days all would be well. Now, however, all was not well, and all I wanted was to crawl back into bed. "Couldn't we go back to the hotel?" I begged Roger, but he only smiled and shook his head. We had to go on. So, he found a cab, got us onto a train, (where I slept). After being dragged along like the zombie I was and changing trains and buses several times, we finally rejoined our group in another mountain town.

I slept for most of the next two days, keeping to the outskirts of our tour group and sneaking off to nap in between travel movements. I was sure that this sickness had come from my communication with the god of the forest, but I had no idea what I could do about it. However, at the subsequent shrines our group visited, I kept a low profile and didn't attempt to interact with any of the deities. I was respectful, but kept a distance. And something about what had happened in the park in Tokyo felt strangely familiar. This experience with the forest god in Japan kept drawing my mind back to an earlier one I'd had with the spirits of nature in Sedona, Arizona. There was something about it….

In Sedona the spirits of the land had been powerful, but distant, and this had surprised me. Now I recalled that the spirits in Sedona had shown no emotion when I'd interacted with them, that they hadn't seemed at all interested in relating to human beings. And somehow the sense I'd gotten from this 'god of the forest' felt similar to that. Slowly it began to dawn on me that in my enthusiasm to be of service in Japan I'd 'rushed' a connection with the god of the forest in Tokyo, hadn't slowed down enough to let him lead. Then I recalled how the Grandmothers had explicitly told me to *go slow* and realized that I had NOT gone slow. So perhaps this was why the forest god had pushed me away—knocked me back, so-to-speak.

A few days later while we were staying at another spa town high in the mountains, I woke in the early morning hours. As I lay on my futon, I began to talk with the Holy Man. He had come in a dream. He'd appeared in the downstairs of a large compound where he was working, and when I saw him there, I was surprised and very happy to see him, but he just looked at me as if to say, "Well, of course I'm here. Of course, I'm working. I'm always here, always working. What did you think?" And, in the dream, again and again, I'd walk past the place where he was working, to check and see if he was still there.

As soon as I woke, silently I began to talk with him, thanking him for coming in the dream. And then I told him about how I'd gotten sick on this trip and didn't know how to talk to the gods here in Japan. And before I knew it, I was pouring my heart out, pouring my heart out to the local gods as well, telling them of my confusion about what had happened and how I didn't know how to ask for their help. As I lay in bed, having one conversation after another, tears poured down my cheeks. It was as if my soul, my whole self really, was lying there, confessing and getting washed clean.

I remember telling the gods that I was ignorant, that I really didn't know anything, and asking for their forgiveness for my lack of understanding. But I also told them that like them, I too loved the earth (a great deal) and was broken-hearted by what human beings were doing to it. "Please help!" I begged them again, and this time I felt them respond.

Soon a great weaving began to take place in that room—a weaving of light throughout the mountains where we were staying, weaving throughout Japan, and throughout the world. This weaving movement was instantaneous, and the connections it made as it grew in strength were stable and steady. *Everything* was now being woven together; everything was being linked in light. There was a rhythm to this interweaving that went on and on like a song, and as I felt my body responding to it and growing stronger, I lay there in awe.

Later that day we visited the famous Zen rock garden in Kyoto where I found just enough room to sit on its edge in order to observe the breathtaking austerity of the place. Each rock had been perfectly placed, set into and bordered with finely patterned gravel. And, no sooner did I sit down there than the weaving, which had begun as I lay in bed that morning, started up again.

This time my connection with it was instantaneous, and as I sat there on that ledge, I felt at one with this interweaving force. The weaving action was having a big effect on me, and I was aware that it wasn't just me. It was affecting the whole world. Now all sense of separation inside myself began to dissolve. Peace descended. Silently, and with great definition, peace implanted itself inside me. Now I was at one with the stones of this Zen garden, and the stones were at one with me. There was no more this, no more that, no more observer, no more observed—no more separation at all. As I sat at the edge of that garden, my spirit flew up and soared.

The last place we stayed before we returned to Tokyo was a monastery on Mt. Koya, where we rose at dawn to meditate with the monks. In the early morning darkness, as we sat in the magic of the prayer room there, candlelight reflected off the many golden statues of the

Buddha, the saints, and other holy beings in the room. It was freezing cold but stirringly beautiful, and the reverberations of the chants and gongs ringing in the candle light went right through my body.

Here again was that now familiar weaving action, and this time it was thorough and complete. A deep connection with the land of Japan was being made, and I understood that from this moment on, those of us who work with the Net of Light would be able to link in with it. Japan, the land of the rising sun, would now contribute to holding the rest of the planet steady. Uluru, Stonehenge, Sedona, Machu Pichu, Mt. Kailash—all of these and more—along with Japan, were now connected within the great Web of Light.

Back in Tokyo in our hotel room, I wrote a brief good-bye, giving thanks to the beings of light in Japan, to the ancient ones of the land, to the Shinto path and the Buddhist path. Deep gratitude to all beings that live in and for the light. *Arigato* from the bottom of my heart.

"Hold Sacred Space. Be mindful of who you are."

After we returned from our trip, it was time to get back to the basics of daily life. The election in America was over now, and the country was terribly divided. As soon as I could, I went to the Grandmothers. I hoped there was something we could do to help with all the trauma and division. "Well, Grandmothers," I said as I stood before them, "now that the election is over, what can we learn? And, if there's anything we can do to help, please let us know.

"**Before we begin,**" they replied, leaning in so close that they were looking straight at me, "**let us explain some things to you. First,**" they said, holding up a hand as if to slow me down, "**you have elected, not a man, but a 'moy' to lead you. He is a boy in a man's body. Moys are a combination of man and boy, but mostly boy,**" they explained. "**They are large and have loud voices so people mistake them for men. But they are not men. A man thinks of what is good for all, while a moy has not yet learned to think of anyone but himself. He has not fully developed. He is still a child.**" "Yes, Grandmothers," I said, nodding as I recalled several years ago their explaining 'moys' to me and how to cope with them.

"**The time you are living in has been called the age of destruction,**" they said, continuing their explanation, "**the Kali Yuga. It is the** lowest point," they said, holding my gaze. "At this time, evil rises to the surface of the earth in order to be destroyed. This dark-age takes place just before the arrival of the in-coming Golden Age, so today you are watching as out-of-balance yang energy creates destruction all over your planet. This IS the Kali Yuga," the Grandmothers declared. "You have heard about it and now it has come.

"Your country has just elected a moy to be its next president. Russia as well as Syria are already controlled by moys while Africa is overrun by them, each moy creating havoc in his area of that continent. The Philippines is controlled by a moy as are so many other countries on earth. Is it any wonder then that the world is lurching from crisis to crisis?" they asked. "The destructive energy that runs these world leaders is also trying to run the world.

"This is what is happening on earth today, and because it is, you must learn to cope with it. You cannot reason with energy like this because it is entirely destructive. Instead, you must hold steady within yourself. Stay within a position of power and observe its wild behavior from that place of steadiness. If you do that, it will not be able to feed on you," they said. "Your steadiness will help contain its rapacious energy so it won't be able to do as much damage as it would otherwise.

"Hold Sacred Space," the Grandmothers said, "and be mindful of who you are. You are a great being. You are here on earth to hold a steady place in an unsteady world. And you can do this," they said. "You are not weak and helpless. Within yourself you carry the great holding power of yin. Call on it now," they said. "Live with it. *Be* as you were born to be.

"We ask one more thing of you," the Grandmothers said, gazing at me with their hearts in their eyes. "Reach out to one another in service. Many are suffering now. Feed the hungry," they said. "Visit people in hospitals and prisons; provide shoes to those who need them; help the animals. If each of you plunges into one activity of service now, together you will accomplish great good. You will turn many hearts to the light," they said as they looked long into my eyes. "We ask this of you because we know who you are," they said. "You are our hands and hearts on earth. You are greatness itself."

They were melting my heart with their words, and their love was overwhelming my mind. But more than that, I realized that they themselves were so selfless that they saw me that way too! They were asking me to be like them, and they were expecting me to do it! They saw greatness in me! Saw it and were calling it forth. Would I ever be able to see myself in this way? The way they saw me? The depth of their love was shaking me and bringing me to my knees.

"A lesser vibration cannot withstand the energy of the SOURCE."

The next time I went to the Grandmothers, however, I was *not* in an elevated mindset. While driving, I'd been listening to a report of the latest terrorist atrocities. "Stories of terrorism and hatred are in the news every day," I said to the Grandmothers. "I heard more about it today, and I have to say that what I heard is overwhelming me. It's so awful. It's subhuman," I said. "Is there anything we can *do* about this?" I asked them, and as I spoke, I heard my voice shaking.

Nodding to let me know that they understood, the Grandmothers then turned and pointed to a group of men, their faces full of rage, who were standing off in the distance. Menacing and full of fury, these men looked like human cyclones, shouting and spinning wildly about. Waving their weapons, they made stabbing motions with them, and as they stabbed at the ground like this, I saw that the impetus of their spin was driving the energies of hate and fear into the earth itself. "They're laying waste," I said to the Grandmothers, "literally laying waste. They're leaving a path of blood and destruction wherever they go."

"Yes," the Grandmothers said, nodding as they watched me with sad eyes. "**People like this are lost. At this point you can do nothing with them or for them, but you *can* do something to de-activate the cyclone energy in which they are caught.**" "What, Grandmothers?" I asked, wanting to be sure I'd heard them right. "What can we do?"

"**Hold yourself very, very steady,**" they replied, and as they spoke, they lifted their hands up in front of them as if to stop traffic. "**Hold stock still, like this, and from this place of utter stillness, let love and light radiate outward from you. However fast they spin in the energy of that cyclone, *this* is how much you must slow your response.**

"*Go slow. Go to ground,*" they said, *"and lock into the planetary grid of light.* **The Net of Light has now implanted itself into the earth,**" the Grandmothers continued. "**It has formed a grid that pen-**

etrates everything on your planet. Lock into that. Think the thought of dropping down into this grid; your energy will follow your thought," they said. "You *will* lock in.

"Anchor yourself there. Then be still, and from this position of oneness with the earth, let light radiate out from you. You already have the potential to broadcast a great amount of light, and when you lock into the grid like this, your potential becomes greater still.

"Go slow when you do this," they said, "and go deep. As you hold steady, light will flood through you and from you—moving outward in concentric circles of power. When you hold steady like this, you tap into a vibration that is so strong and resounds with so much power that the whirling cyclone energy of terrorism with its high-pitched screeching is no match for it.

"Whenever you lock in to the grid of light within the earth, you will feel a thrumming in your heart and body. This," they emphasized, "is caused by your connection with the SOURCE. A lesser vibration cannot withstand the energy of the SOURCE, so hold your place here," the Grandmothers said, "and as you sit in this position of power, begin to call the high pitched, erratic energy of terror and hate home. *Call this energy to come home!*" they said and I looked at them, my eyes huge.

"The energy of terror is spinning out of control. The energy of terror came into being when it allowed itself to spin, and once it did that, it spun and spun—further and further out of control. Call it home now," they said. "Drop into the still point at your center and call this errant force home to the Net of Light.

"You can do this work by yourself or in a group," they said. "It is intensely powerful. *Nothing* can withstand its power. Trust us," they said. "We know what we are talking about."

I took the Grandmothers at their word. Early on they had told me, **"We know what we are talking about,"** and over time I'd learned that they spoke only truth. If they said that anchoring myself to the Net of Light would help calm the terrorists, then I would do it. So, I did exactly that, and though I couldn't vouch for the terrorists simmering down, I could certainly testify that working like this calmed *me* down.

"Our hands are on you."

The next time I spoke with the Grandmothers was on my birthday. I'd decided that I would journey to them as a present to myself. So, I journeyed in the usual way and as I approached their circle, I heard them singing the Net of Light song.

"**Net of Light, Net of Light, floating in the Net of Light,**" they sang, and laughing, they reached out to me. "**See and feel the Net of Light holding the world and holding you,**" they said. "**Feel it touching your skin, upholding your organs while at the same moment it lies on and underneath the earth. The Net of Light IS!**" they cried, their faces lit with happiness. "**And you ARE.**

"**You are not separate from it or from us,**" they laughed. "**You are Divine. Know this now on the day of your birth. This is our gift to you. From now on, accept no substitute identities,**" they said, looking pleased with themselves. "**You are not the past,**" they declared. "**You are not limited. You are light! You are the Fabric of Being of the Universe. No small potato here!**" they laughed and, reaching out their arms, embraced me.

"**You are waking up now, and so is the world,**" they said. "**No more numbness, no more narcotic sleep. You are all coming awake. Rise up and shine!**" they cried, lifting their hands high. "**No more minimizing your worth and hiding your light. Stand forth now,**" they said. "**Shine! Happy Birthday today. Today you are born anew, and we rejoice in your birth.**

"**Even though this is your birthday message, you may share it with others,**" they said. "**Share it and tell them this: 'wherever you live, whatever you are going through, know that our hands are on you. You cannot go beyond our reach. You are our own and we will uphold you throughout everything you face. We are holding you at this minute and we will hold you at every minute of your life.'**

"**You can let yourself relax into our embrace. We are the Grand Mothers,**" they said to me, laughingly, "**and we know how to take care of you. Let your mind relax now and ask it to record what you experience as you let yourself soften into our embrace. The mind too needs rest,**" the Grandmothers said, "**and because there is so much that it doesn't understand, it tends to work too hard. Often the mind falls into a pattern of needless busyness, and when this happens, it does you no good at all.**

"Wisdom will dawn on you from within yourself—not from your mind reaching outward for it," they explained. "You are wiser by far than you know," they laughed. "You are wiser by far than *anyone* knows. Now, let your mind fall back and rest as we begin to teach you the truth of your own being. You will be surprised by this. Actually, you will be thrilled.

"You *are* a thrilling being," the Grandmothers said, grinning with one another as they looked me over. "We can say this because we see you as the magnificent one that you are. We have always seen you," they said, "for we have been with you before what you think of as 'time' ever was. We are the Grand Mothers and you are our own.

"There is a momentum carrying you."

The next time I went to the Grandmothers, the first thing they said to me was, "You have something to say. Speak!!!" and my mouth flew open in surprise. What did they mean? I didn't have anything to say. But because they didn't talk again and remained silent, I finally gave up and sat down. I would just have to wait them out and let them "speak" through me whenever they were ready. But for now, I'd turn within myself, and if they did say something to me inside, I'd write down whatever came. I'd basically transcribe what they gave me. This then is what came.

"Picture yourself on a conveyor belt," they said, and I wrote it down. "You are moving forward, inexorably forward," they said, swaying their bodies to mimic this forward motion. "There's a momentum carrying you," they said, "and this momentum is carrying all beings. All of you are being conveyed, moving forward together." And when I heard this, I felt the force of that motion, felt myself, along with scores of others, being carried forward. "You're doing this together," they said, "so bless your fellow journeymen. You're sharing the adventure; all of you are joined on this ride.

"Each of you has a different role to fulfill at this moment in time," they said, "but you're together on the forward ride. And the momentum of this movement is terrific!" they cried, and I felt it. We weren't just moving forward; we were *racing* forward. Speeding through time and space.

"You're being drawn toward an expanded vista now," the Grandmothers said, and they pointed to something far off in the distance, something very bright out there. **"This place is flooded with light. See it!"** they cried, and my eyes were dazzled by light. Light that seemed to go on and on forever. **"Experience it!"** they cried. **"Big sky and sun on water!"**

An enormous vista of sky and sea was spread out before me now, and the glare from the sun reflecting on the water was so brilliant it was almost blinding. As I squinted my eyes to cut down on the glare, the wind coming off the sea began to lift my hair. Then the conveyer belt we were riding on sped up, and my hair jetted straight back. This journey was becoming intense.

"Don't be distracted by any clumps of darkness you may see up ahead," the Grandmothers called out as we passed a heap of dark shapes on our right. **"You'll see these clumps now and then as you go speeding forward,"** they said, **"but they're nothing to be concerned about. Piles of detritus. Junk,"** they said. **"They have no real significance.**

"Feel the momentum of the ride—how strong and fast it is. You're speeding through time and space," the Grandmothers said as the conveyor belt raced forward. **"This is quite a journey you're taking, so let yourself go with it and enjoy it. But keep your focus on the journey and don't allow yourself to become distracted by anything else,"** they advised, **"including the actions of others who, like you, are also on this ride.**

"And as you journey forward, look for beauty everywhere!" they said. And now my eyes were drawn to the colors, plants and animals that surrounded me here… the parade of people and places popping up all about. The landscape seemed to change every second, and watching it as it shifted and morphed was thrilling.

"Seek beauty and you will find it," the Grandmothers said, their heads nodding in agreement. **"See beauty in nature, see it in people. Seek goodness, too,"** they said, **"and take every opportunity to do good along the way.** *Be* **good and see the evident goodness in the world around you. Look also for the hidden goodness, the goodness that lurks beneath the surface of life.**

"Goodness as a quality is all-pervasive," they said, and gave me a meaningful look. **"Too often in the past you've become distracted by the non-beautiful, the unpleasant, the frightful and the nasty. Let all**

of that go now," they said, flipping their hands up in dismissal. "That stuff is just passing detritus…clumps of darkness. Such things have no real essence and will soon fade into the background and disappear. The conveyor is rolling forward," they emphasized, "carrying you on to the next vista, and then the next—each one brighter and more expanded than the one before it.

"You're on your way to greatness," the Grandmothers said, "on your way to goodness, on your way to a life you cannot begin to imagine. Don't become overly fascinated by those patches of darkness surfacing all over your planet now," they said again and I realized that I *had* become distracted by them. Ugliness was so unusual here in this sea of beauty that my eyes had been drawn to these dark places. "These piles look ugly, and some of them even stink," the Grandmothers said, "but they're only flotsam and jetsam. Passing debris. Let them go. Keep your focus on the great light that's glowing ahead of you. This is where you are going. Bless everyone you meet on this journey," they said. "Bless everyone and everything, and keep on moving forward.

"We ask you to look for beauty and at the same time to give yourself over to the work at hand. Do whatever task that lies before you. Do what needs doing, and do it with a full heart. Beauty and work, work and beauty. This," they said, "is how to live in these times."

"Keep your head up and ride the current."

Several days later I received another message, and this one too was full of encouragement. It was clear that the Grandmothers were going out of their way to help us stay the course. They seemed to understand how difficult it was for us to cope with all the ugliness and negativity that was surfacing all over the world. They wanted us to keep on working with the Net of Light, to lift ourselves, and so they continued to encourage us not to give up.

For this journey I'd gone to the lower world, thinking to find Bear and work on some healing for myself, but instead of meeting him as I usually did, before I could paddle the canoe to shore, I found the Grandmothers standing hip deep in the water of the river, waiting for me. The current was strong here and the eddies swirled around us, but the Grandmothers held me up and we swam through the rough waters together. And there in the midst of all that turmoil, I listened to my wise teachers, swam a little, treaded water, and learned.

"Push upward," they called to me when my feet touched the muck of the river bottom. **"Onward!"** they cried, beckoning me to them. **"Swim forward; ride high with the current,"** they called, **"and as the muck and debris from the bottom of the river starts to surface, keep on moving forward with the flow. Stay on top of the water,"** they encouraged me, **"and ride the waves. Don't try to dive here; now is not the time to explore the depths. The current is rough and the deep so muddy that you won't be able to see anything anyway, so wait on that,"** they said. **"Soon it will be time to examine what's underneath the surface, but for now, wait until it clears. At this moment, it's all swirling eddies and scum.**

"You've never witnessed an upheaval like this before," they said. **"Such a mass of confusing movement is rare—rare and dangerous, so stay out of the roiling foam. Instead, keep on riding the waves and let the current carry you forward. We are taking this ride with you,"** they reminded me, **"and we won't abandon you.**

"The River of Life must cleanse itself," they explained, **"and though you're watching as this takes place, now is not the time to seek understanding of this great cleansing. For now, just keep your head up and ride the current. Ride it with us,"** they said and beckoned me forward.

Now we swam together, and for a while we played in the waves. Then, walking me up onto the sand, the Grandmothers wrapped me and dried me off, and setting me down on the bank with them, they began to talk to me as the wise teachers that they are.

"You think too small," they said. **"You don't understand the immensity of your reach. You still think of yourself as a separate *little* person who counts for nothing." NO!"** they shook their heads emphatically. **"You are immense, and your reach knows no bounds.**

"Because you're living in times of storm and drama," they explained, **"you're struggling to find your footing. And, because we are able to see everything that's happening in the world,"** they said, **"we know what to do. We encourage you to 'stand steady'—right where you are. Wherever you are, stand in *that* place, and from *there*, let love flow. You are a repository of love, a generator and creator of goodness,"** they said. **"That's who you are at every moment of**

life, and because this is your nature, you can do a great deal of good, especially during these times. We will show you how. To begin," they said, "**ask your mind to relax. Ask it to move into receiving mode and to record what we will tell you.**" "Yes, Grandmothers," I replied, and immediately I thought of my mind softening, opening itself to receive and record.

"**Simply think of us,**" they began, "**and imagine that you're breathing us into your body. With each breath you take in, remind yourself that it is WE who are filling you. We are actually breathing you,**" they said, smiling and nodding enthusiastically. "**We're filling you with peace, goodness, and unending love. We're filling you full.**

"**Next, allow the Net of Light to hold and enfold you. It will do that,**" they assured me, "**and it will do it immediately. You don't yet understand that because of your connection to the Net of Light, your reach is boundless.** *Because* **you are linked with this Network of goodness, YOU have the ability to endlessly give and do good. Each act of kindness that flows out from you—to a friend, a stranger, an animal, a condition on earth—radiates throughout the Net. Your smile sends a lift to Egypt, to Australia, to Estonia—everywhere. This is how the Net of Light works.**

"**During the difficult times you're living in, this flow of goodness is especially needed. Therefore, each day ask us what** *small* **thing you can do to feed goodness into the Net of Light. We will show you, and,**" they said, "**what you feed in will not be** *small* **at all. After you've made this request, pay attention to what comes to you. Notice how things happen, who and what shows up, who calls, and what takes place and when. Don't miss the opportunities that will come to you,**" they said, "**for come, they will.**" Then they said, "**We're eager to work with you, and there is much to be done.**

I paid close attention to what the Grandmothers shared on this journey, and I knew that what they'd said about the power of the Net of Light was accurate. The Net, after all, is the Fabric of Being of the Universe, so no matter how my mind might struggle with understanding that I was one with this vast, lighted network, I knew that it had to be true. But knowing something was true and really 'knowing' it (feeling and living it) were two different things. Now and then my mind still pulled me into doubt, and whenever that happened, for a while I might forget. But the Grandmothers were relentless in their determination to hold me to the truth.

"Everything we do, we do together."

As soon as I got the message from the Grandmothers reminding me of the power of the Net of Light, I put it into newsletter form and sent it out. I had to share it immediately; I couldn't stop thinking about what they'd said. They had made me question what I was doing with my own life. Was communicating the Grandmothers' teachings to others enough for me? Was it really helping anyone? Could I be doing more?

In the last few months, I'd sent out message after message from them—sometimes several in a week. When I first started doing this, I heard from so many people who were horrified by what was going on in the world today, and who kept requesting guidance from the Grandmothers, that I put my other work on the back burner and just kept journeying to the Grandmothers. Again and again, I went to them for guidance and reassurance. But this had gone on now for several months, and though initially readership of their messages had risen, as I continued to keep the messages going, responses dwindled. Clearly, I wasn't the only one who was getting tired of hearing the same thing: "Hold tight, stand steady, take the long view."

The drop off in readership made me wonder if I should keep on putting out these messages. Maybe it was time for me to withdraw from feeling so responsible about all of this and instead turn my focus to *my own* learning. Was *I* contributing in the best way *I* could? Maybe I'd gone too far and had lost myself in the Grandmothers' work. Should I stop thinking about their work for a while and instead focus on whatever it was that was MY work? I mulled this over and decided that the next time I journeyed to them, I'd ask this question just for myself.

When I arrived before them, the Grandmothers surprised me by dancing in toward me wearing gauzy, multicolored skirts. Whirling and dipping together as they danced, they enfolded me in their circle and quickly I became one with this dizzying mass of color. Swirling and turning with them made me feel so happy. Happy, giddy…and, after a while, almost nauseated from all the whirling. "Grandmothers," I gasped as I stumbled, struggling to keep my balance. "I'm feeling a bit lost about my own purpose now. I'm sort of off balance in my life, and I'm also not sure your messages are having the right effect any more. Maybe I should be doing something else," I said. "Maybe something just for me."

They took a long look at me then and smoothed my hair back from my face, but I didn't want to be fussed over. I wanted the answer to my question. Now I was feeling hot and dizzy, and this question of mine had been bothering me for so long that it was all I could think about. And before I could even consider what I was doing, I dropped onto my knees before the Grandmothers, and gazing up at them, asked them to answer my question. They smiled at me and continued to dance around, but I was determined, so I stayed there, fastened to the ground, and the longer I crouched before them, the stronger my desire for their guidance became. At last I began to shake with frustration and finally, I burst into tears.

"Listen to us," they said then, **"listen, watch and learn."** And, turning away from me, they began to walk together, each of them carrying a lighted taper. **"We do this together,"** they called over their shoulders as they marched forward. **"*Everything* we do, we do together. We are *The Grandmothers*,"** they said, emphasizing their unity. **"We do NOT work alone,"** they declared, and when I heard this, I really cried. I understood what they were telling me.

"Share *everything* we give you," they said, and as they spoke, I noticed they were eyeing me fiercely. **"Share it all! Why would you hold anything back just for yourself?"** they asked. **"We, the Great Council, have come for all, and you are our mouthpiece. So *share it all!*

"The time for community, the time for communion, has come," they announced. **"Commune with one another; commune with nature; commune with us. Join together. The time of the lone operator is over,"** they said. **"So, open your hearts and share. Share!"** they repeated. **"Seek one another out. Stay in touch with each other. Touch and share all that touches you. More love, more togetherness, more, *more!*"** they spread their arms wide.

"Everyone today is starving," they said. **"People are starved for love, starved for community, starved for sharing. Create opportunities for sharing,"** they said. **"Come together in joy, in song—to share food and to serve. Come together.**

"**Human beings have been too much alone for too long,**" they said, "**and now the technology of the times is isolating you further. Don't allow this to happen,**" they declared. "**No! Seek community. Live in love and spread love wherever you go.**" Then they smiled and looked me over. "**Oh, how we love you,**" they smiled. "**Oh! How we love you.**"

Afterward, as I reflected on this journey, I understood what they were telling me. They were letting me know that I didn't have a separate life any more. That there was no more 'Sharon's work' and no more 'Net of Light work.' None of it was separate. Yes, there was life; yes, there was work; and yes, there was play, too. But all of it was one. I was to share it all. And... I was to let go of my concerns about how well or poorly whatever the Grandmothers gave me would be received. "**Just move forward,**" they said. And when they said this, I happened to think of my name—Sharon. "Share on," I said. "I get it. This is what I will do."

Shortly after this journey, I received this letter from a Net of Light Beacon living in the Netherlands near the border of Belgium and Germany. It confirmed what the Grandmothers were teaching me.

"I would like to tell you what happened to me, she said, "when I answered the call of the Grandmothers to do service to lift the energy for others and for myself.

"I asked the Grandmothers, 'What can I do to serve? Lead me in this,' and within no time a man named Mohammed came in my mind—a man from Afghanistan, living here in Holland in a very bad situation. (I will not bother you with his story.) I had not seen him for some time so I gave him a call and we met in town for a cup of coffee.

"It appeared that since I last saw him, his situation had grown even worse: he was now living on the street without any money so he was very happy to hear from me. That evening I thought, what if I ask him to paint my rooms? (Some time ago I asked the Grandmothers for a solution for how to get my rooms painted since I don't have the money to get it done and I cannot do it myself.) Now I thought, I can give him food and some money for it so maybe it will be good for both of us! So, I texted him with this question and he answered that he was very happy and able to do it.

"The next day I went on a cycling ride with a friend, and out of the blue she said to me: "I don't want to insult you, but I know you have little money and I have too much. Would you like to accept some money from me monthly or once a year for several years?" I was of course surprised by this and so happy, and I quickly assured her that I did not feel insulted at all! So, she decided to give me 500 Euros a year and I told her my story about Mohammed and that I now could give this money directly to him!!!

"I can hardly tell you how flabbergasted and happy and grateful I felt and still feel about how this came about. And all of this magic happened within two days!! For me there is no doubt that this is what the Grandmothers do when you answer their call."

Each time I receive a letter like this one, I feel so lucky. To be on the receiving end of such news, to have a small window into the miracles the Grandmothers and the Net of Light are creating everywhere, creating all the time. This letter was such a gift to me and couldn't have come at a better time. It buoyed me up and encouraged me to keep on sharing and keep on going. "Keep it simple," I said to myself. "Keep it simple and just keep on."

CHAPTER EIGHT
"You are part of this."

The Grandmothers stood together the next time I went to them, not saying anything but just looking at me. When I saw the way they were regarding me, I thought, "Are they studying me again?" But they just stood there, looking so patient that at last, I realized that they were waiting for *me* to speak. "Grandmothers," I said, "I'm sorry. I just woke up, and as soon as I opened my eyes this morning, the desire to help with the Mother's return to earth was the first thing I thought of. It was also the last thing I thought of before I fell asleep last night. That's why I came to you today

"You've told us so many times that you have come at this time to prepare the way for the return of the Mother. And I've noticed that sometimes you refer to yourselves as the Grandmothers, and then other times you call yourselves the Grand Mothers. I know this change in wording is somehow important, and I can't help but think it's a hint from you, to help us prepare ourselves for the Mother's return. "Am I right about that, Grandmothers?" I asked, but again they said nothing.

"We've waited a long, long time for the return of God the Mother," I went on, "and, if it's possible, we want to help you pave the way for Her to come back to earth. We need the Mother and since the moment for Her return appears to be more and more imminent, how can we help? How can we be a part of it?"

"**You *are* a part of it,**" the Grandmothers replied, and when I heard this, my spirits lifted. "Okay, Grandmothers, okay. Good," I nodded, eager now to learn more. "Then how can we do this?" I asked. "Please give us a job to do, Grandmothers. Let us help. We *love* to work."

They chuckled when I said this. Our eagerness to serve made them happy, and for a moment the Grandmothers and I just stood there, grinning at each other. We were in this work together. I relaxed as this thought came to me, and I was enjoying just being with them when I noticed that there was something moving around behind them. And whatever it was, it was distracting me.

I stretched my neck, squinted, and peered hard at whatever was back there. Then I realized what I was seeing was a large head, a female head. As all this started coming into focus, I knew that I was looking at a giant-sized woman, a woman of great beauty with thickly coiled braids framing her face. She was standing behind the Grandmothers, and she was Enormous! Stunning! Her hair was a red-gold color, and those brilliant braids wound round and round her head, forming a magnificent crown. "Oh!" I gasped as I gazed at her.

She looked like one of the women from the cover of the Grandmothers' second book—she was the living image on *Our Love is Our Power*. This is Meinrad Craighead's painting of Demeter and Persephone, mother and daughter of Greek mythology. Demeter, the mother, the one with the red-gold hair, is the goddess of nature whose daughter, Persephone, was kidnapped by the god Hades and taken down to the underworld. And now Mother Demeter was here with us, standing just behind the Grandmothers! A classic beauty in a softly flowing gown, She stood there, gazing serenely out at us. I say 'us,' because now it was no longer just me standing alone with the Grandmothers. I was surrounded by a large number of women and as I observed the women that standing here with me, I noticed that all of us had our eyes fixed on *this* woman. Demeter.

Graceful in Her movements, Demeter began now to walk in our direction. Her elegant arms reached out and encircled our group, and when She drew us in like this, we were flooded with a sense of intimacy with Her and with one another. Our hardened edges started melting off, and as I watched this taking place, I noticed old ideas and old feelings of separation, judgements and loneliness dropping off of all of us. One at a time these things surfaced and then floated off. And as Demeter continued to hold us close to Her heart, we began to soften even more. To expand and grow. Now we were warming and relaxing. No longer a group of individual women, we were fast becoming one being, one 'Us.' Demeter's embrace was bonding us as one.

As all this was taking place, I couldn't take my eyes off of the woman with the glorious hair, couldn't help but notice how natural She was. Perfectly relaxed. And there was something in Her manner, something in the way She reached out so easily and embraced us. A quality of grace and gracefulness.

"Huum.. m… m….," I mused as I continued to study Her. "Her dress is simple, a dusty gold color, the gold of a ripe wheat field. And though it's only muslin, somehow, this dress is elegant. Actually," I said, my voice rising in surprise, "it's not just the dress that's gold—*everything* about Her is glowing gold!" And as I continued to stare at Her, I noticed that *She Herself* shimmered with a warm-colored light.

Now I became aware of all the flowers that were surrounding Her. Flowers were everywhere! Vines, bushes and stalks of them in bloom, and as some of them floated down around us, they sent their perfume through the air. "Flowers are hanging all over the Goddess!" I cried as I watched them drape themselves around Her neck and weave themselves into Her hair. She was carrying even more of them in Her arms and now She began to strew them to the left and to the right of Her. And as She cast them on the ground, She let us know that we were to weave them all into a garland. There were leaves and shafts of wheat, clusters of berries and other grains lying among the flowers, and we were to weave them in too. "All the growing things of earth!" I marveled. "Fruits of the field."

Now we began to weave it together, linking the leaves, flowers, vines and grains and twining it into a chain. "This garland is getting really long," I remarked as we worked. Quickly it had reached massive proportions, expanded to a greater and greater size. Then, as I watched, suddenly, the garland lifted itself into the air, floated upward and draped itself around Demeter's shoulders. And then around our shoulders too.

We got very busy then, helping one another hang it on each other. "This is fabulous!" I cried, amazed as it kept on lengthening. "I wonder what this garland is for," I said. And as we continued to entwine one another, automatically we formed a line until soon we were standing in a long column, each of us connected by the swath of flowers, grains and leaves.

We began to dance then, weaving together in a rhythmic pattern and, as we danced, the garland lifted with our movements, then dipped, lifted again and dipped. We were flowing, moving as one body, and when this happened, I understood that what we were doing was performing a ceremony of some kind. "Oh!" I exclaimed, "this is a ceremony to honor Mother Earth!"

"And oh!" I cried again when I realized that maybe this is *who* we were dancing with! "The woman with the red gold braids! This *is* Mother Earth!" Now I realized that why, as soon as I had seen Her standing behind the Grandmothers, the image from the Grandmothers' book had come to mind. "I don't know why I'd never before thought of Demeter as Mother Earth," I said, "why I never recognized who She really was…" Until this moment, I hadn't made the connection, but now it was obvious that, of course, Demeter is Mother Earth.

"Ohhhh!" I exclaimed then as a different scene began to form in front of us. "I caught a glimpse of this one earlier," I said. "It's the animals!" And it all came back to me. I'd seen these animals when the woman in braids first appeared. "But then," I said, "I got only a hint of them, a flash of animals in my line of vision. But now they're *all* here." Herds of animals had arrived on the scene and now they filled the space before us. Bellowing, growling and lowing, they had come to be part of this ceremony with Mother Earth. I watched them as they milled about, waiting for Her.

As side-by-side cows and bulls came walking toward me, I stood back and observed them. Goats and dogs and horses joined in with them, and other beasts soon followed. Deer, lions, elephants, great cats. And, just like we humans, every animal here was also draped in flowers. "All these animals," I sighed, shaking my head in wonder as they began to move with us in the dance. "They're so incredibly lovely."

Then I recalled other times when I'd seen animals arrayed like this— covered in flowers, bells and vines. "This reminds me of the way they garland the elephants and cows for special ceremonies in India," I said, recalling Sai Baba's elephant, Gita. Festooned in ribbons and flowers, jingling with ornaments, her great trunk swung back and forth as she had come down the road. And with her, had come the village cows and bullocks, their faces painted and their horns also hung with flowers.

"Oh!" I cried, as my gaze moved over all the animals that had gathered around. "Here in this place, we're honoring Mother Earth. And we're honoring everything that's of the earth, including our own selves. Dancing with this garland is really a form of veneration. We're offering our love and gratitude to the earth and to all our brothers and sisters here on earth with us. To the people, the animals and plants, even to the tiny seeds that are woven into this garland. To everything," I said, and I let out a big sigh.

Then the voice of Mother Earth spoke. **"How much I do love you!"** She declared, Her voice so full of feeling that I could hear how happy She was to be able to love like this. And how happy She was to be loved in return. Happy to give and to be given to—I could see it in Her expression. She was utterly *full*.

"This, what we're doing here," I said to the Grandmothers and to myself, "with the flowers and the offerings…. We're making Her happy! We're making *Her* happy. And this is the right way to live," I sighed, nodding to myself. "It's a loving, giving way to live. It's not calculated; it's not even planned. We're not scrambling; we're not in a hurry; and we're not going into the usual mental gyrations we put ourselves through. We're simply loving," I said. "Here in this place, we've all come together just to give. We're here to give to the natural world. And *this* is something we *can* do!" I said with feeling. "This giving to the earth. This is something truly beautiful that all of us can do. And we can do it *right now*."

As soon as I said those words, what came to my mind was the Net of Light Gatherings that were coming up soon. "We can do this in Holland and we can do it again in Chicago," I said. "We can bring something of the earth to the altar. We can offer it in gratitude to Mother Earth and when we hold the Empowerment Ceremony, we can empower Her too. *We can give to Her!*"

I was thrilled with these ideas and was picturing one possibility after another. Songs, ceremonies, offerings. I giggled to myself and then I began to sing and hum as I thought of all the ways we could do this.

"This is something we *can* do, Grandmothers," I finally said. "I understand now. I understand how important it is for us to give back at this time on earth, to give back something to nature. And I want to thank you for showing me! Thank you! Thank you, Grandmothers, for giving us something so beautiful to do. I asked you how we could help, how we could be of service now," I said, "and you responded with *this*! Such a loving offering for us to make." I shook my head in wonder. "I'm so grateful," I said, and noticed that my voice was cracking with emotion.

"This is enough for now," the Grandmothers replied and Demeter nodded her head in agreement. "Yes," I said. I too agreed. This journey was over now. And they were right. This *was* enough.

"Women are the pillars and glue of society."

In the weeks following this journey, I became aware of a quiet happiness living inside me. Now I often woke in the mornings feeling the presence of the Mother inside and all around me. "She really is here," I marveled, really *with* me. No longer external to me, no longer just an idea or a concept. Now I felt Her inside my body. And lately I'd begun to see Her in others too. Clearly, She was beginning to awaken many of us to Her presence, and as I thought this over, I had a sense that this awakening was taking place in people all over the world.

My body, always my best teacher, felt softer to me now, bigger somehow, and wider—as well as calm and smooth. It wasn't that I was physically bigger, or flabby or gaining weight; I guess in some way I was spiritually bigger. One morning while lying in bed, I was observing what I was feeling and letting my attention wander wherever it would, when I noticed that I was continuing to widen out. The sense of expansion inside me was growing—I didn't know how else to describe it. It was like I'd become more connected to everything, more relaxed, more all-encompassing in my reach. Maybe the word I was searching for was *vast*. Yes, *vast* was it. That's what it felt like. I was vast...my understanding was vast. I must have fallen asleep after that because when I woke, I was singing an old hymn from my childhood. And the line I kept repeating was... *"Lord, help us build a heaven here on earth."*

A few days later, I journeyed back to the Grandmothers to ask if it was a good idea to communicate these expansive experiences I was having with others. I didn't know if sharing this stuff would be helpful or whether it might put people off, but as soon as I opened my mouth to ask them, so much emotion came up inside me, that I choked up before I could get the words out. **"Yes,"** the Grandmothers said, nodding as they gazed at me with understanding; they had read my mind.

"Share this, especially with women. Let them know how very present the Mother is! *She lives inside them*," they said, their eyes boring into mine. **"Now is the time for women to awaken to the presence of the Mother, time for them to awaken to their own magnificence.**

They *are* magnificent," they declared, "**because at all times they are closely linked with the Mother.**

"**Women are the pillars and glue of society. They are good,**" they said, "**good at their core.** *You* **are good,**" they pointed to me. "**Take in and own what we're telling you,**" they said, "**and bless yourself. Then go forward wearing that blessing. You are good; you are true; and you are what the world needs.**" And as they spoke, they held my eyes with theirs. "**Be yourself,**" they said then. "**Our arms are around you so you cannot fall.**" I gulped when they said this and nodded to them. Their words were powerful, reassuring. They felt true, and I could feel these words coming to rest deep inside me.

"**Each of you has special strengths, talents and gifts,**" they explained as they looked deep into my eyes. "**And you must never allow these to be diminished by others. Remember that you answer to no one but the Divine, and it is the Divine that made you as you are. Criticism has no place in you. Each of you is a particular manifestation of God,**" they said, watching to be sure I understood what they were getting at. "**Because you** *are* **at one with God, you ooze goodness and love. So, you needn't try so hard to BE good,**" they said. "**Just** *be yourself and let this Self shine forth.* **Each of you is a jewel in the Net of Light, a jewel set in its perfect place and time so that it can reflect the glory of the All.**

"**Shine forth!**" the Grandmothers cried, and as they spread their arms wide, they threw back their heads and laughed out loud. "**Walk forward,**" they commanded me. "**Be who you were born to be. And remember,**" they laughed, "**you are good to the core.**"

After this journey was over, I couldn't stop crying. Their words had stunned me, thrilled me and pushed me past all my self-imposed limitations. And now that this journey was over, I was overcome with awe for what they'd shared with me, so awed that when I got up to blow my nose, I was weak in the knees.

I didn't return to the Grandmothers for several weeks after that session. What they'd said on these last two journeys was so potent that I needed time to integrate it. It was a lot for me to take in. After all, I'd been raised as a good little Presbyterian girl in the conservative Midwest, so, taking to heart what the Grandmothers had just told me might take some time. Granted, I'd been on this unconventional spiritual path for a long time now, but still, learning that God the Mother existed was one thing. Learning that She dwelled *inside me* was a real stretcher, to say the least.

I decided to let all of this settle in for a while, to let it cook on the back burner, so-to-speak while I got on with the business at hand. Our next Net of Light Gathering would be in Holland, and it was coming up the following month. This would be the focus of my next visit to the Grandmothers.

A Man's Perspective

"**This Gathering in the Netherlands will anchor the family, the family in Europe, and integrate it with the family in North America and Australia,**" the Grandmothers said when I asked the purpose of this Dutch Gathering. "**Much community building,**" they added, "**much weaving of the Net of Light. All the group leaders will be with you at this Gathering. Some will come in person, and the rest will connect with you inwardly. Start calling on them now,**" they said, "**and ask them to consciously think of the work you will be doing together in Europe with the Ancestors of the Land as well as with the Great Mother. Invite them to fold in with you,**" they said. "I will, Grandmothers," I promised.

"**At this Gathering, *song-weaving will be strong weaving,*** " they said. "**Music will carry you further than you have yet been able to go; it will strengthen the Net of Light and magnify goodness and power throughout the world. You will have the Native American singer with you this time, the two musicians from Holland, and the singer-songwriters from England. So, sing!**" they cried, "**and when in doubt about what to do, sing some more. Music will carry our work forward.**

"**Sound the Om,**" they said. "**The vibration of the Om will sustain you throughout the Gathering. It will amplify all the good you will do together. Sound the Om on Friday evening,**" they said, "**and do it again on Saturday morning. Do this to raise the vibration of the Gathering and give you a higher platform from which to start.**"

"Yes, Grandmothers," I said. "We will."

"**Establish a lighted field of energy with the spirits of nature in** the forest surrounding this venue in Holland," they said, and I sat up straight, fully attentive. "**There are many nature spirits there in the trees,**" they said, "**so go out into the forest on Friday afternoon and communicate with them and with the individual trees there, too. Ask the spirits of nature to anchor light for the work to be done at this Gathering. Their contribution will make a big difference.**"

"Yes, Grandmothers," I said, "we will do this."

"**You will have an especially willing and spiritually mature group to work with this time,**" the Grandmothers said, "**so together you will be able to do great good.**" And looking me over, they said, "**Call all the Beacons into this work now! Let the family of light support it.**"

"Yes, Grandmothers," I said, "I'm on it!"

Nearly two hundred people came to the Dutch Gathering, and ten of them were men. Things flowed pretty much the way the Grandmothers had said they would, and the music did indeed carry the heartbeat of this Gathering. We joined with one another and opened to the presence of the Cosmic Mother. Women and men blended beautifully and worked in harmony together, and after I got home, I received this letter from a man who had joined us there with his wife. He wrote:

> I want to share something about the Gathering in the Netherlands last weekend. First of all, I and my wife decided to start a new Net of Light group again. We did that years ago but somehow it faded out, but now I strongly feel the call again and I'm very happy that she wants to join in because without her, I can't do it. And that has to do with the experience I had yesterday—the position of men in this work.
>
> This morning we sat on the couch and did the Stone Circle meditation in the Grandmothers' second book, and I asked about the place of men in the Grandmothers' work. They showed me the following. I saw myself, both at the Gathering and again today, as an eagle, and the Grandmothers invited me to take my place in between them. (I still do not know what that means.) Then, there was a spiral movement of many eagles, whirling and whirling till nothing was left, just a blank sky. And then all kinds of men appeared—all of them in full armour. Wars and battles throughout history: in Europe, in Roman times, Native American Indians, etc. I felt the pain of those battles then and it seemed that the men were still stuck in this pain.

After this scene, all the men came into the Circle of Stones with me and together, we were embraced by the Grandmothers. And as the Grandmothers held us, slowly our armour started to melt until we were at last freed from the burden of battle. It was clear that we no longer wanted that burden. Now we men could be ourselves again and, in the end, we formed one circle of men and women with the Grandmothers.

This is what I also experienced at the Gathering last weekend: it was a warm, cosmic, yin bath given by the women. It was a joy to be in it and I felt the melting in me start from the very beginning of the weekend and then go on and on. In that melting and softening process, I felt a new manhood arise in me—as I also felt at the 2011 Gathering. I felt myself lining up—firm, steady, fearless, and gentle—with an open heart.

As the Grandmothers showed me, we men need the women to help us melt so our true male nature can arise again. In 2011 my role as a man was not perfectly clear to me yet, but now it is: we simply have to surrender to the feminine (yin) energy. That might be frightening for some men but the gift we get back is enormous. We get back our true masculine energy as it is meant to be. Without women we stay stuck in the old pattern of yang energy that is always pushing forward on its own. I experienced this weekend that as soon as I was in contact with that true male nature—which stands on its own in that 'yin bath,' I did not feel less or more than the women, but felt together with them. Each of us was playing our role as we were meant to, each of us serving the whole.

Thank you, women, thank you, Grandmothers, for this great gift. And special thanks to my wife for starting a group with me again so we can do something for men and women in this world.

"Here beats the heart of your country."

A month after the Gathering in Holland, there was another one in the rolling farmlands of Pennsylvania, just across the Ohio border. We met at a convent that had been built many years earlier, far out in the countryside where the nuns still grow their own food. Barns, fields, farm animals and lots of trees, glorious trees. People had traveled to this place from all corners of America and a few had even come in from Europe. The atmosphere at Villa Maria was a comforting one and the sisters there welcomed us to their home with open hearts.

It was good to be back in the Midwest again, near the place where I had grown up, good to be in touch once again with my own roots. And, after the Gathering was over and just before we were to leave the peace of the convent, I lay down on my bed to rest a little. I was lying there, enjoying the quiet and reflecting on the kindness of the people at this Gathering when suddenly the Grandmothers spoke.

"**Here, in the center of your country, in the midst of woods and farmlands runs a river of connection,**" they said. "**Here the bonds of humanity converge, cross, bless and enrich one another. Here is yet another place of coming together.**

"**This part of the world is sometimes overlooked,**" they said. "**It's seldom in the news. It's not on the front pages of fashion and enter- tainment, so it often slips your mind. However, this part of the world is steady and stable. Here beats the heart of your country. An even, strong beat, not one fractured by the momentary events of the day. Steady yourself here,**" they said, and I breathed a deep sigh, nod- ding in agreement. "**Anchor yourself here and rest,**" they said. "**Let the land of your birth support you now. It *loves* you; it holds out it arms to you; and it waits to enfold you. Come home,**" they said, and I felt myself giving over and relaxing.

"**Here you were born,**" the Grandmothers said, smiling sweetly. "**The land remembers you and has waited for your return. Always when one returns to the land of their birth, there is the potential for great good to occur. Here in this place you belong and will always belong,**" they murmured, patting me gently. "**So, rest easy. You are home.**

"**You have *many* homes,**" they said, and I looked at them in sur- prise. "**We are speaking to you now,**" they nodded, "**but we are also speaking to everyone. The world loves you,**" they continued. "**What we mean is—the REAL world loves you. The world of fad and fash- ion loves no one. But what abides forever, what is deep and always founded in truth, *loves* you. You too are deep,**" the Grandmothers said. "**You are part of the foundation of all that lives. Ergo, you are at home in the earth, you are at home *on* the earth.**

"**When you travel, wherever you go, you feel the great love of the earth. You don't feel it so much in the cities, but amongst the trees, looking out over the fields and canyons, you know that you are home. Know it now,**" they said, looking at me to be sure I was following them. "**Home. You are home. The earth holds few places that will feel foreign to you,**" they said. "**And those places will be man-made, not made by nature.**

"**Be happy in your home,**" the Grandmothers said. "**Be happy here on earth. And,**" they smiled brightly, "**we thank you for returning to the land of your birth. This journey brings with it a great healing— for you and for the earth Herself.**"

I sobbed softly when I heard this and then lay quietly in my room for a while and let myself feel all that I was feeling. "Yes, I'm crying," I said to myself, "but these are tears of happiness."

"Whenever a great movement is called for, so is a great steadiness."

The next time I went to the Grandmothers, before I could say a word to them, they fastened their eyes on mine and spoke. "**Listen to us,**" they said, and I gulped, "Yes, Grandmothers," wondering what's coming now?

"**Today we begin to fill you with light,**" they said. "**More light than you have ever known. And little by little, we will increase your capacity to receive, hold, and give light and love to others. You are growing in power now,**" they said, looking me over and nodding their approval, "**and, if you wish, you will continue to grow.**

"**This is happening because you are needed to hold light steady. Soon,**" they promised, "**there will be no more stuck, static energy left on earth. No more of the battles and struggles that have gone on for far too long, no more cycles of fear and hatred. We have come to infuse the energy of yin back into your planet, to return it to balance with the energy of yang. And you,**" they said, speaking to all of us, "**are the vessels for our work. You are our hands, eyes, and hearts on earth, our partners in light.**

"**For a long time now, the world has been stuck in a state of non-expansion, of endless repetition. Although you see activity around you and a great deal of to-ing and fro-ing, for many years on earth there has been no real movement forward. But now it will be different,**" they announced. "**Everything will begin to change. *Everything*,**" they repeated. "**And whenever a great movement is called for, so is a great steadiness. *Those we have called to this work will hold and store*** *this steadiness for this planet.* **You,**" they said, pointing to all of us involved with the Net of Light, "**have been called.**

"**Begin now,**" the Grandmothers said, "**to prepare yourself to receive, to receive,**" they emphasized, "**more than you have ever imagined. Hold still while we pour light and love into you. Say** *'yes'* **to expansion,** *'yes'* **to reception,** *'yes'* **to us,**" and under my breath, quietly I murmured, "*Yes.*"

"**Receiving more and more love will give you abiding joy,**" they said. "**Your heart will swell to the point where it will automatically reach out to everyone you meet. And while this love will give you great joy, it will give others rest. Your presence will create a holding tank for peace on earth,**" they said, and when I heard this, my eyes spilled over with tears. "**You will become an ever-greater holding tank of peace and love for this planet. Therefore, we urge you to say** *'yes'* **to the down-pouring of light and love that's going to quickly inundate your world.**

"**From now on, more and more goodness will be given to you, given according to your capacity to receive it. You were born for this,**" they assured me, "**and to prepare yourself for this influx of light and to avoid being overcome by sudden downpours of love, read our books and messages. Come together with those of like hearts to discuss our teachings. These activities will help you ease into the increase of power that's coming and to be able to do it in a gradual way. We are calling you to this work,**" the Grandmothers said. "**The need for steady, steadying anchors of light on earth is great, and you were born for exactly this. We ask you to step forward now and say** *'yes,'* they said. "**We are waiting for you.**"

Then they stood back and studied me. "**We want you to expand the power of your reach,**" they said, "**to be more inclusive when you work with us, to feel how supported you are, not only by us, but by** *all of life.* **Everything on earth is here for you,**" they said, giving me a meaningful look, "**and it's time for you to also be here for everything.**

"**Each time you cast the Net of Light, cast to** *all life,* **everywhere,**" the Grandmothers said. "**No one and nothing should be left out of this. Include the waters of the planet, the land masses, the air and the atmosphere of the earth, as well as all the moving and growing things upon it. Include the spirits of nature each time you work,**" they said.

"Through their roots, the trees on earth have the potential to be deeply connected," they said. "Trees are born communicators. You can learn a lot from them. It's time to honor their skill in communication, time to ask the trees to help strengthen the Net of Light. Ask them to amplify the reach and depth of the Net throughout the earth by moving with it through their great root networks. Trees are gracious and giving, so they will gladly comply. They are ever-giving," the Grandmothers said, and I noticed that they looked thoughtful as they said this. "You would do well to emulate the trees," they said at last. "Trees continuously reach out, succor, feed and heal one another. Ask them to teach you how you too can start to connect like this." "Oh! Grandmothers," I said, surprised by what they were telling me. "We will!"

There was a long pause after that, and I wondered if perhaps this journey was over, but the Grandmothers had something else to say. "The world weighs heavily on you," they said, and, "Yes, Grandmothers," I admitted, "it does." I was often upset and overwhelmed by the ugliness now showing up on earth. Looking me over as this came to my mind, the Grandmothers said, "We see how you suffer as the miseries and hidden evils of life rise up to the surface on earth. Cruelty is rife now," they said, nodding their heads in unison. "Anger is flaming up everywhere, and fear is lurking in the shadows of the night. The world today is not," they shook their heads, "a pretty picture. We understand how you feel.

"But there is more to it than this. Much more," they said, and they drew themselves to their full height. They shared secret smiles with one another then and said, "Underneath the sneaking deeds of those who would *run* the world and *ruin* the world, lies the Fabric of Being of the Universe. This Fabric has been woven with great power," they said. "It upholds life everywhere and is able to withstand tremendous force and wear. This fabric provides the ground of all being. Without the foundation of the fabric of light that supports the world, mankind and all life on earth would be destroyed. You would fall into the darkness of the abyss. However," they said, and I noticed that they'd folded their arms tightly across their breasts so that as they stood together, they formed a powerful blockade. "We assure you that this will *not* happen.

"No matter how loudly the voices of the foul ones may bray," they said, shaking their heads in disgust, "no matter how wildly they may swing their arms, they cannot destroy the foundation of life on earth. They will continue to try," they said, shrugging their shoulders as if to say, 'Well, what do you expect?' "but they will never succeed.

"Beneath the horrors that are showing up on the surface of the earth today lies the radiant Net of Light. Brilliant and growing stronger by the day," they said as they threw their heads back. "THIS is the Fabric of Being of the Universe. Formed of light and made of love, the Net of Light connects all living things. It is the largest construct in the universe, and *this fabric is empowered each time you think of it. Empowered each time you link your heart with it.*

"Call on it now," the Grandmothers commanded. "Affirm and magnify the power of the Net of Light. We have told you, 'This is the Net of Light that will hold the Earth during the times of change that are upon you,' and we assure you that this time is *now. The changes are here.* So do not wait another day," they said. "Call on the Net of Light. Always."

"Yes, Grandmothers, yes," I assured them, and I bowed and took my leave. I was deeply moved by what they'd said, so moved that I made the journey back to ordinary reality like a sleep-walker. I don't even remember how I got there, but when at last I gratefully climbed the stairs to my room, I went straight to bed. "Rest and integration," I said to myself. "That's what I need now. Rest and integration." And that's what I did. I rested and waited for everything inside me to come into balance again.

Earth Speaks

A couple of weeks after that encounter, one morning while sitting underneath the avocado tree, observing how the blooms on the trumpet vine were climbing it, I realized that I was waiting for something. I was admiring the brilliant orange of the trumpet flowers and listening to the birds, but at the same time I was aware of a sense of anticipation. It was a crystal-clear morning in early summer and there was nothing unusual about that. "So what?" I wondered, "am I waiting for?"

Finally, I realized what it was. I was waiting to hear the voice of the land. Somehow, I knew that today the earth was going to speak to me. I don't know how I knew it, but I did, and I'd even brought my laptop with me, ready to write down whatever Mother Earth might say.

"What?" I asked myself, "makes me think that this is really going to happen?" But before I could mull it further in my mind, I heard myself say, "That which dwells within and underneath everything I see here has something to say to me."

My pronouncement startled me. My language! I sounded a bit like a prophet, even to myself! But after that, I sat myself down in the shade of the avocado tree with my computer on my lap and simply waited.

I wasn't sitting there long before I heard what sounded like laughter. And when I looked around to find the source of it, through the lavender bushes growing underneath the tree, I glimpsed a pair of happy faces. Rosie faces with smiling eyes, faces of small people wearing jaunty hats and colorful clothes. Childlike spirits were at play under the avocado tree! Running around underneath the branches and exploring the garden. These little ones reminded me of pictures in story books of leprechauns or gnomes. But whoever these small people were, they seemed to be coming up from the earth itself. And as I watched them running about, I immediately saw how *full* of joy they were. And, as I continued to watch them, quite suddenly, so was I!

I wasn't especially surprised by them appearing in the garden like this, although I don't think I'd ever before glimpsed nature spirits. But I was surprised to notice that as soon as I saw them, I was as happy as they were. The joy inside me was instantaneous. It was thrilling to come upon them like this, and when I laughed in happy surprise, they dodged forward, hugged me and then skittered off again. Back and forth they dashed like this, daring me to play with them. And so, I did! Soon we were all chasing one another around the tree, dodging, hiding, laughing and grabbing at each other in a tagging game. We were children at play!

These happy souls were so full of fun, joy and freedom that the old woman I had thought I was quickly disappeared, and now I too was a kid. It was a colorful world I found myself in now, this world of play. There was no gray, no black or white here—only sparkling color. Now the sunny radiance of the day broke through to everything. "Ah…h…," I breathed out in joy, and "Ah.. h.. h.. h," I breathed in again. "I'm so happy to be here," I shook my head in wonder, "simply to be here. Being here is enough for me!" I declared. "All I could ask for."

"Draw on us," the nature spirits responded. **"Draw on our energy, draw us in,"** they explained and when they said this, I noticed that my breathing had slowed down. Now I was breathing in synch with them. I *was* breathing them in!

"We are here for you," they said. **"We are here to be *with* you— always. You are surprised to see us, but we assure you that we are as real as that dark, sober world *you* think is the real one,"** they laughed. **"We are real too!"** they declared, **"so you can live your days in black and white or you can join with us in living color."**

Their words made me laugh out loud, and I realized how much fun it was to play like this. Way more fun than thinking all the time, thinking and worrying. Way more fun than being *so* serious. "I never liked those old black-and-white films of the 50's anyway," I said to myself, "so why am I living my life in a Noir world? I've always preferred the colors in Cinderella and Snow White, in all the musicals and fun stories, not the black-and-white of the grim 'Who Done Its.' And lately," I said to myself, "I've been living twenty-four hours a day in a gray, black-and-white world. Somber, dark, and harrowing." And, as I thought this over, for some reason, now it made me laugh. "Ridiculous!" I declared, "simply ridiculous."

I sat quietly after that realization hit, reflecting on it all over again, and when I looked up, my little friends had gone. But there I was. I was still in the garden, still under the avocado tree. I chuckled to myself as I sat there, and then I laughed out loud and shook my head in amazement at this crazy, wonderful play of life. "What an experience! What a marvel," I said. "I think I'll start spending more time in the garden. I need this joy."

And no sooner did I say "I need this joy" than I felt a movement. It was rising upward from the earth under my feet. A back and forth weaving motion was stirring down there, and soon I felt a rocking rhythm rising up toward me. A connection was being activated, and it was coming from inside the earth. A force, a fabric of sorts, something alive was waking up down there. And by my response to it, I could tell that this force was both tender and potent. And as it began to rise upward toward me, tremors of aliveness fluttered, skittered and ran through my body. I was responding to it.

"This that I'm feeling now is the Fabric of Being of the Universe!" I gasped. "It's coming fully alive within the earth now. That's what I'm sensing!" I cried, my voice full of conviction.

And when I looked down at the ground underneath me, I saw the many layers of earth stacked one upon another under my feet. The first thing I noticed was how different the Net of Light or Fabric of Being looked in these various regions of the earth. In some layers of earth, the Net of Light glowed brightly while in others, it was hard to make out.

I wondered about this for a moment but now I began to rise upward. Soon I had a birds-eye view of our planet and now I could see that in some places, the connection of this fabric of light to the earth appeared to be tenuous. This was the case in the Middle East and also in a few of the crowded urban areas of the planet. I'd seen the seeming fragility of the Net of Light in the Middle East before but I'd never before witnessed the tears in the Net of Light in urban areas on earth.

As I became aware of how fragile this fabric of light linking all aspects of the earth together was sometime, I also glimpsed something that looked like connective tissue. And as I watched, this tissue began to build up inside the body of the earth. The build-up was especially apparent in the areas that encircled the Middle East, and as I watched, a mass of connective, connecting tissue rose up out of the sands of the Sahara. Here it formed a fibrous structure, and the fibers began to reach out in all directions.

I peered at it in fascination, and now I saw new tendrils springing forth, sprouting and connecting with one another like an ever-strengthening network of vines. The tendrils were solidifying the Fabric of Being, helping it to anchor deep, and as I watched, tendrils of light penetrated the crust of the earth right down to its core. The Net of Light or Fabric of Being of the Universe was alive! And it was growing! Anchoring itself everywhere.

Whatever these tendrils touched, they drew together, and now these fibers were linking all parts of the earth together. This was happening all over the world, and I could see that now there were no more separate *parts* of earth, but only *one whole earth*. One earth body, upheld, strengthened and linked throughout by the radiant Net of Light. The earth was an indivisible Being, one being, woven into a body of light. The Fabric of Being that penetrated and held the earth was now vibrating with a palpable rhythm, and as I stared at it, transfixed, I said, "What I'm seeing here is the Rhythm of Life. This pulsing, rhythm of life runs throughout all of Mother Earth. With no exceptions! It's humming and singing in Her fibers."

I continued to stare at this scene as excitement built up inside me.

And then, from deep within the earth, the Great Mother Herself began to stretch. I saw Her! And watched, not breathing, as She lifted Her head, raised an arm, and flexed Her muscles. "It looks like She's preparing to rise up," I whispered to myself, and then I heard a voice intone, **"And rise She will! And soon."**

"Oh!" I gulped, "Oh! And when She does," I whispered to myself, "She will shake the earth. She will shake each one of us," and I shivered, as I tried to release some of the energy inside me. Chills were running all over my body now, so I took in some deep breaths in an effort to calm myself. But I couldn't stop the shaking and I finally had to give up the effort. "If this is how it's going to be," I said, my voice as well as my body quivering, "well, then, this is how it's going to be. I'll just shake like this. This stuff, whatever's happening to me, is way beyond *my* understanding anyway. So, I give up," I said at last, and then I closed my eyes. I didn't want to see any more.

It was quiet for a few minutes after that, and when I opened my eyes again, I was still sitting in the garden, still underneath the avocado tree. And my laptop was still balanced on my knees. "Oh -h-h-h!" I breathed out slowly. And I didn't say any more after that. I was stunned and didn't have anything else *to* say. But after a while I heard myself speaking. "I guess I'll just stay here in the garden," I said, "rest here in the garden. I mean, I'll rest here in *Her* garden. This is *Her* garden," I corrected myself. I was tired now, feeling groggy. I wasn't myself yet. I was too astonished, too gobsmacked by what had taken place here under the avocado tree.

A few minutes after this, I looked up and saw that before me was standing Mother Earth and the Grandmothers. They were standing there quietly, just looking at me. "Thank you, Mother," I said to Her, bowing in reverence, and She smiled at me as if all of this was the most normal thing in the world. "Thank you, Grandmothers," I then spoke to all of them together. And after that, I bowed and stumbling, I took my leave of them. Then I started my journey back to 'ordinary' reality.

"So much energy moving now," I murmured to myself as I trudged along, slowly walking back into the house. "Energy is moving in the earth, it's moving in me, moving everywhere," I said to myself." And all this movement is taking place simultaneously. It's too much, really," I said, "too much for me to take in. I really can't handle any more than this," I said to myself as I climbed the stairs.

"Oh, well," I murmured as I stretched out on the bed., "I'll just give it all over to the Grandmothers. They know what's happening, even if I don't and anyway," I sighed, "all I can do is just keep on breathing and keep on going. They'll guide me wherever I need to go. Everything will eventually shake down the way it will," I said. "The Grandmothers will have to lead. I certainly can't."

"Weave and connect. Weave and connect."

This journey had been another of the Big Ones, one of the earth-shaking lessons, so when it was over, I took a three-week rest from all Grandmother-related work to recoup. I busied myself with the ordinary things of life and spent a lot of time out in the garden with the dog. But it wasn't long before the familiar urge to learn more from my teachers began to build in me, urging me to return to them. So, after a short hiatus, I journeyed back.

When I went to the Grandmothers, they took one look at me and without batting an eye said, **"The Net of Light is a structure, a structure that you are building."** I noticed that they were taking care to pronounce each word deliberately, and I stared at them, wondering *Why are they being so careful with their words?* **"You are building and strengthening the Net of Light each time you use it,"** they explained; **"you're doing this for yourself and for everything that lives. This is important,"** they said.

"The Net of Light provides a framework, a skeletal structure, for the entire body of life on earth, and as you work with it, this structure is getting thicker, stronger and more closely woven." "Yes, Grandmothers," I replied. "The last time I came to you, you showed me how this strengthening was taking place in the Middle East and all over the earth."

"Without the structure that the Net of Light provides," they continued, **"human beings would flail about in space and float aimlessly. You would be constantly seeking for the ground under your feet."**

And to illustrate, as they spoke, behind them I glimpsed a crowd of people doing just that—bobbing through the air, grasping and reaching out to one another, even grabbing at the air itself as they tried to latch on to something. And as I continued to observe, I became aware of how many more men than women were floating along like this, trying desperately to grab hold of something—anything.

The Grandmothers caught my eye and laughed. "**By nature,**" they explained, "**men are not as spiritually grounded as are women, so, men need your help in linking themselves to the Net of Light.**

"**Because of their intrinsic connection to the Net of Light,**" they continued, "**women are more anchored to earth as well as to one another. However,**" they said, "*linking with the Net of Light quickly changes everything,* **so as soon as a man connects with the Net of Light, he also becomes anchored. Immediately, he too is held safe and secure within it.**

"**Many times,**" the Grandmothers said, "**we have told you that woman must lead the way. Woman must lead in drawing humanity together into the Net of Light. And woman must do this because she** *can* **do it,**" they emphasized. "**She can do it because she is** *already* **connected to the Fabric of Life. Each time a woman is born, she is born at one with the Mother. The human female is always at one with the Mother, and** *it is the Mother,*" they explained, "*who generates the Fabric of Being.* **Women are naturally at one with Her,**" they said, watching me to see if I understood what they were saying. "**You came in this way! You came in at one with the Net of Light.**

"**Just like Grandmother Spider of the Native American teachings,**" they laughed, "**you too spin the threads of the Fabric of Being—into** *being,*" they emphasized. Then they smiled broadly and said, "*We...,*" *gesturing* with their arms to include all of us within this 'we,' "**We are** *She.*

"**This Net of loving support that we call the Net of Light or the Fabric of Being will link all life together,**" they said. "**The Net of Light calls humanity back to family, brings it back to oneness. This work you are doing with the Net of Light was ordained to take place** *now,*" they said, "**so weave, women, weave! Embrace and connect with one another, and while you are at it, remember that We, the Great Council of the Grandmothers, are holding you steady. We will supply you with everything you need in order to perform this task.**

"**Work on!**" they cried. "**Weave and connect. Weave and connect!**"

CHAPTER NINE

"Now is the time to fulfill women's mission on earth."

From years of work with the Grandmothers, I learned to vary my monk-like spiritual existence with some social life. Dip an oar into the waters of the so-called 'real' world every now and then to keep myself from getting too isolated. Mix some 'normal' life in with the intensity of the Grandmothers' message to help keep me grounded. So, Roger and I would join with pals for dinner and a movie, or I'd have lunch with a friend, go to a book group meeting, or show up at the garden club. I also dabbled in painting, pottery and sculpture in between working on the Grandmothers' books and seeing clients. Because I spent so much time alone, it was good for me to get out into the world.

I was having dinner one night with a group of women friends when we started talking about what we, as women, were experiencing in our day-to-day lives. Most of the women in this group were high achievers who'd 'made it' in a man's world. They were pretty proud of their success, but on this evening, they spoke of how shocked they were by the direction society seemed to be taking now when it came to the treatment of women.

"It feels like we're dropping back into the 1950s," one of them said. "What I mean is, I never thought I'd see a repeat of this sort of behavior toward women." Another said, "I thought that since the '60s, society had become more enlightened, but it doesn't feel that way today. I didn't like the '50s the first time around, and I'm not liking it any better now." This started a discussion about sexism and the way it was showing up in today's world.

These were smart women who had a lot to say, and though I enjoyed being with them, I'd been around them long enough to know they saw themselves as tough-minded intellectuals—i.e., not the sort of women who would be interested in the Grandmothers' explanation of the times we were living in. Consequently, instead of offering any hard-won spiritual information from the Grandmothers, I just listened and observed as they talked. But as the evening wore on, I determined that the next time I journeyed to the Grandmothers I would lay this subject before *them*.

"Grandmothers," I said when next I stood in their circle, "so many countries today, including our own, are run by men who treat women as 'less than.' In fact, they treat women so badly that today, instead of the status of women rising, it appears to be sinking downward." I then asked these wise teachers, "What are we as women supposed to do at a time like this? We want to be ourselves and we also want to help uplift our planet," I explained. "But feminine values are being thwarted now. Today women are threatened by bullying men, and many women are being harmed by them." As I continued to explain the situation, the Grandmothers patiently regarded me and when I finally realized that they didn't need my explanation because of course they already knew it, I stopped talking. It was then that I became aware of just how important this issue was to me—when I felt how heavily it had been weighing on my heart.

I paused a moment when I felt the pain of it lying like a boulder in the center of my chest. The Grandmothers gazed at me then with compassion in their eyes and said, **"In your many lifetimes you have played the roles of both male and female. But now,"** they added, **"you must learn how to *truly* live as a woman. This is not a time to act like a man,"** they said, and I gasped.

"Grandmothers," I cried, horrified. "Am I acting like a man?" I was so surprised by what they'd said that I was afraid of what their response might be. **"No,"** they said, shaking their heads emphatically and waving their hands in dismissal. **"What we mean when we say, 'It's not time to act like a man,' is that, as a woman, you have special gifts and strengths that men *do not have*. It's time now for you to live from *these* strengths and trust in *these* gifts. It's not a time to imitate men as so many women have done,"** they said, **"but to be your own powerful self.**

"**Come close to us,**" they said, and beckoning me forward, they made room in their midst. Then wrapping their arms around me, they looked me in the eyes and said, "**You don't yet know the power of yin.**"

"I don't yet know the power of yin?" I parroted back, shocked that they would say this. Why *would* they say this? "After being with you for more than twenty years?" I asked. "Grandmothers, I *still* don't know the power of yin? *Still*?" I repeated, incredulous.

"**That's right,**" they said, "**you *still* don't understand yin,**" and when I heard this, I swallowed hard. "Wow!" I whispered, staring at them in disbelief.

"**You are *still* struggling to understand the power of yin,**" they said, and patted me on the back to reassure me and calm me down. "**It's hard for you to grasp the power of yin because of the way you've been conditioned,**" they explained, "**conditioned to believe that you are the 'weaker' sex, not powerful enough, not mentally acute enough, et cetera, et cetera,**" they said, a disgusted expression on their faces. "**You've been so deeply conditioned by these old beliefs that you've only *just* begun to scratch the surface of that conditioning.**"

"**We will help you grow in understanding,**" the Grandmothers said as they eyed me with compassion, "**but you must realize that you can move forward only from where you are now, not from where you wish you already were.**"

Bewildered by all of this, I stared back at them, but when they remained silent and continued to thoughtfully regard me, I had to think again about their words. Maybe they *were r*ight. Maybe in spite of all my years with them, I was still green as grass when it came to understanding the feminine principle. I sighed deeply as this thought surfaced, and they sighed, too, and smiled at me, gentle smiles.

"**You hear the way men speak about women,**" they said, "**the day-to-day sexism in your culture, the degrading jokes, the dismissive political speeches. The world is thick with the devaluation of women—full of those who infer in subtle ways that women are 'less than' as well as the flat-out sexists who come right out with it. Most men don't have any idea that they're sexist. They would be shocked to hear themselves described that way, but sexism is ingrained in every society on earth. *And...,*"** they said, drawing the word out to make sure I was paying attention, "***it is deeply resistant to change.* You** react to sexism in anger," they said, "which does no good, because the resistance to recognizing and confronting it is dug into your culture. Locked down deep," they gestured with clenched fists. "You will break your hearts over it if you struggle to shift this resistance.

"Let us explain more," they said. "There is another way to approach this issue, and we will help you. First, because men do *not* understand the power of yin, they do not understand what a woman is. And," they said, "because their absence of understanding makes it impossible for men to help you reclaim feminine power, you must perform this task alone. YOU must reclaim this power.

"However," the Grandmothers said, holding a finger up in front of me to get my attention, "as you approach this task, you come to it with a built-in advantage. You," they pointed to me with big smiles on their faces, "have already experienced the power of yin. You know what yin feels like because you carry it in your body, and so you know what this power can do. So, what you must do at this time is *stand firm in what you know*. Stand firm in what you know deep down in your core. No matter what!" they said, and they pounded one hand into the other for emphasis.

"Do not go to war with men over this," they said, shaking their heads, and waving their hands to dismiss the thought. "Don't waste your time on that. In fact," they said, giving me a thoughtful look, "leave men alone. Let men dwell on the outside of this issue of feminine power. At this time, that's all they *can* do.

"Instead of focusing so much on men," the Grandmothers said, "reach out to your sisters, to your mothers, daughters and friends. *Now is the time to fulfill women's mission on earth.* You, as women, are needed to uphold one another and uphold Mother Earth. We, the Great Council of the Grandmothers," they said, drawing themselves to their full height, "have come to call women and men to selfless work. All people are welcome to our work, but we primarily count on women because we know women will respond.

"Women are the ones who naturally serve society. Generosity and compassion are basic to a woman's character. After all," they pointed out, "who rears the young, nurses the sick and sits with the dying? Only a rare man does any of these things. Women," they called, "we have much to teach you. Are you ready to learn?"

I looked hard at them. I'd thought I'd already learned the lessons of yin, but it was clear that I hadn't yet mastered them. "Yes, Grandmothers," I said, pointing to myself, "this woman is ready to learn."

Holy Mother

The question the Grandmothers posed at the end of this journey kept reverberating in my mind. **"Women, are you ready to learn?"** they'd asked, and my answer was an emphatic *'yes!'* And as soon as I realized just how strongly I felt about this, I journeyed back to them, eager to learn more.

"Grandmothers," I said, bowing as I greeted them, "since I was here last, I've rediscovered how strong my commitment to you is. And...," I said, drawing out my words as I thought about it all over again, "I've become aware of just *how* much I want to learn. Not learn things just so I can pass them on to others," I said, shaking my head. "No! I'm standing here before you, aware that the times we're living in today are even more dire than they were when you first appeared that morning by the beach. These times are desperate, and *I* need more understanding.

"The teachings you've given us so far have done us a world of good, Grandmothers," I went on, "but now I'm asking you to give us even more. With all my heart," I said, my voice breaking, "I'm asking for *more* knowledge, *more* wisdom, and *more* information about how we can be truly powerful as women. Because of the way things are on earth today, we *must* be the powerful women you tell us that we are.

"We're watching as dictators and oligarchs sprout up all over the earth," I said, "as they take control of governments everywhere. These are lawless men, quick to dish out injustice and violence to anyone who opposes them. And they're focusing a lot of their anger on women. So, speak to us, Grandmothers," I said. "Speak to women about what we can do at this time. Give us something you haven't given us yet."

"These times are not for the faint hearted," they said, and as they spoke, I noticed that they were looking straight at me. "Yes, Grandmothers, I know," I nodded. "We're becoming aware of that fact and we're struggling to stay strong," I said, shivering a little.

"Please teach us how to live," I said, "during *these* times that *aren't* for the faint hearted. I'm asking because I recognize that lately *I've* become discouraged. All this negativity is having an effect on me. I'm feeling tired, longing for peace and escape from the horrors here on earth. But escape isn't the answer," I admitted, "not really. What I really want is to be fully engaged; I want to serve with every breath in my body. I *want* to be strong. Please, Grandmothers, speak to me clearly, and I'll live your message and pass it on. How can we as women live in these times?"

As I waited for them to respond, suddenly I began to feel the presence of the community of the Net of Light around me. So many people were surrounding me now, and as I felt their comforting presence, I became aware of the importance of women's support for one another at a time like this. The sense of being part of a loving community washed over me, and the Grandmothers whispered in my ear, **"Yes!"** But when they said nothing more after that 'yes,' and again there was only silence, I began to wonder if my question was the right one. Maybe I should ask them something else. But when that thought popped into my mind, they shook their heads 'no' and motioned for me to wait. So I waited.

As I sat there, I began to ruminate on all the reaching out I'd noticed happening in the Net of Light community. Women from different cultures and countries connecting with each other, groups building community in their regions, and the number of women who went out of their way to enfold new people into the Grandmothers' work. "Every bit of this is so good," I said to myself, "SO good! Thank you, Grandmothers, for all of it," I said, and as I spoke, I heard a catch in my throat.

After I voiced that 'thank you,' lines of light began to appear in front of me. Suddenly they were just there, vibrating and floating in the space before me. And as I watched in fascination, they began to fan out in all directions—in front of me and behind. I noticed then that some of the lines were linking people to one another; some were linking people to earth; and some were linking people to the heavens. And when I tilted my head back and looked up, I noticed even more lines. Many of them were reaching into the sky. Some were even linking to the stars.

Then I noticed that the lines of light in the sky were connected to vast numbers of beings who seemed to be stationed throughout the heavens. These beings looked a lot like people, but they were *very* big. "What *is* this?" I asked the Grandmothers as I squinted, trying to make out what was up there. "Are these people?" And as I continued to study them, they certainly looked human, but whoever or whatever they were, they were standing all over the heavens. There was something about them....

"What is it that they are wearing?" I asked the Grandmothers, and, unable to believe what I was seeing, I squinted again. "Oh, my God!" I whispered. They're all women. Every one of them! They're different forms of the Goddess!" There were masses of them, and when I realized how many there were, chills raced over my body. What in the world *was* this? A convocation of goddesses? Hundreds of figures of the Great Mother were standing everywhere. Hundreds—maybe more! As far as my eyes could see, that was all there were.

I was able to recognize a few of the goddesses, but I had no idea who most of them were. Still, I somehow understood that each one was an embodiment of the Mother. There was Kwan Yin, elegant and graceful in flowing robes, and near Her stood a group of others. By the lion She was riding, I recognized Durga, and near Her stood Brigit with a white cow or bull. I saw Isis on Her throne, and there was the Virgin of Guadalupe! These particular goddesses were familiar to me, but most of the figures gathered here I didn't recognize. And everywhere I looked was yet another embodiment of the Mother.

So many goddesses had come together, and each one was SO beautiful! Each Mother was covered in jewels, cloaked in shimmering fabrics and ornaments of every kind. Some were draped in gold or silver, and many were gowned in silks—of all the colors of the rainbow. "Oh!" I cried, agog, "All these forms of the Feminine Divine! I don't know most of them, but each is the Mother! Every one! I'm witnessing the Mother in ALL Her forms. She's really here!"

"It's good to call out the names of the holy ones," the Grandmothers said, interrupting my stupefied state. And I was *so glad* to hear their familiar voices. **"It's good to call the names of the Goddess,"** they said. **"There is power in the name. There is always power in the name of God,"** they said, **"and God the Mother has been absent from your planet for far, far, far too long."**

I listened as the Grandmothers spoke those three *fars,* aware that what they were telling me was important. That the Mother *has* been absent from earth for too long. And that She needs to be named, needs to be welcomed and called by Her name. All of this made perfect sense to me, and catching my eye, the Grandmothers nodded, **"Yes."**

I was straining to pay attention to everything that was happening around me—to the Grandmothers and this massive parade of Mothers. And paying close attention to *this* scene wasn't easy because I was so moved by everything passing before me, utterly gob-smacked by it. I was determined to remember it all.

"I will not allow myself to become so flooded with emotion that I end up forgetting this," I said, willing myself to attend to everything before me. Though even as I 'willed it,' I knew that I *was* flooded with emotion. Still, I kept on trying to be calm, to remember to breathe slowly and relax, and I thought I was doing a pretty good job of it until I heard myself sobbing. And when I became aware that it was *me* that was sobbing, I gave in, threw up my hands, and sobbed some more.

When at last I was able to calm myself down enough to take in a couple of deep breaths, I spoke to the Grandmothers. "We'll do just as you've asked, Grandmothers," I said. "We'll call out the names of the holy ones. We'll start right away with naming the goddesses. Yes, Grandmothers, yes," I said, "I know it's important to honor the Mother in all Her forms." And then, under my breath and without any conscious intention, I heard myself praying. "Holy Mother," I implored, "Holy Mother, come to us. Holy Mother, enter our hearts. Holy Mother, enter our lives. Speak to us, Mother. Speak through us, love through us, breathe through us, work through us, Holy Mother."

The Grandmothers let me go on like this for a while before they interrupted my litany. **"*The timeline for Her return is escalating,*"** they said. **"The time for the return of God the Mother is coming on faster. From now on, call Her, and when you gather together, share images you have of Her. *It's time for you to get to know the Mother.*"** "Yes, Grandmothers," I said, nodding to them, while under my breath I continued to whisper, "Holy Mother, Holy Mother." The words kept running in my mind, automatically and in a continuous stream.

"At our next meeting, I'll put up all the pictures I have of the Black Madonna, Grandmothers," I told them, "and we'll talk about what prevents us from recognizing our oneness with Her." Then as an afterthought, I said, "That meeting will be a week from tomorrow," and hearing the ridiculousness of my prattle, I stopped myself from saying more. "I'll just sit quietly now," I told myself. "There's nothing more to say. I'll just sit here and wait for the Grandmothers to lead."

So, I did, and there was a long silence after that. But when the silence had gone on for a while, again I heard myself speak. "I'm waiting, Grandmothers," I said. The prolonged silence had made me wonder if they'd forgotten about me. And after that, I must have zoned in and out of a dreamlike state for a while until, out of the corner of my eye, I glimpsed something that was moving off to my right. I turned my head a little to give whatever it was my full attention, and when I did, I saw that it was the Mother Herself.

"Oh!" I gasped, "She's here. Right here!" A towering figure was walking in my direction, a woman so massive that it took me a moment to register that it *was* a woman. A woman covered in roses. She carried masses of them—pink and red roses—as well as an enormous bunch of lilies. "Oh!" I said as I realized who She was. "She's Primavera, the Goddess of Spring! I've seen Her in paintings, in books and museums. All these cascading flowers in bloom, all these colors!" I cried. "And the scent!" Now I was feeling woozy, and almost swooned as the fragrance of a blooming garden enveloped me.

"She's laughing!" I marveled as I watched Her approach, surprise in my voice. "And She's tossing flowers as She comes." Flinging roses to the left and right of Her, tossing them to everyone. As She progressed, flowers flew through the air and cascaded around Her. "Oh!" I gasped as She went by me and brushed my face with a rose. It was the softness of it, its faint perfume, and the fact that she had done it on purpose that made me take in a quick breath. "Oh my, oh my," I exclaimed.

Now another towering figure walked forward, a golden-skinned woman, draped in gold fabric. "Gold, gold, and more gold!" I cried, "covered in gold!" Bangles stacked up her arms, necklaces hung from her neck, and as She progressed, in Her hands She carried several golden objects. Here was the Goddess Lakshmi, Maha Lakshmi in a sari-like garment, but not like any sari I'd ever seen. This one was form-fitting and hugged Her curves while it left her midriff bare. "I never saw anything like this in India," I whispered, and as I eyed Her voluptuous beauty, my gaze was caught by something else.

"Headdresses!" I exclaimed. "She's wearing a headdress, and carrying more of them!" I watched then as this Goddess of Wealth and Prosperity reached up and removed the headdress She was wearing. She held it out. "She's giving it to me!" I croaked, and though I was astounded that She would do this, I accepted it, took it and held it in my lap.

Then as I watched, She gave away headdress after headdress to woman after woman. Gave them all away. And the headdresses multiplied as one after another, She handed them all out.

Lakshmi was clearly relishing this great 'give away,' laughing and smiling all the while. She shared every one of them, and I was so stunned by Her behavior that I just sat there, gawking at Her, with the headdress in my lap.

When I looked away from Her for a moment, my eyes were caught by a movement in the great crowd of women. A figure in sky blue was gliding across the floor. It was the Blessed Mother! "Ah," I sighed, "Mary is here, the Blessed Mother in Her beautiful blue. How sweet She is," I murmured as She lovingly reached out and touched those who were standing around Her. Then "Oh!!!" I exclaimed. "There are lots of them now, *lots* of goddesses! Legions of them!" I gasped, as everywhere I looked were goddesses in motion.

"And all of them are coming this way now!" I said, and suddenly the space around me became inundated with goddesses. "Innana, Cebelle, Artemis, Venus, Quan Yin, Tara…," I stopped naming them when I became overwhelmed by their numbers. "They're pouring in from all directions, coming in from the front, from the sides, coming from everywhere, just flooding in. It's a convocation," I said, my voice breathless. "It's the Holy Mother in all Her forms. All of them are here," I gasped, and as I watched, hundreds—maybe thousands—of goddesses converged in the space around me.

"Oh, my God! The Beauty of it! And the variety!" I exclaimed. "I didn't know there were so many forms of God the Mother. She's of all races and all cultures of humanity. And She's wearing all the costumes on earth. She's *so varied, so overwhelmingly beautiful…*" I murmured, and then my voice trailed into silence. I had no more words to describe the sights before me.

There was a long period of quiet after that until again I heard myself speak. "They're filling up all the space here," I said. "It's so crowded with goddesses, so packed with them that I can't help but touch them, and now I'm even breathing with them. I'm taking them in with my breath, and I can't help but do it!" I noticed. "And," my voice was very quiet now, "because they're all here, and because I'm breathing them in like this, I'm feeling very close to them. Very close," I whispered. "It's happening," I squeaked, barely able to get the words out. "They're filling me with themselves. And, because it's happening like this," I said, my voice shaking, "because it's taking place like this, because I'm breathing them in now," I stammered, "*all women* are also going to be able to breathe them in.

"Oh, my god!" I whispered as understanding of what was happening began to dawn on me. Wave by wave, comprehension was coming now, and I cried in amazement as it came. "It's happening like this; this merging with the Mother is taking place now because of the Net of Light!" I cried.

"Because I am so fully linked with the Net of Light, and because *I* am having this experience with the Mother, now *everyone* can have it. Because I'm having this holy connection, now everyone can access this holy connection through the Net of Light! It's possible because of the Net of Light! The Net of Light is making this happen."

I was stammering and struggling to put my observations into words. This unimagined miracle was taking place *because of* the Net of Light. And as this thought came to me, I glanced up at the Mother, and she nodded and smiled, happy I was aware of what was going on here.

Because of the many years I'd spent working with the Grandmothers and the Net of Light, I'd come to understand what the Grandmothers mean when they talk about human beings being *the plug in the wall*. They'd pointed this out to me many times in the past, but now, not only was I *the plug*, this time *I knew* I was the plug! And now the electrical outlet for this work that over time I'd become, was connecting to the Mother as well as to the Net of Light. 'My' outlet was linking these two magnificent sources of Light. And because the human woman that I am was present at this specific moment, it was possible for *all* human women to access the Beauty and Power of the Great Mother. Because *my outlet* was connected, through the Net of Light, *all* women could connect.

The enormity of participating in such an 'electrical link' stunned me into silence as I sat there watching, the Mother continued to smile at me. As I gazed back at Her beautiful face, I understood that I didn't need to say a word about this. I didn't have to 'explain it' to anyone.

"I can speak of this if I want to," I said to myself, "but whether I say anything or not, it's still taking place," and when I said this, the Mother nodded her head in agreement. "It's taking place right now within every woman on earth. Every woman everywhere, whether she knows it or not, from this moment on will be able to connect with the Mother.

And it's all because of the Net of Light, the radiant Net that connects us all. It gives each woman the same access it's given me.

"I never imagined anything like this could be possible," I said, shaking my head in disbelief. "I sure didn't expect this; I never expected to be absorbed like I am now in communion with the Great Mother. And this *absorption* that I'm feeling runs really deep," I said, shaking my head in wonder at just how true these words were. "This holy recognition, or whatever you want to call it, is anchored down into the center of me. And…," I added, shaking my head in disbelief, "I can feel it going into everyone else too. Holy Mother, Holy Mother," I whispered as I continued to stare at Her beautiful face.

After that, I must have dropped into a light sleep because when I came back to myself, the Grandmothers were sitting beside me. **"You asked,"** they said as they peered deep into my eyes. And as I looked back at them, I remembered that I *had* asked. This miracle had taken place because when I'd come to them, I'd asked them how we could live as women in these difficult times. But when I'd asked that question, I never dreamed their answer would look like this.

"You asked," they said again, and "Yes, Grandmothers," I agreed. "I asked and you responded. *I am so grateful to you*," I said, dropping to my knees before them. "Thankful to you for myself and thankful for everyone else too," I said. "Thank you, thank you, beloved Grandmothers. Thank you, Holy Mother." And when I gazed up at the Mother and the Grandmothers who were standing together in front of me, my heart was so full, I could barely breathe.

They smiled at one another as they watched me struggling to assimilate the gifts I'd just been given. And by their compassionate looks, I knew they understood that this was a lot for me to take in. And as they continued to regard me, I noticed that they were breathing very deeply. "Oh!" I said, and took in a breath with them. This deep, relaxed breathing of theirs was infectious, and before I knew it, I was breathing in rhythm with them—deep, slow breaths—in and out, in and out.

They nodded encouragingly, smiling as they calmly waited for me to come back to myself. And after a few minutes had gone by and my breathing had returned to normal, they turned and gestured outward to the space in front of us. I followed their gesture with my eyes.

There, spread out far into the distance, was our entire planet, looking like a map drawn out flat. As I ran my eyes over its contours, over all the continents on our beloved earth, I saw that the awareness of the Mother's presence on Earth was beginning to awaken. I could see movement in Europe as well as in Asia. Then I watched as She awakened in Vietnam and Cambodia, in Italy, in China, and in Siberia. I watched as She embraced the people of the First Nations, all the tribal peoples and indigenous beings on earth.

Then I saw groups of suffering women responding to Her loving presence. All over the globe now, women were feeling a change, feeling the return of the Mother. There were women who'd been locked in prisons, veiled women in the Middle East, indigenous women in the Western Hemisphere, impoverished women, and even the so-called 'trophy wives' of the rich. All of them were responding to the Mother.

"Whoa...," I said as I observed. The presence of the Mother was now infusing the entire energy field of the planet. "The connection to the Mother is coming alive everywhere," I said, and "W o w!" I whispered to myself, as I felt the awakening taking place inside me too. A new vibration was moving deeper into the cell beds of my body, anchoring itself fully inside me.

"Grandmothers!" I exulted as I threw my head back. "What a blessing this is!" And my heart was so full of gratitude that I could hardly find the words to describe what I was feeling. "A great boon has just descended on us," I said at last. "Descended all over us," I declared, "and what a blessing for humanity! This awareness of the Mother is going to be soaking into us for a very long time," I declared, and the Grandmothers nodded in understanding. "This," I repeated, "will be soaking in for a *very* long time.

"Thank you, Grandmothers, thank you for bringing this gift to the world. The Mother *is* returning," I marveled. "This is for real!" But there was only silence after that, and then once again I heard myself chanting, "Holy Mother, Holy Mother, Holy Mother."

It took me weeks to absorb this lesson from the Grandmothers. This journey had made me realize that though this definitely *was* the time for the return of the Divine Feminine, I was still pretty ignorant about Her. It was clear that in spite of all that I'd read, studied and experienced with the Grandmothers, I knew next to nothing about the

Divine Mother. I was now in over my head. So far over my head that I wasn't comfortable sharing what had happened to me on this journey. Not with anyone. How in the world could I explain *this*?

And, as it turned out, I *never* did tell anyone about it. What had happened to me on that journey, what I'd seen and gone through that day was too BIG for me. Too much to share with anyone. In fact, I didn't feel capable of explaining it at all—not until now.

"Share the news of my return. I am coming for all."

I took a little break from journeying after this and didn't return to the Grandmothers for over a month. And when I did come into their presence again, I said, "Grandmothers, I don't know *anything at all* about God the Mother. I don't know anything," I admitted, "and I really need to learn. If now *is* the time for her return, if there is something that would help me and others better understand these times of transition that we're living in, I would be so grateful if you'd show me. I want to learn and if you teach me this Grandmothers," I said, "I promise I'll pass it all on."

"You really do know nothing," they said, confirming what I'd said. Then they seemed to study me. "That's true, Grandmothers," I admitted as I waited for them to continue, "utterly true."

"WE will teach you," they said then and gave me a ready smile. "Okay," I responded. "Thank you, Grandmothers. I'm relieved." But then something caught my eye—a movement behind them. Again, something was moving around back there. "Oh!" I said, "This is looking familiar."

There were now large numbers of female figures walking around behind them. And as they got closer to the Grandmothers and me and converged, I saw that, as before, they were goddesses. "This is like my last journey, Grandmothers," I said. "Here they come again."

Droves of goddesses poured in. Some were again wearing sari-like garments. Somewore togas and somewere wrapped in cloaks or 'cauls' that covered them completely. And no sooner did they walk close to me than I choked up and burst into tears.

As they drifted by, several of them reached over and patted me on the back while others paused to cradle me for just a moment. **"There, there,"** they murmured as they gently rocked and tried to comfort me.

"It's all right," they said. **We are here. We ARE here,**" they affirmed, and they looked deep into my eyes. But that only made me cry harder.

As they continued to move forward, I noticed that some of them were holding animals nestled in close to their breasts while some walked along beside larger animals. These goddesses were caring for the animals, and as I watched them, I recalled that certain animals are said to be special to certain forms of the Mother.

And as if to make this point, Athena came forward now with an owl on Her wrist, while Artemis walked along beside a stag and Saraswathi carried a swan draped over Her shoulder. Goats, bears, lions, snakes, horses, dogs, and other animals were present, as well as every type of bird. And it was clear by the way She treated them that every one of these animals was precious to the Mother. And as I observed their tender bonds, I cried some happy tears.

Then I noticed the fish. Fish were swimming in so close to the shore here that they'd begun to pile up on one another as they pushed to get closer and closer to Her. Straining to catch a glimpse of the goddesses, they swam as near to land as they could. Every form of life present was as entranced by the goddesses as I was. "SHE is really here!" I whispered to myself, still struggling to believe what I was seeing. "Now!" I declared, striving to convince myself. "She is here. Now!"

Then speech deserted me. And as I watched the Mother interacting with Her animal family, their communion with one another continued to soften my heart. "No one knows about this," I murmured to myself. "No one knows about this love! This bond! And no one knows that the Mother has returned. I didn't know it either!" I squeaked, shaking my head in disbelief. "But it's real. The Mother *is* back…now! Now! Now!" I repeated to myself, and as I did, I began to shake.

"**Bless you, my daughter,**" She said. Together, all the goddesses spoke these words as one. "Each one of them is 'Her,'" I whispered to myself, "and now they're even speaking as one." "**Thank you for being our voice,**" they continued. "**Thank you for hearing us, for being our messenger. Thank you.**" But I only shook my head at them. Flooded with emotion and unable to reply, I simply cried on. "Overcome," I mumbled, "I'm overcome."

I took a few deep breaths when I realized I had to calm myself or I wouldn't be able to continue to hear and see them. I had to stop being so surprised by all this, to accept that they *were* here, to accept that this *was* happening. Really happening. The goddesses smiled at me then and began to do deep breathing with me, just as they'd done before. Nodding and smiling, they breathed in synch with one another to help me get a grip on myself. And when I realized how dear their behavior was, how loving and how funny we all were, I began to laugh, and they laughed with me. "The wonder of it!" I said, shaking my head as I laughed on. And so too did they.

"Okay," I finally said to them, "Okay. I think I can pay attention now."

"**Good,**" they smiled. "**We have come to speak to you,**" one of them said, and when I looked closely at Her, She looked familiar. *I think this is Durga,* I said to myself, and "**Yes,**" she laughingly nodded, "**I am Durga. It is time for the great Warrior Mother and so I am here.**" And as She spoke, the other goddesses nodded. "Clearly, they are one with Her," I said. "At this moment they are One Being with many forms and only one voice."

"**Align with me,**" Durga said and swung a leg over her mount as She spoke. She motioned me to join Her and do the same, but I couldn't make myself move toward Her. She beckoned me again, but I just stood there, frozen in fear. Her mount was a lion.

"**Don't be afraid to take this ride with me,**" She said, speaking to my fear. "**You are ready for this and all will be well. You are brave and strong and nothing can harm you.**" "Nothing can harm me," I repeated Her words, trying for reassurance, and She nodded at me. I swallowed hard then and said, "Okay, I'm willing. I'll do whatever You guide me to do."

"**Come with me,**" She beckoned, making room for me on the lion's back. So, I got on, carefully threading my legs across his broad posterior. Now both of us were riding on the lion, and as he padded forward and we swayed with him, I could feel the power of this magnificent animal. His fur was warm and soft under me, and when I recognized that it felt something like my golden retriever's, I smiled.

Riding on the back of a lion was strange, but oddly it wasn't scary. "I'm comfortable here," I said in surprise as the great cat moved forward with Durga and me swinging with the rhythm of his gait. As I relaxed into this bizarre mode of travel, I said to myself, "I can hardly believe this is happening. And I will never share this information with another soul. No one could possibly believe this."

The sun was beating down on us, and everywhere growth was springing up and flourishing. Everywhere I looked, I saw animals moving about over the land, and people too. "This is the glory of the natural world that I'm seeing," I said to myself, and as I reveled in its beauty, I realized that even though man has done great damage to the earth, there is still the great beauty of the natural world. It is still present. **"Yes,"** Durga nodded.

"This is the earth *as it is*," Durga said. **"The damage that man has inflicted is not permanent. The forces of earth are greater than man's mind. Man is limited,"** She said. **"Know this and rest easy."** I looked hard at Her when She said this. I knew She was trying to tell me that nature is stronger than man's behavior, stronger than his destructive tendencies, but... "I don't know," I said to Her. "I want to believe what You're telling me, but I'm not sure I do. The damage that man has done seems pretty pervasive to me."

She laughed at my response and shook Her head. **"Align yourself with the growing things,"** She said. **"Put your heart into the living things of earth—the plants, animals and people of earth. These are real. It is the things of the mind that are not real,"** She said, and I understood what She was getting at. "Yes," I agreed with Her, "yes, I understand," I said, "and I will."

"Speak out," She said, and I sat up a little straighter. **"Speak out to every woman who is willing to hear you. Speak also,"** She added, **"to the men who are willing to hear. Share the news of My return. I am coming for all,"** She announced.

"*All* are my children," She said, **"and many of my children will be comforted by knowing of My return. So, let them know. Let each one open to the form of the Mother that speaks to them. Tell them to listen and wait, listen and wait for Me. I will come. And as for you,"** She said with a sly smile, **"get busy with your art. Go to work with it. All the drawings and paintings that you're doing now have to do with My return. Did you know that?"** She asked. "No, I didn't," I said, surprised by her reply. "But now I will look for You in the work."

"Take this ride with me," She said, and I looked up with a question in my eyes. "Now She's talking about more than riding on this lion," I said to myself, and She laughed out loud.

"Call on Me," She said. **"Be with Me. And when you give your love, give it to that which is capable of loving you back. Ideas are**

ephemeral, and money has no life in it," She said. "Don't go there. Go instead to your heart. That is where life is. Trust your heart. That is where *I* live, and from your heart, I will speak to you. Wait on Me now and listen for My guidance," She instructed. "You will know My guidance by the feeling of love that wells up within you when you hear that guidance." And smiling benignly, She said, "Trust in that."

"Yes," I replied, bowing my head in reverence. "I will. I will do that." And then I noticed that I was no longer on the lion with Her; in fact, She was riding away. She lifted her hand then and waved goodbye to me. "Goodbye for now."

Who is She?

After these last two journeys to the Grandmothers, and especially after talking with the Divine Mother Durga, I realized what I was learning wasn't just for me. I had to find a way to share this with others.

For thousands of years, we humans have been told, "There IS no Mother. There is only a Father." Long ago patriarchy set up the mechanics of this story so that this one-sided narrative would be all anyone would ever know. Patriarchy basically erased the knowledge and history of the Mother. Every organized religion on earth is patriarchal as are all the world's institutions. They're about men—focused on the male perspective, controlled by men and run on a hierarchical, top-down system. "So," I asked myself, "who is going to believe that suddenly the Mother has returned to earth? And even if someone should be open to this idea, how in the world will they relate to the Divine Feminine? They don't even know who She is.

"Who *is* She?" I asked myself. "What does She look like? What is Her name and what is Her story?" As I mulled this over, once again I realized that if I were going to introduce the concept of the Mother, for most people I would need to start from ground zero. So, not knowing where else to look for help with this task, I began to scour the internet, searching for images of the Great Mother in all Her guises. Searching for information on the Divine Feminine. Had others also been looking for Her, I wondered? And had they had success?

Initially, I didn't find the internet a treasure trove of information. For starters, I had to wade through hordes of images of sex object goddesses—from comic book covers to pinup girls. But I kept on going and finally found sacred images—ancient art, myths and stories that had originated in cultures from all over the world. Most of these had sprung from before recorded history, and though many details of these myths and stories had been lost over time, eventually my search for God the Mother *did* yield a treasure trove.

As I pursued my quest, I noticed that all goddess stories shared a common theme. In each tale, whether or not She was an actual, *physical* mother, the goddess invariably embodied qualities of the Mother. She was powerful. She was loving. And She invariably went out of her way for *all* her children. She might be young, old, red, white or black, but She was unwaveringly brave, powerful and true. And in every tale, *no one* messed with The Mother.

Working with the women in the Net of Light groups, we printed up these goddess images, hung them on the walls at our Gatherings, and asked the Grandmothers to give us activities and ceremonies to help us build a connection with the Mother. We were eager to form a strong relationship with the Feminine Divine: we were looking for a personal link with the Mother. We sang the Grandmothers' songs, meditated with the Mother and asked for Her guidance. And as we did all this, we grew in steadiness and confidence, and the Feminine Principle came more and more alive inside us.

The Grandmothers, who had themselves come to earth to pave the way for the return of the Mother, showed us the way. Patiently, they taught us how to relate to this, our formerly missing parent. And as She made Her way back to us, we shed many tears and together bloomed in joy. We were taking part in a reunion, a *family reunion.*

"Ask us for a taste of your true self and then savor what it's like."

I was beginning to feel my way now, starting to get comfortable meditating with the Goddess and calling on Her. Each time I recalled the expression on the Mothers' face as She stood with the Grandmothers, a great warmth suffused my body. In my mind's eye I could see Her and the Grandmothers standing together, and my heart filled up. Each time the feeling of Her embrace and Her look of loving kindness came back to me, God the Mother became less and less foreign.

One day I went to the Grandmothers and asked them for a message for myself and everyone else too. It was time to put out a newsletter with a teaching from the Grandmothers. They looked carefully at me when I made my request and seemed to be thinking about something. **"You are a tree,"** they said at last, and I stared at them. **"Not the sort of tree you see in parks or along the street,"** they explained, and now I really stared. What were they getting at?

"Not a tree in your garden, one that lives for a while and then is gone," they said. **"No,"** they declared. **"You are the World Tree. You are one life, one indivisible life. The life *you* are,"** they declared, looking hard at me, **"the force *you* are, underlies every tree, every person, every body of water, *everything* on earth. You are the life everlasting that the scriptures speak of,"** they said, smiling contentedly as they regarded me. **"There is nothing impermanent about you. Nothing at all,"** they added, and now I was speechless. I continued to stare at them, open-mouthed.

My head was swirling with disjointed images of trees and quotes from the Bible, but the Grandmothers weren't finished with me yet. **"You often confuse the 'you' of you with your body,"** they explained. **"You also confuse it with your personality and with the various thoughts that go flitting through your consciousness. But you are not things that are here one moment and gone the next,"** they said. **"You're beyond all that flux and flutter. *Vast!*"** they declared then, throwing back their heads at the word. **"You are vast!**

"Right now, the world around you is changing at a pace so fast that you can't accommodate it," they explained. **"You're shocked by the way things are taking place,"** they said. **"All the sacred cows of your childhood are dropping to the ground. *Everything* is in flux,"** they declared, and as they spoke, I could feel the rapidity of this change. I was shaking now and could hardly breathe. **"Change is moving at warp speed,"** they said; **"you can't keep up with any of it. Don't even try."** They shook their heads. **"Just watch it. Be the one who observes.**

"And you can do that," they nodded, slowly wagging a finger, **"because you are the one who never changes. The 'you' of you underlies everything that you think of as 'reality,'"** they said and I took in a breath, straining to understand what they were getting at. **"You are more than any of this,"** they said, gesturing to everything around me. **"So much more. So, let all the busyness of life simply go on as it will,"** they said as they lifted their hands in dismissal.

"**Just sit quietly. Call on us. Slow down,**" they said then, motioning with their hands, "**and when at last you feel yourself becoming quiet inside, ask us to give you a taste of your 'real' reality. Just a taste,**" they said. "**We will give you just enough.**

"**Ask us for this taste of your true self and then savor what it's like. Take the time to own the changeless core of what you think of as 'you.' You need a dose of reality every now and then,**" they affirmed, "**a dose of who you really are. You need this so you can more easily cope with the topsy-turvy world you are living in. You need it, and we are happy to give it to you. And all you need do to receive it is to quiet down inside, ask us for it, and then simply observe what happens. Try it right now,**" they said. "**It will do you good.**"

I was taking in what they were saying, but what I was most aware of now was how full of information I was. Full up! Ideas and questions about what the Grandmothers had said were bouncing around inside my head. I wasn't sure I understood all they'd just explained to me, but understand it or not, what they had conveyed had a ring of truth to it, and truth was what I wanted. So, in spite of the jumble of thoughts that were vying for my attention, I did as the Grandmothers were asking. I slowed down and gave over my need to understand all that they'd said. Then I waited. It felt like I was waiting for my mind to catch up with the truth the Grandmothers had spoken. Or maybe I was waiting for my body to open up and own this truth. Anyway, I waited. I sat still and willed myself to simply receive whatever it was they wanted to give me. Waited and watched.

And as I sat there, I became aware of a peaceful feeling starting to awaken in me and noticed that my perspective was changing. All the drama in my mind was still going on. In fact, the rush of thoughts and ideas was just as fast paced, demanding and crazy as ever. *But I wasn't.* Now I was able to simply observe. Maybe sitting quietly like this had allowed the drama to be diluted somehow. Anyway, the busyness and drama had now receded into the background, and I was able to observe everything from a place with a l…o…n…g view. *I liked this.* It was peaceful. It was quiet. This was a perspective I could live with. Now I could see everything, but I wasn't being affected by any of it. This waiting and receiving was good for me.

A few weeks after this experience with receiving, I returned to my wise teachers, and as soon as they saw me, they said, "**This is an open-**

ing time." And when they spoke, something out in front of me moved, something colorful. I looked at it and realized that here was a flower, unfolding before me. As its petals slowly and gracefully folded back, I could see that the center of the flower was full of light. And the deeper into the center of this flower that I was able to see, the brighter it got. The flower was lit from within, and its center point had great depth. Like an ever-brightening funnel, the center dropped deeper and deeper into the light, so deep and so blindingly bright, I wasn't able to see to the bottom of it. And as I continued to observe, the flower continued to open.

"**This is where we are leading you,**" the Grandmothers said; "**this is where you are going. Deeper into the light.**" "Oh!" I exhaled, surprise in my voice. And then, somewhere far off in the distance, I heard a beautiful voice singing, "World without end, amen, amen."

"**Yes!**" The Grandmothers declared after that second 'amen' sounded, their faces radiant. "**There is no end to this light; there is no end to this beauty.**" And locking their eyes on mine, they said, "**There's no end to the beauty that** *you* **are. Who you are is expanding now and you are going to continue to expand. Far beyond your wildest dreams,**" they said, and I noticed they were holding my eyes with theirs.

I watched them, surprised, stunned by their words and by the look they were giving me now. "**Don't worry,**" they said. "**This will come about gradually. The expansion we're talking about won't overwhelm you. In fact, you'll LIKE it,**" they reassured me. "**Your capacity for feeling good, for doing good, and for being good will continue to grow and grow now. And this increasing store of goodness inside will give you tremendous joy. Ever-expanding joy.**"

I started to laugh then. "I think maybe I'm feeling a little bit of it now, Grandmothers! Listening to your words just now brought this light, happy feeling up in me, and this is *nothing* I could have come up with myself," I said, shaking my head. "This is…is…so different.

"I guess I'm not accustomed to feeling this sort of lightness. I'm more accustomed to just kind of going along, Grandmothers," I explained, "to sort of slogging along through life, and life, well…," I sighed as I thought some more, "life has been so *difficult* lately. So many people are suffering now, and all over the world," I explained, "there's so much anger and fear. Everything is really unstable now, and no one, including me, seems to know what to do about any of it." At a loss for words, I then just looked at the Grandmothers.

"**We know!**" they laughed. "**We know all this! And though what you're saying is true, all of that is ending now. Not much longer to wait,**" they said, holding up their hands to stop me from worrying. "**Soon, everything on earth will start opening up,**" they said. "**And** *you*" they emphasized, "**are already starting to open up. More of that will follow,**" they promised me, smiling conspiratorially at one another.

"**Think of that opening flower we just showed you,**" they said, "**and hold it steady in your mind. Remember the depth of light at its core.** *This* **is where you are going,**" they confirmed. "**Deeper, wider, bigger. MORE light!**" they announced, and then they burst into laughter. "Okay, Grandmothers, okay," I said. "I'm beginning to feel it now. I'm beginning to sense the light up ahead of me, and you're right. This *is* where I want to go. So, lead on, Grandmothers. Lead on."

After I said that, I took in a long, slow breath, and when I let it out again, I said, "Teach me about God the Mother, Grandmothers. I know so little about Her, and it seems important to understand Her. If I'm right about that, please teach me what I most need to know about Her."

The Grandmothers stood together in silence, just observing me. "**God the Mother is over all,**" they said. "**She lies under all and She is within all. Your body is** *Her* **body,**" they said, which startled me. "My body?" "**Your work is** *Her* **work,**" they continued. "**There is no separation, none at all, between you and God the Mother.**"

They stopped speaking then and looked me in the eye. "**Do not pray '***to***' Her,**" they said, and I blinked, startling a little. "**Call Her up from within yourself,**" they said, nodding slowly to confirm the truth of what they were saying. "**What we are saying now about God the Mother is also true about God the Father. The presence of the Masculine Principle also dwells within you,**" they said, and I sat up straight when I heard this. This was something I'd never considered, and hearing the Grandmothers speak out about it so clearly now actually sounded a bit blasphemous.

"**We understand your confusion,**" they said, laughing together at my reaction, "**but long ago, God the Father was co-opted by patriarchy for patriarchy's gains. And at that time patriarchy separated God from humanity. This 'take over' of God the Father has caused untold pain to humankind, and besides that,**" they added, "**it made** it difficult for people to understand the true nature of the Masculine Divine.

"Those who separated man from God," the Grandmothers said, "did so for what they thought of as their own benefit. If man was separate from God, they reasoned, then how could man hope to reach God? Through the structures laid down by patriarchy, of course," they answered. "No one could come to know God by themselves alone; they had to go through a middle man—a priest.

"Every one of the world's religions have this in common," the Grandmothers said. "Man must be *taught* how to behave with 'God.' And in most cases, man must be tutored and controlled by human men, *special* men who *know* how to reach God. Patriarchy was set up to separate man from God," the Grandmothers said, "to separate man from man, man from animals. To separate man from life. Patriarchy," they said, "is utterly opposed to the all-pervasive truth of Oneness. It does not understand the One Love.

However," the Grandmothers said, and as they spoke, they pulled themselves to their full height, "the time of patriarchy is over. There is no more life left in patriarchy, no juice," they said. "It's a dead system, and though for a while yet it will try to control humanity, it will no longer succeed. Its time has passed," they said with finality. "With the return of God, the Mother, wholeness and wholesomeness is returning to life. The flow of love that's pouring forth from the Source to all forms of life now is irresistible. And who," they asked, "can resist pure love?

"God, the Mother, must return at this time," the Grandmothers said, "because man can no longer live without Her. Here on earth for far too long there has been too much of the mind and not enough of the heart. It is the Mother who feeds the heart, and the heart of humanity today is dried up; it is starving for food. *Real* food," they said.

"More than twenty years ago, we told you that we, the Great Council of the Grandmothers, had come to pave the way for the return of the Mother. Well," they fixed their eyes on mine, "we have done that. In these twenty plus years, many of you have learned about the Feminine Principle, learned about the qualities of Yin and how to work with the Net of Light. We asked you to 'Live our message,'" they said, "and this you have tried to do. You have been good students, and over the years we have drawn enough of you together to help us lay a foundation for the return of the Mother. You have worked steadfastly with us, and together we have accomplished what we set out to do. Now," they said, and paused meaningfully, "*She is coming.*

"Look for Her in your heart," the Grandmothers said, "and look for Her in your mirror. When you stand before your mirror and gaze deeply into your own eyes, you will make contact with the Mother. When you allow your heart to open and soften toward others and toward yourself, too, *She* will come alive in you. Enjoy all the images of God the Mother that you want to enjoy. Speak the many names of her form—Maria, Brigit, Quan Yin, Athena, Fatima, Durga. And hundreds more," they said. "Light candles before an image of Her that you love, sing Her songs, love Her in all Her magnificent forms, but do not be deceived that She dwells 'out there' somewhere. *She does not live outside you.* That simply is not true. She lives within you. Within you," they repeated, murmuring low.

"Welcome the Mother into your life just as you have welcomed us," they said, "just as you have welcomed whatever form of the Divine you love. She is real and She is here now," they said. "No more absent Divine Mother," they shook their heads. "No!" they cried. "She is alive and well—in you," they said. "Believe it!! We are telling you this," the Grandmothers said with feeling, their hearts in their eyes, "and we never lie.

"This is enough information for now," they said. "Take it in and rest in it. Breathe deeply, think of Her and take it all in. We are very happy for you. You have waited a long time for this."

CHAPTER TEN:
The Grandmothers' Meditations

"These are tools for furthering individual empowerment."

'Knowing about' something, even 'knowing' it, is not the same thing as living it. The Grandmothers' meditations are designed to give a visceral understanding of the truths they have come to impart. They're gathered here from all four of the Grandmothers' books for easy access.

These **"tools for furthering individual empowerment"** contain layers of meaning. Whether or not you have chosen to receive the Grandmothers' Empowerment, these tools will help you put their work into practice. **"These meditations anchor our teachings,"** they say, **"allowing our lessons to go deeply into the viscera of your body/ mind and be held there. They will become your own truth. When you have owned and taken in these truths, they will no longer be thoughts that pass through your mind, but will be deeply known."**

The Grandmothers' meditations create change. Not just intellectual exercises, they are opportunities to experience another way of being. This is a workbook for those who seek active participation with the Grandmothers. Some meditations are simple, while others are more complex, but all are designed to help you heal, balance and expand your awareness and consciousness. As this happens, you will, by your very being, bless all life on earth. You can, if you like, record these meditations so you can listen directly to the power in the Grandmothers' words.

PRELIMINARY RELAXATION EXERCISE

If you are unfamiliar with meditating, this simple method will bring you to a point of relaxation, enabling you to work with the Grandmothers. Use it as needed to precede the following meditations.

To begin, find a place where you can be alone, take a seat and once you have, think of why you are doing this. What is it you want from this experience? You may be curious about these so-called Grandmothers, or you may want to open yourself to the presence of the Divine. Be clear about what you are seeking as you approach this work. Your clarity honors them and you. *This is your intention.*

Once you have taken your seat, let your body assume an open position. Uncross your hands and feet, unless you are sitting cross-legged on the floor, and take a moment to notice how perfectly the chair or the floor supports you. They hold you at every moment, though you are seldom aware of it. Feel your contact with the chair or floor and notice how comfortable or uncomfortable you are.

How is your body occupying space? Where is your weight placed? Notice your entire body. Are your feet heavy on the floor? Do you feel your feet? Take the time you need to settle in and observe your total self with a somewhat disinterested air, like taking inventory. Is your heart beating fast or slowly? Is the rhythm of your breath regular or irregular? *Just notice.*

Take in a slow, deep breath and as you exhale, think of letting go of the old (old thoughts, attitudes, and air) and when you inhale, think of taking in the new. Close your eyes and do this for three or four times, feeling your breath moving in and out with a deep, slow rhythm. *Letting go of the old, opening to the new.*

Observe your heart beating and notice its rhythm. Is it slowing down? Speeding up? What is the temperature of your body? Your heart may beat fast or steadily. Your body may feel warm or cool. You may be tense or relaxed as you begin, but don't try to change anything about yourself. Don't force yourself to 'try' to relax. Simply observe without judging. *Observe and take your time.*

Notice where your body feels tight and where it feels softer, if you are holding your breath or breathing fast or slowly. No judgment. No hurry. *Just keep observing* without evaluating yourself and when you are ready you can let the Grandmothers know you'd like to begin.

MEDITATION ON THE NET OF LIGHT

"The light that illumines the net originates in the heart of each one."

We begin with a meditation on the Net of Light. The Grandmothers ask us to do this meditation often in order to extend the grace of this lighted support system to everyone and everything on Earth.

"Begin to work with the Net of Light," they say, "by thinking of a vast lighted fishing net spread over the earth and stretching into the distance, as far as your eyes can see. This is the great Net of Light that will support the earth and all life on this planet during the times of change that have come. The Net of Light covers the earth from above, from below, and permeates the earth like a great grid. It penetrates, holds, and touches everything. This is the Net of Light that will hold the earth while the energies of yin and yang shift. And they will shift; the change has already begun.

"Walk forward and take your place on the Net of Light. Somewhere where two of the strands come together forming an 'x' or a 't' is a place that will feel just right for you. Walk forward and take your place there. Here you can rest and allow the Net of Light to hold and support you while at the same time you support it.

"Many times, we have said that the Net of Light is lit by the jewel of the heart. This is true. Experience now as the radiant jewel of your own heart begins to open and broadcast its light along the strands of the Net. Every person who works with the Net of Light is linked in light with others who also work with it. Experience your union now with people all over the globe who are connected by the Net of Light. Some call it a Web of Light, a lighted grid, the Cosmic Web, or Indra's net, but whatever they call it, it is the same construct.

"Call on the Net and find your place on it and think of receiving and sending light throughout this vast network. As soon as you think this thought, your energy will follow it, and you will feel the Net of Light working in and through you.

"Experience your union with us and all who work with us. There are thousands of you all over the earth. Experience your union with the sacred and holy places on this planet and all the sacred and holy beings—the great saints, sages, and avatars who gladly give their lives in service and who have come at this time to avert the catastrophe that looms over the earth. Experience your union with those of good heart who seek the highest good for all life. Know and feel the power of this union and let your body experience this force of and for good.

"Once you have strongly felt this power, begin to cast the Net of Light to those who don't know about it. Cast wherever there is suffering, to human beings, to animals, to conditions of every kind, to all forms of life, and to Mother Earth herself. Magnify the presence of the Net of Light for people who are longing to serve, but haven't yet found a way to access the Divine. As you cast the Net of Light, many who have, until this moment been asleep to the fundamental connection we all share, will begin to awaken and feel the spark of Divinity coming to life within them. Ask the radiant Net of Light to hold all life in its embrace and know that each time you work like this, you are adding to the reach and power of the great Net.

"Cast the Net to all women and men everywhere. Cast to the leaders of this world to remind them that they are a precious part of the Net of Light that holds and supports life. Cast to the animal kingdom, asking that every animal receive what it most needs. Cast to the plant kingdom and to the mineral kingdom. Cast to the Ancestors, to the elemental spirits and to the elements of Earth Herself. Cast to everything that lives, and when you have done that, ask that everyone in all the worlds be happy.

"This is how to work with the Net of Light. There is no greater service you can perform. We ask you to give from your heart and work with the Net of Light every day. Do it for yourself, and for the sake of everything that lives. We bless you."

THE PITCHER AND THE CUP
"We do the Giving. You do the living."

To experience what it's like to have the Grandmothers fill you full of the Source, begin the same way you did in the previous exercises. Go to your quiet place and make yourself comfortable. Then call on the Grandmothers and ask them to take you to a sunny room where you can become acquainted with the Pitcher and the Cup. As soon as you make your request, a particular room will come to mind. Once it does, think of or see a table where the pitcher and cup sit. Sunlight streams over everything, pouring through a window, a doorway or another opening. See, sense, or imagine this. Notice the pitcher—its size, shape, weight and color—and how full it is, full to the rim. Touch it if you like and feel its curves.

The cup, many times smaller, sits next to the pitcher. Take in the details of this scene as if you were an artist, capturing the size and shape of the table, the quality of light, color and shape of the cup and where it sits in relation to the pitcher. You may feel the warm sunlight, smell the air or hear the sounds of birds outside the window. Use your senses and imagination to create this scene and let it implant itself in your consciousness. Mark how you feel in this scene of light, grace and plenty.

Now watch as the contents of the pitcher pour into the cup, filling it full. When the Grandmothers gave me this exercise, the pitcher was full of cream but it can be full of any good thing. The Grandmothers may do the pouring or it may seem to take place by itself but as soon as the cup is full and the pitcher at rest, look inside it. This pitcher *cannot be emptied*. It is kept ever filled by the Source.

Let yourself resonate to this truth. There is an endless supply here and you, at one with the sun-bathed pitcher, are filled to the rim too. A container of abundance and every good thing, that is what you are. You *cannot* be emptied because the Grandmothers will keep you ever filled.

"All you have to do to be filled is think of us," the Grandmothers say. **"As a result, you will find yourselves filled and, like the pitcher, there will be no room in you for emptiness. From this fullness, giving to others will take place so easily you won't even think of it as giving. There will be no separation between giver and given to. What you give will flow from the source of which you are a part."**

From a position of fullness, life flows effortlessly. The Grandmothers say, **"As you practice this exercise your life will become easier and easier—as it should be. We do the giving. You do the living, and let us give to others—through you."**

THE TREE OF LIFE
"You are related through this Tree."

To strengthen the relationship between women and men and balance yin and yang, the Grandmothers give us the Tree of Life meditations. **"The Mother cares not only for the branches or roots of the Tree but takes care of the whole Tree."** These meditations help us receive what we need from the feminine aspect of creation. With the re-emergence of yin comes an automatic increase in steadiness.

These meditations balance relationships and create harmony within individuals. They promote healing for the one meditating and for all life. **"The Tree of Life exercise is for everyone—men and women. Let yourselves experience the peace of this Tree."**

This meditation has three parts, each one valuable. But probably its greatest service lies in balancing the flow of yin and yang within oneself.

This is the world Tree, an archetype or symbol for unity and interconnection, a subject of folk art around the globe, revered by indigenous peoples everywhere. I saw my first Tree of Life in Mexico—made of clay, with animals and people perched on its branches—but I have seen it since in many cultures.

"The symbol of the Tree serves a purpose. Its roots support everything in the world while its branches cover the earth. All beings are related to one another through this Tree. That is why 'Love everyone' is practical advice."

We are deeply joined with and by the energy of the Tree, which personifies our connection to God and one another. Although we live in a material world, we are more than base material. **"As you open to the support of God the Mother through the Tree of Life, you will have more to give. And as you learn to give in this way, you too will become a living and giving part of the Tree of Life."**

Balancing Yin and Yang

"You must realize that the Tree is a unit. Both above and below, roots and branches are one."

Because most people have a limited view of life, the Grandmothers teach us how to see the Tree not just as the sum of its parts, but as a whole. And to correct our perspective and awaken us to a balance of yin and yang, they give us a breathing meditation that harmonizes masculine and feminine energy. They use the symbol of the Tree to bypass the limitations of our rational minds.

After you have relaxed, call on the Tree and observe as it comes to mind, being especially conscious of its canopy and roots. If you're not good at visualizing, *just call on the Tree.* Think of, imagine, or feel yourself leaning against its trunk as you breathe deeply from its roots. Be aware of the entire Tree and notice your connection to it. You can do this sitting, standing, or lying down.

"Draw the energy of the earth up into your body with each breath, and do this three times." Receive what you need from Mother Earth with these three deep breaths—security, steadiness, and comfort—and observe as these gifts, specific qualities of the Great Mother, infuse your body and mind. Give yourself time to absorb them.

"Now breathe from the leaves and branches of the tree, drawing the energy of the sky down into yourself with each breath. Do this three times." Draw in what you need from the masculine principle of energy—strength, protection and clarity. Although we inhale first from the roots, and then from the branches, it is not necessary to direct our exhalations to anywhere in particular. **"Your exhalation will go to wherever it is needed. Your inbreath carries with it a gift to you, and your out-breath carries a gift to the world. These gifts will go where they are needed.**

"Since breathing like this creates harmony within the self and forms a harmonious atmosphere, it will be beneficial for women and men to do this exercise together. It is absurd for men to ignore the feminine aspect of life or for women to ignore the masculine. If all of the branches of the Tree were cut, the Tree would die. If all of the roots were cut, the Tree would also die."

"The Tree needs attention and it needs care *now*." We can't afford to waste more time in power struggles; we must begin to view one another with new eyes. "The whole Tree needs care—both roots and branches. Great benefit will come from working with the Tree of Life. When you breathe like this, Earth and Sky meet in the great embrace of the Mother/Father, Father/Mother, yin/yang."

EXPANDING THROUGH THE ROOTS OF THE TREE

"This is the root/route for your life— the Source for your individual life."

Following the relaxation procedure, visualize, imagine or think of the Tree's network of roots and branches, spreading farther than the eye can see. They encompass the earth, all peoples, their countries, and their customs. *Simply think this thought, let it go and observe* your response to it.

"**Visualize or imagine these roots like the veins of rivers, that touch every part and place on earth—Europe, Asia, Africa, the Americas, all islands and the poles. The roots intertwine throughout the earth while the branches shelter the entire planet.**" Move into the roots of the Tree. Dive down, reach throughout this vast network and explore.

The roots are anchored in and anchor you to Mother Earth, feeding you just as they feed the Tree. As you breathe in and receive what the Great Mother is giving you, know the depth of your connection to this Mothering Source who holds you secure within Her network of roots. Let your body feel its connection to Her and to earth.

You may sense a place within this network that feels like your own. You have a root (route) that connects you to the Tree in a special way. This is yours alone and will feel very comfortable to you. Look for it now and once you find it, rest there. "**This is the root/route for your life, the source for your individual life.**"

Explore your root—its shape, circumference and placement within the underground system of the Tree.

Each time you practice this meditation, your root/route and your connection to all other roots will be strengthened. Since every person connects to the Tree of Life via its roots, "**It is impossible to help yourself without benefiting everyone. As you strengthen your root/route, everyone's connection to the Divine gets stronger.**"

The Tree exercise is helpful to men and women, but something special happens for women when they work with it. For many years women have been cut off from the source of feminine power, and one way to access this power is to work with the Tree of Life. The Grandmothers say, **"It is time for women's roots to be established; the roots of the Tree are like women who stand steady and supportive in their power.**

"As women work with the roots of the Tree of Life, each root will reach out and touch another. Together these will form a web of support that will hold the earth steady. This is another way for people to open to the Net of Light."

FRUITS OF THE TREE
"Each fruit is necessary for the overall health of the Tree."

"In human lives and in the Tree of Life, energy travels from the Source, up the root/route and into the body. There it manifests as fruit—the fruits of one's actions and the fruits on the Tree of Life." In both cases, fruit ripens gradually.

This exercise allows us to see ourselves in a new way while honoring our specific gifts and challenges. **"Each fruit is necessary to the overall health of the Tree. It is *this* fruit, chosen from the Tree of Life, that gives each life its savor. The fruit on the Tree reflects the special identity of each."**

If we think of our fruit as symbolic of how we live and who we are, we can take the lesson of the Tree to a deeper level. Our lives reflect our individuality. Some of us are achievers some are contemplators; some are survivors, explorers, evaluators—the list goes on. In time our life will manifest these intrinsic qualities (our gifts, challenges and character) just as fruit will manifest whatever is intrinsic to it (its sweetness, color and texture).

To begin this exercise, follow your usual method for relaxing, then call on the Tree of Life and notice its canopy, laden with fruit of every kind. Hanging from its branches are mangoes, bananas, guavas, grapefruits, every fruit imaginable. Walk up to the Tree and be aware of the fruit you select, or rather that which selects you.

Whether or not the significance of your fruit is apparent to you is not important. The fruit is a metaphor for your life, so treat it with respect to see what you can learn from it. The Grandmothers purposefully give 'lessons' in this non-linear way to help us sneak up on ourselves.

Once you have chosen or been chosen by your fruit, get to know it. You may be tempted to exchange it for another, but resist temptation and study its color, texture and size. Feel its weight and shape, its smoothness or roughness. Smell it, taste it. Take a sensory inventory.

As you explore, you will more deeply own this fruit, and as you claim your fruit you may also choose to claim the special being that you are. The fruit is a teacher, given to help you value your unique qualities.

"The more you let yourself embody your fruit, the truth of your individual manifestation of being, the more you will step forward into the world to be who and what you are. This particular fruit from the Tree of Life is yours. This particular life is also yours. Your fruit, your life, is a gift from yourself and from the Source itself."

To serve and connect with the great cycle of life, we must own who and what we are. The Tree of Life, a metaphor for God/Source, shows that just as each fruit comes from and is part of the tree, we also come from and are part of God/Source. We, the fruit, belong to the tree.

Once we claim our gift from the Tree, we can live out the fruit of our lives and when we do this we bloom. Anyone who has witnessed a friend 'come into her own' knows the thrill of seeing this awakening. This part of the Tree of Life meditation nudges us toward 'coming into our own.'

Fruit inevitably follows flower, so after you bloom, you bear fruit. Once we become ourselves, own our strengths, flaws and talents, we have something to give back to the world. What we give is determined by the fruit we are given and by what we do with it. The fruits of the Tree represent both the hand we are dealt and how we play it. The saying, "Who you are is God's gift to you, what you become is your gift to God," sums it up.

By living out the truth of our Self, we give back to the Tree of Life and complete the cycle of giving and receiving. **"The Tree of Life supports everything that lives by continuously giving of itself. This meditation will help you own, and then use the gifts of your particular fruit. Then you too will have something to give to the world."**

FABRIC OF BEING

"You are much more than you have conceived. You are as the night sky."

This meditation expands consciousness by dissolving fears and the illusion of separation from the Divine, as well as separation from one another. By dissolving false barriers, it counteracts loneliness and isolation. Liberating, breaking through constrictive beliefs and mindsets, the Fabric of Being frees us to enjoy an expanded state. This is another symbol the Grandmothers use to teach about the Divine and our relationship to it. The Fabric of Being breaks us out of the confining identification with our individual problems and our small selves and moves us into contact with the greater Self. Since it is the sense of separateness from the *whole* of life that creates loneliness and isolation in the first place, here we experience joy. This meditation gives a body-mind understanding of union with the Source and union with each other.

The Grandmothers say, **"You *are* the Fabric of Being. Think of the night sky and let yourself move into the indigo blue of this sky. Here there are many stars and moons and a glow from all of these."**

After you reach a state of relaxation, think of the expansive nighttime panorama of moon and stars. If you live where you can see the stars, walk out your door and look up. If not, think of a time when you did look at the deep blue of the night sky, and as you gaze at it with your physical or inner eyes, think of the Grandmothers' statement that you are not separate but part of it all.

Gently breathe, and with each inhalation, draw the starry sky into your body. Then merge into it as you exhale. As you breathe in, the sky enters you. As you breathe out, you flow into the sky. Continue to breathe like this and to explore this expanse. Let yourself be supported by the firmament. The mantle of sky wraps around you, and as you rest enfolded in it, you touch everything—stars, earth and air. **"You encompass all this,"** the Grandmothers say; **"you are the indigo blue night sky. You surround everything and throb with life. The stars and moons in the sky pulsate within you just as your physical heartbeat echoes inside your physical body."**

Be aware of the sky moving in and out of your body to the rhythm of your breath. The life force of the universe *is* inside us. It is underneath our skin, as well as over and around us, but this exercise will allow you to feel it. As you breathe like this, notice the temperature of your body, the rhythm of your breath and your heartbeat.

"If you were only your body, if you were only your breath or your thoughts, you would have no recognition of any of them. But you are much more than any of these, and because you are, whenever you turn your consciousness inward, you can be aware of them all. You are much more than you have ever conceived. You are as the night sky. Vast.

"We give this meditation to move you beyond the sense of limitation and smallness. The Fabric of Being will move you beyond mental divisions of 'me' or 'mine,' 'you' or 'yours.' These are tiny concepts— not even pinpoints—and are not what you are. You are great; you are the deep blue, ever-reaching blanket of the night sky.

"Meditating on the Fabric of Being will heal worry, nervousness and release stress. It releases negative mental and emotional states because the Fabric of Being is the truth of who you are."

ROSE OF THE HEART

"Begin by sensing the center of your chest," the Grandmothers say. **"What we are doing here is 'a before and after.' This is the before. Notice the texture of this area of your body, the temperature, softness or hardness, perhaps the color you sense inside your chest. Observe what it is like in the heart area of your body. What is it like?**

"Get an actual rose so that you can look at it. Not a tight bud nor one that is fully blown open, but a multi-petaled rose, partially opened. Look into this rose and take your time. Smell it. A natural rose that hasn't been hybridized will have a scent. These are best because scent is intrinsic to a rose.

"Feel its skin, the petals, of the rose, and smell it again as you examine the intricacy of its petals. How beautiful these petals are! Study how each relates to each. Observe the pattern that lies on top and underneath each petal as well as the petal's delicate edge. Notice how the rose circles round, folding and enfolding, right to the very heart of itself.

"Dissecting a rose will not show you what a rose is because a rose is formed in relation to its petals. The miracle of the rose exists because of its scent, texture, its variation of color and the relationship of its petals.

"How perfect this flower is. How perfect you are. If you only knew! Every part of you relating perfectly to every other—your organs in harmonious conversation with each other; your essence permeating throughout. Like the rose, the human body can also be dissected; the personality can be dissected and diagnosed. But your essence, which is within every part of you, cannot be touched. As is the rose, so are you.

"Now close your eyes and focus on the heart area of your body. Again, notice how it feels, what the sensation is like here, and then think of bringing the rose, the beautiful rose you have been studying, into your heart. The rose is now within your heart.

"Watch as it opens slowly. Opening…opening. As you inhale, the rose opens as if it's stretching, and as you breathe out, the rose also breathes out and closes a bit. Breathing in, it opens further; breathing out, it closes a little. And at the next breath, it opens more, casting its fragrance into the atmosphere.

"As the rose opens, so does your heart. With your in-breath, both the rose and your heart open; with the out-breath, they close a little; and in the next inbreath, they open further. Because the rose/heart follows your breath, this gradual process serves to expand your heart. Breathe now with the rose of your heart, opening a little more each time you inhale.

"Next, expand the rose so that your chest is contained within its petals. Experience this enormous rose of your heart. Now the rose swells throughout your body until it contains your entire body. Feel yourself surrounded by and filled with the rose.

"Expand it further to fill the room you are sitting in and further still to fill the area where you live. Let it expand to saturate your part of the country.

"This enormous heart/rose is now expanding to fill your entire country. Onward, outward, ever outward, it is filling all the countries of the world, holding all the peoples, all bodies of water and landmasses of the earth. The great heart/rose now holds the earth within its petals and continues to expand until the sun is contained within it—then the galaxy and the universe. Everything. Everything is now contained within your enormous heart/rose.

"Far into space this vast rose of your heart expands until it holds and contains everything. Feel this. Sense this." Rest in this place

for a moment and notice what it is like for you to be in such an expanded state before you continue.

"Now the return journey begins, a much faster journey. The Rose of the Heart is beginning its return to you. It is coming in now; it is rushing back, contracting back to your country, to your city, to your home, contracting into your body, and last of all, into your own physical heart.

"Take a moment to rest in this space within your heart and observe this area of your body. This is where the rose/heart lives and will always live.

Notice if any changes have occurred since we began this exercise. What is this area of your body like now? How does it feel here in your heart? Notice the size of your heart, its weight, its temperature, color and texture. Compare your heart now to the way it felt before you did this exercise.

"Such is the beauty and massive magnificence of your own heart," the Grandmothers say. **"Rest here."**

THE CONTAINER THAT YOU ARE

Perhaps one of the strongest and most telling qualities of yin energy is its ability to hold, accept and nurture whatever presents itself. When we don't push against something, don't exclude or judge anything or anyone, but instead bring whatever comes onto our lap and hold it there so it can settle into itself and find its place, we allow yin to work through us. Not dramatizing the challenge of the moment, but simply being *with* the moment. This quality of nurturing acceptance belongs to the Mother, and we ourselves can open like this to the Feminine Principle and deal with people, ideas, and situations—in short, with everything—in this way. Accepting, accepting. Initially this may seem a strange idea to you, a foreign one, but that's only because this concept has been missing from our world for a long time.

A position of openness and acceptance creates a force field of harmony. There is an undeniable greatness in what the Grandmothers call the *Container*. "She who holds" accepts what is, and this acceptance allows everyone and everything to relax and be who and what they are. Held by and at one with the Container, we become 'real.' And because this is so, this meditation creates a foundation for harmonious relationships. It harmonizes women and men, seeming opposites, yin and yang.

"It's time to experience the container that you are," the Grand-mothers say. **"You are the container that holds love, that holds life, and supports everything that lives. Your capacity is enormous. Become aware of yourself."**

To experience yourself as this Container they speak of, begin by moving into a state of relaxation, sitting with your arms and legs uncrossed and your spine straight. Place your hands palms up on your lap and notice what it's like for you to sit in such an open posture. How does your body feel as you sit this way? How do you feel? As you do this, don't judge yourself or try to change anything about your-self—just notice. As you sit, you will find yourself dropping into a deeply receptive state, the position of the Container. Open and recep-tive to whatever comes. This position evokes the presence of the Great Mother—She who accepts all life and holds everything. As you sit this way, you may become aware She is with you, holding you, and at the same moment, She is sitting inside you. Take a few minutes to enjoy your powerful connection with the Great Mother by being open, receptive.

As you sit, you may also become aware of the chair underneath you and the support you are being given by both the chair and the floor. At this very moment you are in your right place.

Now take a moment to invite in whatever comes onto the screen of your mind. Let it come up as it will, and when something appears, quietly hold it there. Simply hold whatever shows itself. Don't move toward it, and don't move away from it. Let it come to you and be with you for as long as it wants, and when it gets up and leaves, accept and hold whatever comes next.

You will find you're able do this because you are a container and this is what a container does. It holds. A container is not the least affected by what fills it. If you pour water into a pot, the pot is unchanged. If you pour milk into it, it is still unchanged. Become aware of how it feels to simply hold like this—just for this moment, unaffected by whatever comes to your mind. No judgment, no evaluation, and if judgment should appear, well, hold judgment in this nonjudgmental way too.

The Grandmothers are performing this action with you—holding you and holding with you so that you can learn what it's like to be the container that you actually are. **"In the vastness of your being, you can do this,"** they say. **"You are great enough to hold everything."** You may become aware of the truth in their words: that just for now you *can* accept and hold everything.

A succession of people, problems, and stories may parade through your mind. Let them. You can simply sit there, and knowing the Grandmothers are present with you, holding you, relax and watch the parade. It's a lot like being at the movies. Scenes come and go, rise up and fall away, and should a scene stay on for a while, hoping perhaps to become the main feature, let it. Simply hold. **"Hold, hold, hold,"** the Grandmothers say, for as long as is needed, and while you're holding, be aware of your body and notice how you're feeling. What is it like to be a container?

"As you go through life," the Grandmothers say, **"stay within the awareness of the container that you are and hold whatever comes to you. Hold it as a basin holds water or as a planter holds earth. Water does not change the shape or color of a basin. Earth does not alter the size or shape of a pot. A container is. It holds. *You* hold. You can encompass all this because *it is your nature to be the container. This,"*** they say, **"is Yin."** Feel it.

Blooming as the Flower that You Are

As with all of these meditations, first give yourself enough time to reach a relaxed state. Then as you begin, ask the Grandmothers to come to you so you know they are there, knowing that as soon as you make this request, the Grandmothers will swoop in and surround you.

They are all around you now. In front, behind, above, below, as well as to the sides of you—cradling you in their loving embrace. Among the Grandmothers are all forms of the Divine. All forms of the Divine are with you in joyous numbers. Invite whatever form is dear to your heart to come close to you now and as you breathe, breathe *with the Divine* so the rhythm of your breath becomes a deepening into oneness with the Source. As you do this, love will permeate your body, penetrating your skin and the organs inside you.

"This is your natural state," the Grandmothers say. **"You were born to love and be loved. Everything else is simply a diversion from this.**

Joyous, happy presence is your home, and at a time of so much darkness and horror on earth, it is true joy to be at one with what is real.

"**Here there is a joyous bloom of love, you are blooming. Each time you breathe with the Divine as you are now, you expand, soften, and become more of who you really are. Not that brittle, busy person the mind tells you, you are, but who you *really* are. The core of you that is limitless, the you that knows and feels the truth.**"

After you have breathed with the Divine a few minutes, the Grandmothers will move inside your heart and take up residence there. You may see or sense them sitting inside your expanding heart. "**We come into your heart,**" they say, "**and as we do, your heart opens more fully. It blooms.**"

Notice what you are feeling at this point, and if you like, invite them to enter your heart more completely. If you say 'yes,' they will. As they anchor their energy inside you, you will feel a change. Any nonsensical stuff your mind may be entertaining will quickly fall away. All the worries, fears, and labels will also disappear. The presence of the Grandmothers will create such a force there will no longer be room for that.

Breathe with them as they sit inside your heart. You breathe with them and they breathe with you, and with every breath, you draw them more deeply into yourself. Also, each time you breathe out, old blockages that in the past may have prevented you from receiving their presence, will leave effortlessly.

Love is beginning to bloom inside your heart. Notice how you feel and what it's like to be centered here, observing while your heart continues to expand and deepen. This beautiful organ is beginning to form a pattern now; it's taking on the shape of a flower. Watch and enjoy the transformation taking place inside you.

As your heart moves into the form of a flower, pay attention to the color it takes. Its hue will resonate, and as its petals form, notice the movement, shape and direction they take.

While the flower of your heart expands, become aware of its softness, its living quality—how big it is and how resonant. Soft and yet strong, it will begin to surge and swell. And as it expands, the hard and hurtful places inside you begin to fall off. Throughout our lives, most of us have taken a lot *to heart,* and these things have formed blockages that obstruct the flow of love inside us. As your heart opens now, these blocks begin to drop off—no need to hold on any longer, no need to hold back. With each beat, your heart is becoming stronger and softer, and from the center of your heart where they have taken up residence, the Grandmothers smile at you.

Notice how you feel as this takes place. Do you feel warm? Cool? Soft? Tight? Sad? Peaceful? *Just notice,* and open to the freedom that's coursing through your heart at this moment. New energy is lining the walls of your cells. So much old material is sluffing off now that new energy is flowing into places that haven't seen the light of day in a long time. You are filling with joy. In fact, the room where you are sitting is filling with joy. Again, notice how you feel. Observe your body and the way you're breathing. Just notice.

You may also see and sense color as the flower that you are comes into full bloom. **"Each flower, each bloom is perfect,"** the Grandmothers say, so once you become aware of the flower at the center of your chest, place your hands over it to honor it. Your heart—this beautiful organ. There is a pool of sweetness here, sweetness and depth.

Whenever you work like this, you will become aware of painful places, too, as little corners where energy has been blocked off begin to awaken. Don't worry about these pockets of pain, but let them reveal themselves. Know that this is a normal occurrence, temporary, and a sign that your heart is opening.

The capacity of your heart is growing. Now it can receive more love, and because you are enlarging the place where they live, your capacity for radiance and beauty is also increasing. These qualities live in your heart and spread throughout your body, your mind and then out into the world. Here is where the core of your beauty/power lies, and as soon as you recognize it, you will feel it. Power/Beauty *is* one, and *this* is what you are. In fact, this is *all* you are. Everything else is a passing show. The flower of your heart is perfect, and now you are beginning to experience it.

Turn your attention to the special beauty of this flower within you— its color, movement, shape, and petals. What is it like? Observe it again, and then take a moment to express your gratitude to your heart for being the repository of so much glory. And as you do this, you'll feel how grateful your heart is for being recognized. It's been waiting a long time for this—this lovely flow of love and gratitude from you to your heart, from your heart to you.

The Grandmothers, say, **"As you focus in your heart, every breath you take in enables this organ to grow in beauty. The petals of your heart/flower will open wider while its color becomes deeper and more vivid. Each of you is unique in your beauty/power, unique in your expression of the Divine. In a garden every flower is unique, so with reverence for this divine unfolding within, experience the quality of the flower that you are."**

Stay with this experience long enough to register how you feel, and then see yourself standing tall and walking forward in your own distinctive beauty. As you step forward, notice how the glow of your radiant heart precedes you. Brightness goes before you, and after you pass, this brightness leaves an afterglow. This is your signature, the specific way that God expresses through you. Feel it, and as you walk forward be aware of the shimmering trace you leave behind. This is one way the flower that you are expresses itself on earth.

Take a breath now and as you exhale, reverently bow to your own preciousness. At this very moment you are truly blooming as the flower that you have always been and always will be. How does it feel to recognize *yourself*? Notice your response. *Feel it.* **"We salute the beauty/ power, the power/beauty that you are."**

Holding a Sacred Space

"This is what each of you must do," the Grandmothers say. **"Tell all who work with us to hold a sacred space, to claim and hold it."** They ask us to do this at all times, wherever we are and by so doing, re-sanctify not only our lives, but the very earth itself. **"There is no mundane world. *This* world,"** they emphasize, **"is sacred and the commitment to hold a sacred space is *everything*. It is primary."**

First, we need the commitment to hold and claim sacred space, so to begin this meditation, give yourself permission to relax, and once you have, call on the Grandmothers. Sit tall, uncross your arms and legs and place your hands on your knees. As you take this posture, you convey your readiness to make this commitment. While you sit quietly, think of your desire to take this step and then let the Grandmothers know that you're ready to live your life in sacred space, in touch with and at one with the Divine not just some of the time, but *all the time*.

When the Grandmothers showed me how to claim sacred space,

they stood directly in front of me and stepped forward, with their left foot and then their right. As I watched them, I remembered that the left side of the body is the feminine or receptive side, so it made sense to initiate this movement on the left.

"The thought while stepping forward," they said, **"is to send energy downward through your foot so it sinks into the earth. Take only one step with each foot, and as you do, think and say, 'Here I hold a sacred space.' You may also say, 'I hold a sacred space for the good of myself and all beings.'"**

When you're ready to do this, let the Grandmothers know you want to hold a sacred space. Stand up then and, when you feel firmly balanced, take a step forward with your left foot. As your weight transfers, think of energy pouring through the bottom of your foot into the earth, diving down through the subterranean layers of the planet, anchoring you deeply to Mother Earth. Down, down, down the energy plunges. You have begun the process of holding sacred space.

After you've taken the first step, turn your awareness inward and notice how you feel. How does this act register in your body? *How* do you feel and *where* do you feel it? Observe what's happening inside you and ask your brain to record the process.

Now the right foot, and after you have taken that step, stand quietly, and again notice how you feel. What is your body telling you? At this moment you are rooted in and to the earth. This stance anchors force, and as you feel it, you may be surprised to note that all fear has left you. *Fear cannot withstand the power of sacred space.*

Breathe in deeply and own the space you've claimed. You are anchored to the Mother now, steady and secure. Feel it and declare it. You may say, "Here I hold a sacred space," or "I do this for the good of myself and all beings." Let this be your vow, as you own the power of sacred connection.

"Do not forget to take this step," the Grandmothers say. **"In the times that are approaching, many will panic, but you need not. Simply choose to hold sacred space, and then do it. Hold,"** they say, **"and tell others to do the same. Now is the time to step forward and claim sacred space. Once you consciously make this commitment, no matter what happens around you, no matter where you find yourself, you will not forget that you are holding sacred space."**

This is an active meditation—one that involves the body as well as the mind. You can, of course, perform it only in your mind, but bringing your physical self into the act makes for a stronger experience. Many say it strengthens their commitment. And for this reason, holding and claiming sacred space is a potent exercise to perform in a group.

"**Taking the step to hold sacred space, and doing it in a public way, will strengthen your resolve and make you conscious of having taken a stand,**" the Grandmothers say. "**It's a decision not to be caught in the ephemeral activities of daily life, but to claim sacred space now and forevermore—for yourself and all beings.** *This step* **can only be taken in selfless love.**" This meditation strengthens us. It is also an offering.

This **is what it means to become a Grandmother,**" the Grandmothers say. "**And this is what is needed now.**"

THE CIRCLE OF STONES

When people began to have difficulty using the shamanic method of journeying to the Grandmothers, I asked for a simple, safe, and easy way to use to work with the Grandmothers. This was when they gave us the Circle of Stones.

The Grandmothers sat themselves down on the ground and formed a circle with a large, smooth stone facing each Grandmother. "**This circle is a sacred space, an opening to the great below and the great above,**" they said. "**You need no longer journey in the old way, unless it's something you enjoy,**" they said. "**Instead, you can let** *us* **call the spirits to you.**

"**This way of working will be easier, because people won't have to work alone. They can journey to different levels of non-ordinary reality under our guidance and protection. We will show them the way and help them get to where they want to go. We will work with them, and they will work with us.**"

To experience what it's like to journey with the Grandmothers, think of them sitting directly before you, each Grandmother's place in the circle marked with a stone. Then walk forward until you are standing in their midst. "**Feel your own place in this circle,**" the Grandmothers say, "**and remember that all forms of the Divine are with us as we work together. You are an integral part of this circle, and** the fact that you are *part* of this circle, and not separate from it, is important. You are one with us, one with the Divine, and this is true for everyone who chooses to work with us. And, once you step into this circle, you will become the focus of the entire circle. Your questions will be answered here.

"Ask only one question each time you step into our circle, and everything you hear, see, and experience after your question will be in response to it. So, pay attention to what happens after you ask, and do not stray from your question." I've learned that you can easily 'journey' to the monotonous beat of a drum, to the swish/swish of your windshield wipers, or to any repetitive sound. However, you don't actually need any sound in order to journey and somewhere between ten and thirty minutes will give you enough time.

To form your question for the Grandmothers, ask about something you have already put some energy into. Don't ask a 'yes' or 'no' question since a response to a yes/no question won't give you much information. We go to the Circle of Stones to learn, so ask the Grandmothers something you *really* want to know. And let me suggest that you begin your journey to the Grandmothers in humility, asking something that will help others in addition to yourself. The Divine *is* compassion and therefore operates on compassion. So, if your question has to do with being of service to others, it is much more likely to be answered.

You will be able to enter both the upper and the lower worlds from the middle of the Circle of Stones. But since journeying is not the subject of this book, I will not go into what working in these worlds is like. The Circle of Stones is designed to make journeying simpler, safer, and easier and as I mentioned, everything in non-ordinary reality can be explored by starting from the center of their circle.

Once you have formulated your question, think of stepping between two Grandmothers seated near you and walk into the middle of the circle. Greet the Grandmothers, then humbly and sincerely ask your question. After you've done that, notice what comes to you. What do you see? Hear? Touch? Think of? The Grandmothers may tell or show you something, or they may give you an experience. These journeys can be emotional events and surprising as well. The Grandmothers know how to circumvent the limitations of your mind and go directly to your heart. They know exactly what it will take to bring you to an understanding of the question you have asked, and that is what they will give you.

After you've asked, open your mind wide and *observe.* Be curious about the process and while you're noticing whatever you're noticing, remind yourself not to judge your experience, the Grandmothers, or yourself. *Just observe.* The Grandmothers are consummate teachers. They know what they are doing, so let the good student you are turn your awareness to whatever comes to you. It may be helpful to speak your journey into a recorder so you won't have to try to remember everything that happens. And, if you record it, you can go back later and listen to what transpired during your adventure.

When you make the decision to step into the Grandmothers' circle, you enter the realm of non-ordinary reality and when you step out of their circle, you make the decision to return to ordinary reality. So, after your journey is over, thank the Grandmothers and then respect-fully step out of the Circle of Stones.

When we journey to and with the Grandmothers, we do so to learn how to be of greater service in the world we live in. Working with the Grandmothers is not meant as an escape from the pain of the world but as a means of being of service *in* and *for* this world and all worlds. To be effective in the world, you must keep your feet on the ground so I suggest you journey to the Grandmothers no more than two or three times a week.

POWER IN THE WINGS

The power of yin energy is entirely different from the power of yang, which for most of us, is the only 'power' we have ever known. For or several thousand years our world has been dominated by yang, so it can be difficult to get beyond our conditioning and experience what the power of yin is. But by teaching us how to work with symbols, and thus with our subconscious minds, the Grandmothers show us new ways to experience yin. As they activate the power of our 'wings,' they awaken the power and dignity inherent within us.

To experience the power in these wings, begin this meditation as you always do. Take time to get yourself to that relaxed state, and when you have, begin to think of the power of eagles and other raptors. What must it be like to rise into the air, to swoop and glide on mighty wings? Imagine it.

Allow yourself to possess a pair of wings like these, wings that attach at your shoulders and back. Just think the thought, and then playfully and with a great deal of curiosity, open to the idea of having wings of your own. Focus on the area of your shoulder blades. **"As you focus on your wings,"** the Grandmothers say, **"you will feel *our* light shining and filtering through them. We will support you in the work you do, happy to see you explore your potential.**

"What we are doing here is play," they say, **"but it is not idle play. Because our work is based on service,"** they explain, **"the power in these wings will serve the greater good. The wings we speak of are vehicles for power and care-giving on earth. We are happy to see you getting to know this aspect of yourself.**

"Few have sensed this power within themselves," they say, **"so if we were to talk with most people about opening to the power of the wings, you can imagine the reception we would receive. But only certain ones will be drawn to our work."** And since the Grandmothers *have drawn us* to their work, we will go where they are leading. To experience the power inherent in your wings, the Grandmothers ask you to be brave and for a minute or two, throw caution to the winds. Experiment. We will work together with our 'wings' to experience them as vehicles of power.

"Think of a great raptor," they say. **"And when one comes to mind, stand up and stretch your arms out to the side, as wide as you can, making a 'T' with your body."** Try this posture on for size and see how it feels to stand like this. Be sure to space your feet wide enough so you're balanced and comfortable as you hold the position.

When I first began to own the power of my wings, I extended my arms out and then flexed them in a waving motion, just as a bird would. For me, this movement was back and forth, rather than up and down, but either way is fine. I noticed that each time I flexed like this, the center of my back seemed to grow more supple, to open wider, while my neck rolled forward and backward, forming a graceful arc. And as this took place, I became aware of the grace and power in this movement. Take a few minutes now to play with *your* wings. Up and down, back and forth—play.

Breathe in rhythm with your flexing wings, and as you breathe, a nimbus of light will begin to glow inside and around you. Your back will stretch wider until the reach of your arms begins *to feel enormous.* The Grandmothers tell us, **"There is power in the wings; this work will stretch your idea of who you are. It will stretch you into greatness."**

After you have expanded your wings and your idea of who you are for a minute or two, rest quietly and observe your body. How do you feel now? How's your breathing? If you were to describe what this is like, what would you say about the state you're in at this moment?

Once you have the feeling of these wings, try something else. Stand with your upper arms extended to the side, and bend your elbows so your hands face the sides of your head and point upward. Keep your spine straight and your head up. This commanding posture speaks of queenliness. You may have seen it. This is the posture of the ancient goddess of Crete, the one standing in power with snakes wound around her arms.

Feel the power in this stance. This position is another testament to the Grandmothers' statement, **"There is power in the wings."** It is difficult, perhaps even impossible, to disparage or demean yourself when you stand in this position. A posture like this, challenges you to be the great one you were born to be.

PERSONAL POWER SOURCE

The Net of Light permeates all life and holds the energy on Earth steady. It is everywhere and so at the same moment it holds the macrocosm (i.e., the Universe) as well as the microcosm (you). You are accustomed to calling on the Net of Light to hold places and people on earth but you often forget to ask it to hold you. If you would like to personally awaken to this force of light within you, you can call on the Net of Light to assist you.

Begin by thinking of a source point of light that sits five or six inches above your head. And as soon as you think the thought, the Net of Light will focus there like a star or a small sun. A source of clear light. You may also see it as white, or golden. This point of light is the essence of purity, a piercing brilliance, casting radiance in every direction. Although you will be working on yourself, remember that because you are part of the Net of Light, this 'personal' work will benefit not only you, but everyone and everything. The Grandmothers say, **"You cannot help yourself without helping all beings."** And, like all work with the Net of Light, this too will take place effortlessly.

Think the thought of this radiant light downpouring over you now, covering you. You are under a shower of light that's washing away everything that is *not* light. Any garbage or confusion, any of the 'stuff' that may have accumulated in your mind and personality, is now effortlessly being flushed away. This downpour is so powerful that nothing but light can withstand it. Observe as old thoughts, feelings, memories and energy rise up and are effortlessly washed away. Watch as they show themselves, are flooded with light and are flushed out. Away they go!

Light is streaming through your hair, scalp, the skin of your face and head, and the bones of your skull. It's flooding the membranes in your cranium and the brain itself. Flushing through all the glands. Everything in you is being radiated, along with your eyes, ears, eustachian tube, gums, teeth, mouth, tongue…. Inside and all about you now is a cascade of radiance and it's purifying everything it touches, washing away whatever doesn't belong to you, and the only thing that *belongs* to you is light.

Now the light is streaming into your upper chest and back and down your shoulders. It's flooding your lungs and purifying your heart. It's washing the organs and energy systems of your entire body now—purifying, healing and blessing everything it touches. All organs, joints, bones and vertebrae. Everything. Every part of you is being washed clean with this purifying light. Notice how you feel now. You are radiant, lit from within.

You are a conduit for light! And now light is pouring in through your head and out through your hands and feet, giving radiance to the Earth Herself. Light is pouring into all layers and strata of the Earth, all bodies of water, currents of air around the earth, to all the elements on our beloved planet as well as all the systems of your own individual body.

You are working simultaneously in the small and in the large, in yourself as an individual human and in the planet itself. The microcosm and the macrocosm are overrun with light. And all of this is taking place at the same time—effortlessly.

Experience as you continue to sit in this cascade of light and observe the energy of the downpour as it washes away everything within you that is ready to go. *There is nothing you have to hold on to. There is noth-*

ing you have to figure out. It's all just 'stuff', and the light is now purifying every bit of it. Washing away everything that's ready to go. Become aware now of how the light is touching you, how it is holding you in perfect equanimity. All of your parts are folding together into perfect harmony…. They are singing in happiness. And throughout the cosmos, throughout the Net of Light that upholds everything that is, is ringing the song:

"Oh, how we love you, oh how we love you. Oh, how we love you, oh how we love you."

This song is reverberating throughout your cell beds, throughout the universe, through all bodies of water, land masses and growing things, through all trees, grasses, and mosses. It's echoing through the Earth Herself—the air currents, breezes, and winds. The song vibrates throughout the Fabric of Being of the Universe.

"Oh, how we love you, oh how we love you. Oh, how we love you, oh how we love you."

Feel your body now. Notice what's it's like to be in this vibration of clarity, of radiance. *This is home base for you.* THIS is your home. All the other stuff—the chitchat in the brain, the rushing about from activity to activity, the anxious feelings, the sad feelings and mad feelings—that stuff is only passing show. It does not stick to you! It's not real. It is not who you are. This vibration of radiance is who you are.

HEALING THE ANCESTRAL LINES

Ancestral work magnifies the power of all we do with the Grandmothers. We invite the ancestors to join us each time we work with the Net of Light. We've learned that because there really is no actual 'time', whatever is helpful to us is also helpful to the ancestors. Whatever heals us can heal them.

Whenever we pass the Grandmothers' Empowerment on to others, we also offer it to their ancestors, who, in turn, may pass it further down the ancestral lines. And, each time this happens, not only is life in the present moment healed, the whole of life is healed.

We work together to heal our own ancestral lines, and we encourage those who are interested in this, to join with a Net of Light group near them. Forgiving and healing the pain of the past benefits us and everything that lives.

We will end this chapter with the Grandmothers' Ancestral Declaration. The Grandmothers ask us to honor both our ancestors and ourselves by thinking of casting the Net of Light, and then speaking these powerful words.

THE ANCESTRAL DECLARATION

from the Great Council of the Grandmothers

- I call upon the Net of Light and affirm my union with the Divine.

- I honor my loving connection with those living today, those who lived in other times, and those yet to be born.

- Love is not limited by the calendar or by the clock.

- Each of us is an eternal being, part of the One Love.

- Recalling this truth now, I bow my head in gratitude, saluting the Love within my higher consciousness and within the higher consciousness of everyone else.

- I invite the Ancestors of my family line and the Ancestors of the land where I live to join me in this blessing work, and I welcome all who love and serve the light to connect now within the Net of Light.

- As we gather together, I ask forgiveness for my past ignorance and small-mindedness; I no longer wish to judge and criticize others; nor do I wish to judge and criticize myself.

- I also gladly forgive anyone who ever judged or criticized me.

- I am able to do this with ease each time I remember that it is the breath of the One Love that breathes through me, and the beat of the One Heart that pumps life through me.

- My immortal self exists outside the limitations of action and beyond the circumstances of time and place. So, as I turn to this presence within me, all pain from the past as well as any fear of the future falls away. All is forgiven.

- With my heart open wide, I offer blessings to all beings everywhere.

- And as we joyously embrace one another, together we sing:

- "May all the beings in all the worlds be happy."

Printed in Great Britain
by Amazon

64534635R00139